Hockey Hall of Fame

Hockey Hall of Fame

TRUE STORIES

Eric Zweig

FIREFLY BOOKS

A Firefly Book

Published by Firefly Books Ltd. 2024
Copyright © 2024 Firefly Books Ltd.
Text copyright © 2024 Hockey Hall of Fame and Eric Zweig
Images copyright as listed in the photo credits

First printing

Library of Congress Control Number: 2024935011

Library and Archives Canada Cataloguing in Publication
Title: True stories 2 / Eric Zweig.
Other titles: True stories two | Hockey Hall of Fame
Names: Zweig, Eric, 1963- author. | Hockey Hall of Fame.
Description: First edition. | Includes index.
Identifiers: Canadiana 20240350391 | ISBN 9780228104971 (softcover)
Subjects: LCSH: National Hockey League—Anecdotes. |
    LCSH: Hockey—Anecdotes. | LCSH: Hockey players—Anecdotes. |
    LCGFT: Anecdotes.
Classification: LCC GV847.8.N3 Z842 2024 | DDC 796.962/64—dc23

Published in the United States by
Firefly Books (U.S.) Inc.
P.O. Box 1338, Ellicott Station
Buffalo, New York 14205

Published in Canada by
Firefly Books Ltd.
50 Staples Avenue, Unit 1
Richmond Hill, Ontario L4B 0A7

Cover and interior design: Hartley Millson

Printed in China | E

Canada ♦ *We acknowledge the financial support of the Government of Canada.*

PHOTO CREDITS

Hockey Hall of Fame
Alain Brouillard: 50, 65
Chris Kelke: 193
Craig Campbell: 107
David Sandford: 13, 155
Doug MacLellan: 192
Graphic Artists: 26, 131T, 162
James Rice: 20
Le Studio du Hockey: 17, 19, 36, 73, 84, 86, 89, 120, 151, 154, 184, 198
Matthew Manor: 11, 18
Michael Sr. Burns: 35, 158, 160
Miles Nadal: 190
Paul Bereswill: 189, 194
HHOF: 15, 16, 25, 31, 32, 41, 63, 68, 71, 76, 77, 80, 97, 98, 99, 102, 110, 112, 125, 137, 159, 173, 178R, 181, 191, 195, 203
Robert Shaver: 42
Turofsky: 7, 34, 39, 40, 43, 48, 49, 56, 74, 83, 157, 171, 178L

Orillia Museum of Art & History
134, 135

SIHR
145, 146

Victoria and Valerie Ross
123

COVER: (L to R) HHOF: Paul Bereswill, Dave Sandford, Paul Bereswill, Graphic Artists, Steve Baineau
BACK COVER: HHOF: Turofsky

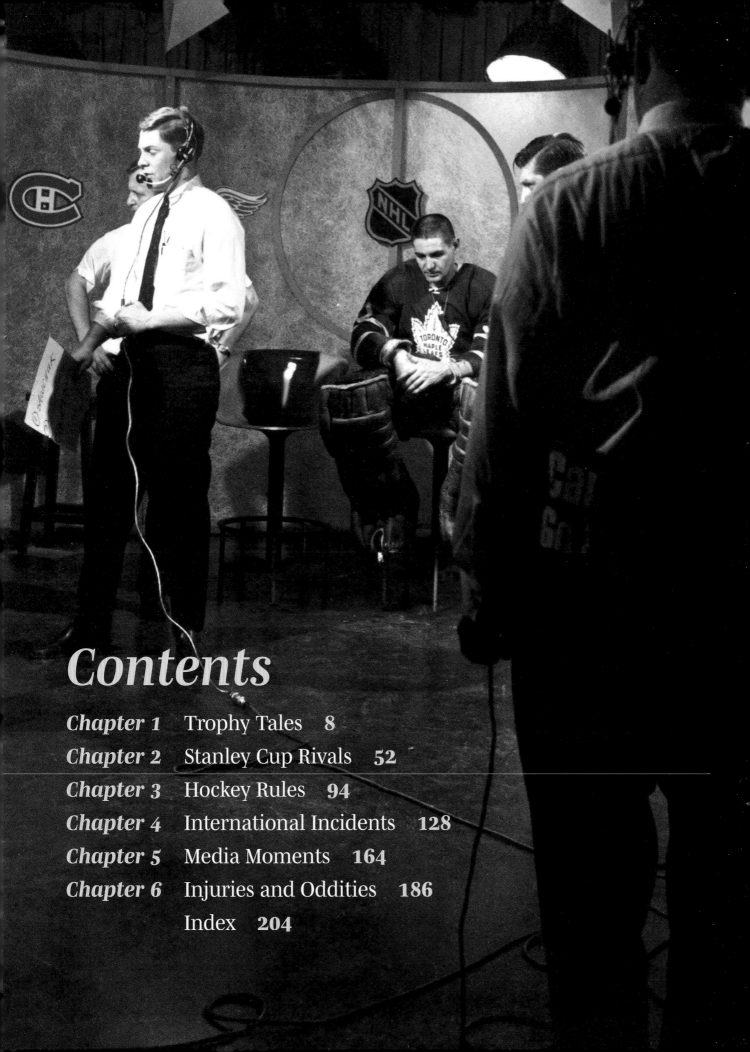

Contents

Introduction and Acknowledgments

▼

Getting to write a sequel is a unique challenge. Of course, it's very gratifying to know so many people bought the original version of *Hockey Hall of Fame True Stories*. Enough that Firefly wanted a follow-up. If you're one of those buyers — or someone who received it as a gift — thank you! But doing this a second time was a little bit daunting.

When Firefly editor Darcy Shea asked me to write the first book in the spring of 2021, we were under a tight deadline. So, I basically put together what I thought of as all the true stories (hence the title!) behind every old hockey myth I could think of, and scrambled to find many more. Though we met the deadline, pandemic-related setbacks meant a book originally scheduled for the fall of 2021 didn't come out until the fall of 2022. But, I never expected they'd ask me to do it all again.

Fortunately, there are a lot of hockey stories to tell.

I have a fondness for stories from the early days, so that first book — and this one — certainly have an oldtime-ness about them. I've been fascinated by the NHL trophies since I was about 10 years old. We touched on the origins of the Vezina Trophy in the first book, but in this one, there's a whole chapter dedicated mainly to the stories behind the Hart, Lady Byng, Calder and Art Ross trophies. The early history of the Stanley Cup is one of my strongest hockey interests, and so there's a chapter that touches on the trophy's earliest days but focuses mainly on the quirky era of the 1920s, when the Stanley Cup was a battle not just among NHL teams, but among the champions of the Pacific Coast Hockey Association and the Western Canada Hockey League too.

I was still about six weeks away from my ninth birthday when Team Canada faced the Soviet Union in September of 1972. I'm sure that watching the drama of that series unfold is a huge reason why I became the hockey fan I am. There were a few stories about Team Canada '72 in the first book. In this one, we'll trace Canada's international hockey adventures all the way back to 1912.

In the introduction to the first book, I thanked many of my fellow writers and researchers for their help: Stan Fischler and Brian McFarlane, who have been writing these kinds of books for decades; the late Bill Fitsell, who was the driving force behind the Society for International Hockey Research (SIHR); other SIHR stalwarts Ernie Fitzsimmons and Glen Goodhand; and contemporaries Kevin Shea, Paul Patskou, Stephen Smith, Todd Denault, Mark Durand, Mikael Lalancette, Richard J. Bendell, Craig Bowlsby, Robert Lefebvre and Stephen Harper. Unfortunately, I left out Jean-Patrice Martel — another longtime friend who (like many of the others) I met through SIHR. J-P is a past-president of SIHR. Current SIHR president Andrew Ross probably deserved a thank you last time. He definitely did this time.

Also for this book, I wish to thank Phil Pritchard

Linesman George Hayes is breaking up a fight between Boston and Toronto combatants.

and Craig Campbell from the Hockey Hall of Fame, who I'm sure I should have thanked last time too. Phil had some excellent suggestions when I was running into a few roadblocks, one of which led me to reconnect with Julie Young. Julie is now a senior director of communications for the NHL in the Toronto office, having been a mere director in the days when our paths used to cross more regularly while I was working with Dan Diamond, James Duplacey, Ralph Dinger and Paul Bontje back when the NHL relied on books to get the word out instead of a website. Both Julie and Stuart McComish, senior manager of statistics and information with the NHL, helped with all sorts of interesting archival information about the donation of the NHL trophies. The stories I've written would not have been nearly as complete without their help.

Finally, thank you again to everyone who read and enjoyed the first *Hockey Hall of Fame True Stories*. I wanted to call this one *True Stories Too* ... but Firefly opted for the more traditional sequel style and went with *True Stories 2*.

I suppose that leaves the door open for *True Stories 3*.

CHAPTER 1

Trophy Tales

The NHL has the greatest collection of silverware
in sports. Individual awards have now been
handed out for more than 100 years, and the true
stories behind some of the oldest NHL trophies
are as unique as the prizes themselves.

▼

You Gotta Have Hart

The NHL has the greatest collection of silverware in sports. Some of its impressive trophies are named in honor of the game's greats. Some for those who made their mark off the ice. Others are simply named for the men and women who donated them.

The award for the NHL's most valuable player isn't the Heart Trophy, but the homophone for the name of the trophy still seems fitting. Heart has long been seen as a key attribute for hockey players, particularly by Canadians, who — since the days of the 1972 Canada-Russia series — have often believed their players "want it more" than others. But the NHL's first individual award was named in honor of the man who donated it: Dr. David Hart of Montreal.

Andrew Ross, who works as a government records archivist at Library and Archives Canada, is a historian of sports and business and the author of *Joining the Clubs: The Business of the National Hockey League to 1945.* Ross has researched Hart and his trophy and notes that little is known about the early life of David Alexander Hart. He was the great-grandson of Aaron Hart, who was likely born in England around 1724. Wikipedia's entry for Aaron Hart says August 16,

1724, and notes that his parents had come from what is now Bavaria in Germany. Aaron Hart arrived in Canada with the British Army from New York around 1760 and would settle in Trois-Rivières a year later. If he wasn't the first Jewish settler to arrive in Canada, he was certainly among the first.

David Hart may have been involved in helping to repel Fenian raiders in Canada in the 1860s. He attended Bishop's College and became the second Jewish doctor in all of Quebec. He was a prominent physician in Montreal, and he and his wife, the former Sarah Matilda David, were the parents of six boys. It was because of one of those sons — Cecil Hart — that Dr. David Hart donated his trophy to the NHL.

Cecil Mordecai Hart was born on November 28, 1883, in Bedford, Quebec. Baseball was his first sporting love, and he played as a pitcher and a shortstop. The day after his death, in his obituary in the *Gazette* on July 17, 1940, the Montreal paper said this of Hart: "His genius for organization and leadership was first made manifest in 1897, when at the age of 14 [given his November birth date, he was probably only 13], he formed what was to become his famous Stars baseball team which competed in the City Senior League." The

Stars would play for some 20 years, winning championships, the obituary notes, in 1906, 1907, 1910, 1911, 1916 and 1917. Among the stars of the Stars were hockey heroes Art Ross and Sprague and Odie Cleghorn. Prominent opponents included Lester Patrick and his brother Frank.

According to Andrew Ross, Cecil Hart was playing hockey by about 1900 on a team in the Montreal Manufacturers Hockey League. In November of 1910, Hart's Stars entered a hockey team in the Montreal City League. Hart played for the team through 1913 while also serving as secretary to the league. His obituary states the team won championships in 1916 and 1917.

It was around that time that Cecil Hart met up with Léo Dandurand and Joseph Cattarinich, who were in business together importing tobacco. They also ran gambling operations at local racetracks, and Ross states that after World War I ended and American states began legalizing gambling, Dandurand and Cattarinich began expanding into the United States. Cece Hart, as his friends called him, doesn't appear to have been involved directly with those businesses (according to the 1919–20 Montreal City Directory, he was an insurance broker), but the two men still relied on him to represent them and a third partner, Louis Létourneau, after Hart informed them the Montreal

National Hockey League trophies:
Presidents' Trophy, Vezina Trophy, Conn Smythe
Trophy, Prince of Wales Trophy, Stanley Cup, James Norris Memorial Trophy,
Frank J. Selke Trophy, Hart Memorial Trophy and Lady Byng Memorial Trophy.

The Montreal Stars ice hockey team of the Montreal City Hockey League in 1912.

Canadiens would be up for auction on November 3, 1921. George Kennedy, the team's owner, had been stricken with the Spanish flu during the ill-fated Stanley Cup Final between Montreal and Seattle. He had never truly recovered, and the team was being sold in the wake of his death on October 19, 1921.

There were two other bidders for the Canadiens. One was Thomas Duggan, who had built the Mount Royal Arena in 1920 and worked with Kennedy promoting events there. The other was an unnamed Ottawa bidder represented by NHL president Frank Calder. Author D'Arcy Jenish sets the scene in his book *The Montreal Canadiens: 100 Years of Glory*, originally published in 2008:

Duggan bid first. He pulled from his pocket ten bills, lay them on the table and declared, "I have ten thousand dollars in cash to pay for the club." Calder matched him. Hart asked for time to call Dandurand, and reached him in Cleveland. "Listen closely, Cecil," Dandurand said. "Just make sure you outbid the others. I'm giving you a free hand."

Hart duly offered eleven thousand. Duggan collected his cash and snapped, "If you're playing me against Léo and his partners, I'm through." Calder was finished as well.

Hart had won the day for Dandurand and his partners, and he would help run the Canadiens, with some sources calling him a corporate director and others calling him managing director — although that was also a title given to Dandurand. One of the biggest contributions Hart made to the team came in the summer of 1923, when Dandurand sent him to Stratford, Ontario, to sign Howie Morenz to a professional contract. Hart left the team, briefly, in 1924, to run the new NHL club in Montreal, but with the soon-to-be-named Maroons struggling, he was fired in February of 1925. Hart returned to the Canadiens on September 28, 1926, when Dandurand hired him to replace himself as coach of the team. He would guide the Canadiens to back-to-back Stanley Cup titles in 1930 and 1931 before falling out with Dandurand in 1932. Hart would later return to the Canadiens from 1936 to 1939 but wouldn't enjoy the same success. When he died in Montreal on July 16, 1940, after an illness of three months, he was only 56.

Cecil Hart is one of only 19 coaches to win two or more Stanley Cup titles in the NHL. He was the second in league history (after Pete Green of Ottawa in 1920 and 1921) to win them back to back. Even so, the trophy that bears his family name does so not because of Cecil Hart's success but because it was donated by his father, Dr. David Hart.

Hart of the Matter

The story of the Hart Trophy begins a few months after Cecil Hart signed Howie Morenz for the Canadiens. On the night of November 29, 1923, friends and admirers of Hart gathered at the Reform Club in Montreal to celebrate his 40th birthday. "Members of the Bench, Bar, and Parliament, and prominent representatives of every walk of metropolitan life attended," reported the *Montreal Star* the next day. "There were

speeches and toasts from nearly all the friends of Mr. Hart," added the *Gazette*, "all eulogizing him for his hard and painstaking work in connection with the local pro hockey club and the league generally."

A highlight of the evening, noted in both newspapers as well as in the French-language *La Presse* (and no doubt other city papers as well), was the speech by Hart's father, Dr. David Hart, who said he intended to donate "a cup" to the NHL.

In the biography *Léo Dandurand: Sportsman*, written in 1952 by Rosaire Barrette, David Hart is

The original version of the Hart Trophy as donated to the National Hockey League.

described as "un partisan des canadiens enragé" (a rabid Canadiens fan). The book claims that a few days before the dinner for his son, David Hart asked Dandurand about donating a trophy for the NHL's highest scorer. (The *Montreal Star* account of the party notes that Dr. Hart had made a similar donation, for the top goal-scorer, to the Montreal Hockey League when Cecil "was the backbone of that organization.") Dandurand recalled advising Dr. Hart to change the objective of the award. While an award for the highest scorer made sense, Dandurand argued that it would be biased against goalies and defensemen. More importantly, it would encourage individual play and discourage team play, as the forwards might be egotistical and no longer pass the puck.

Interestingly, the *Star* reports that while Hart's previous cup donation had been "for the best goal average in the Montreal City League," he had made up his mind this time "to present a similar cup to the National Hockey League for the same purpose, in which competition, however, not only the scorers, but the assistants will be counted."

Although the wording is awkward, the point is obviously that not just goals, but goals and assists, would count toward Hart's new trophy. And yet, when Hart informed the NHL of his plans — perhaps with Dandurand's thoughts in mind — he no longer intended his trophy for the league scoring leader. In a letter to NHL president Frank Calder on January 16, 1924, Hart notes his understanding that both his son and Dandurand had already spoken to Calder about a proposed trophy for the league's most valuable player and that, if accepted by the NHL, he would "have much pleasure indeed in offering a Trophy for this purpose."

It would appear that Calder replied immediately to David Hart, for in a letter dated that same January 16, 1924, he writes:

David A. Hart, Esq., M.D.,
296 Sherbrooke St. W.,
Montreal.

Dear Sir:-

I have to thank you for yours of the 16th, in which you offer a Trophy to be donated to the most valuable player in the National Hockey League.

There is not the least doubt in my mind that the Governors of the National Hockey League will accept with gratitude the kind offer you make.

I am putting it before them immediately and should hear from them in the course of a few days.

It seems Calder immediately sent letters to the governors of the four NHL teams, and they may have discussed Hart's proposition at a special session of NHL executives held in Toronto on Saturday, January 26. The main reason for the meeting was to discuss Ottawa's protest of rough play by the Montreal Canadiens in general, and Sprague Cleghorn in particular. No action was taken, except to discourage teams from using talk of rough play to promote ticket sales. That decision was reported in newspapers on Monday, January 28, with word the following day in the *Ottawa Journal*, and at least one other paper, stating that Dr. David A. Hart had donated a trophy for the most valuable player.

Interestingly, it wasn't until February 12, 1924, that Calder wrote to Hart telling him that "the Governors of the National Hockey League have accepted with many thanks your kind offer of a Trophy to be held each year by the player who shall be deemed the most valuable man to his side." A week later, he wrote a series of letters to newspapers in the four NHL cities

(Montreal, Ottawa, Toronto and Hamilton) to recruit two sports writers from each city to vote for a winner. "The system of balloting is very simple," wrote Calder. "You will be asked to name eight players in the order in which you think they are most useful.... The first player placed at the head of the list will be allotted eight points, the second player seven points, the third six, and so on.... The player scoring the highest number of points in all the ballots will be awarded the trophy."

By at least March 5, David Hart had obtained a large vaselike trophy mounted on a square wooden base. There doesn't appear to be a surviving record of whether or not Hart commissioned a new piece of silverware or bought an existing cup and had it suitably engraved, but the trophy was formally presented to Frank Calder on behalf of the NHL by Cecil Hart, Léo Dandurand and Canadiens president Athanase David in Montreal on March 8, 1924, prior to the first game of the NHL final between the Canadiens and the Ottawa Senators. On March 11, 1924, in Ottawa, before the start of the second game in the two-game, total-goals series, the trophy was presented by Calder and the Governor General of Canada, Julian Byng, to Senators captain and star center Frank Nighbor as the first winner.

The First Hart Vote

Frank Nighbor of Ottawa won the first Hart Trophy by a single point over Sprague Cleghorn of the Canadiens. The final tally was 37–36. In writing to David Hart on the day the award was to be presented, Calder informed the donor of the trophy: "You will be interested to know that seven newspapermen of the four cities which comprise the National Hockey League circuit acted as judges in deciding the award of the Trophy. Their various decisions placed Frank Nighbor,

Frank Nighbor.

of the Ottawa Hockey Cub, at the head of the list with thirty-seven points, Sprague Cleghorn, of the Canadiens, second with thirty-seven, and John Ross Roach, of the St. Patrick's team, third with thirty-five."

Andrew Ross speculates on the possibility of Calder having cast a deciding vote himself to break the tie, but he believes it more likely that Calder made an error, as there is no other record of a tie vote. The *Gazette* in Montreal noted the vote totals as 37-36-35 and gives the rest of the contenders in order as George Boucher, Ottawa; Billy Burch, Hamilton; Howie Morenz, Canadiens; Jake Forbes, Hamilton; Goldie Prodger, Hamilton; Cy Denneny, Ottawa; and Babe Dye, Toronto, without providing any further point totals.

Support for Sprague

Elected to the Hockey Hall of Fame in 1958 (two years after he and his brother Odie died two days apart, on July 12 and 14, 1956), Sprague Cleghorn is generally

Sprague Cleghorn, 1924.

considered to be the toughest, meanest and dirtiest hockey player of the 1910s and '20s ... and perhaps of all time. He was also the best defenseman of his era, while his brother Odie was a top-scoring center — and only slightly less mean and dirty.

"If some of the longhairs I see on the ice these days met Sprague Cleghorn," said Red Dutton, another star player from the same era, in Trent Frayne's book *The Mad Men of Hockey* (1974), "he'd shave them to the skull. Jesus, he was mean. If you fell in front of Cleg he'd kick your balls off."

Still, the tight vote for the first Hart Trophy is evidence of how highly regarded Sprague Cleghorn was in his day. On March 6, 1924, the *Ottawa Journal* ran a story from the *Montreal Herald* in which sports writer Elmer Ferguson of the *Herald* explained why he voted for Cleghorn over Frank Nighbor for the Hart Trophy:

> Frank Calder, president of the National Hockey League, was good enough to ask me to be one of the judges in Montreal to make nominations for the trophy donated by that fine old sportsman, Dr. David Hart, of this city, father of Cecil Hart, well known director, scout, entertainer, etc., of the Canadiens team....
>
> The trophy, it will be noted, is not for the best player in the league, but to the player most useful to any one team, and I am probably committing no breach of faith or etiquette when I state that Sprague Cleghorn was my choice for first position.
>
> I do not consider Sprague Cleghorn the best hockey player in the National Hockey League, but rate him one of the best. But I do consider him of far more vital importance to the Canadien team than even Frank Nighbor is to Ottawa, while neither of the other two clubs, in my estimation, possess any one

player of nearly such outstanding importance to the team as either of those named.

Sprague Cleghorn I consider is more necessary to Canadiens to make them a winning team than is Nighbor to Ottawa for these reasons.

1–Nighbor's best and most effective hockey is played in Ottawa. Cleghorn plays equally well "on the road" as at home.

2–Canadiens, without Cleghorn, lose morale. They were badly beaten at Ottawa this season by a score of 4–0 when forced to do without the services of Cleghorn. In other matches at Ottawa they were beaten only by the margin of a single goal. Ottawa, on the other hand, won numerous games without Nighbor.

3–Cleghorn is a more effective puck-carrier in relation to his position [defense] than is Nighbor [a center], and makes comparatively more "scoring plays" for Canadiens than does the Ottawa forward.

These reasons, the fact that Cleghorn is not so fragile as Nighbor, is a more robust player on all kinds of ice, gave him my vote.

Three of a Kind

An original suggestion made by David Hart when discussing the Hart Trophy was that should the trophy be won three times by a player (not necessarily in order), it would become his permanent possession. This was a fairly common term for many team and personal trophies of this, and earlier, eras. The suggestion seems to have been adopted by the NHL, and yet this never happened.

The first three-time winner of the Hart Trophy was Howie Morenz of the Canadiens, who won it first for

Howie Morenz poses for a portrait as a member of the Montreal Canadiens no later than the 1927–28 NHL season.

the 1927–28 season and then again in 1930–31 and 1931–32. Morenz and Cecil Hart (who never married and had no children of his own) had an almost father-and-son bond, so if anyone had ever been given permanent possession of the Hart Trophy, Morenz would have been a fitting recipient. As to why it didn't happen, the regulation was obviously changed, or just forgotten about, at some point. Perhaps it was after David Hart died, just a little more than a year following the first presentation of his trophy, on June 30, 1925, at the age of 81.

The Hart Memorial Trophy

The square wooden base on the bottom of the Hart Trophy had room for nine small silver plates to engrave the names of the annual winners on each of its four sides. That meant that after the 1958–59 season, when Andy Bathgate was awarded the NHL's MVP, all 36 nameplates were filled up. In more recent years, when the nameplates on the bases of other NHL trophies were filled, larger bases have been added beneath the originals. But sometime during the

The Hart Memorial Trophy awarded to the Most Valuable Player of the National Hockey League.

1959–60 season, when then NHL president Clarence Campbell noticed there was no room for more names and noted the general deterioration of the original trophy itself, he thought it was time for a new one.

Various newspapers on February 10, 1960, reported on the NHL Board of Governors meeting going on in Palm Beach, Florida. Most prominent among the items on the agenda that day was the fate of Red Kelly. The Detroit Red Wings had recently traded their star defenseman to the New York Rangers, but Kelly didn't want to go. When he refused to report, Detroit tried to trade him to Toronto. But the NHL governors decided Kelly had to remain in Detroit, where Red Wings officials were saying he had to report or go on the retired list. He would eventually be traded to Toronto.

The governors also listened to a delegation from Los Angeles suggesting expansion beyond the then six NHL franchises to the West Coast. No formal application was made, but it was said to be the first time the league owners formally discussed expansion. What they did vote to expand was the league pension plan, extending it beyond players and referees to include junior club executives. A building committee was authorized to proceed with plans to construct a Hockey Hall of Fame on the grounds of the Canadian National Exhibition in Toronto, with hopes of opening up in the summer of 1961. Finally, "the league owners voted to retire the Dr. David A. Hart trophy to the Hall of Fame and buy a new trophy."

According to documents in the NHL archives, the NHL received an invoice for eight sketches relating to the new Hart Trophy on July 7, 1960. The balance owing of $175 appears to have been paid on July 15. Three days later, Campbell received a letter from Eric Boffey on the stationery of the jewelry company of the late Alex Falle, a company that specialized in watches, clocks, diamonds, silverware and trophies. They had long been used by the NHL.

Gordie Howe, Ed Chadwick and Rudy Migay in game action between the Detroit Red Wings and Toronto Maple Leafs no later than the 1959–60 season.

Dear Mr. Campbell

With regard to the proposed new Dr. David A. Hart Trophy, the full scale drawings have been submitted to the silversmith and the following factors emerge.

The trophy will have an overall height of approx 30 inches and contain about 300 Troy ounces Sterling silver.

The main pear shaped cup of the Trophy will be of satin finish whilst the flame superimposed portions will have contrasting finish of electroplate gilt. The remainder of the trophy as far as the base will be bright finish....

The silversmith informs me that this will constitute one of the most outstanding trophies that he has ever made up and proposes to use his utmost skill and imagination on the flame portion.

Delivery on the Trophy would be approx 7 weeks whilst it would take another week to have a suitable carrying case made up.

My price to you on the completed Trophy including Engraving and Carrying case would be 2450.00. This price includes Fed and Exc Tax whilst Provincial tax would be extra.

Hoping that this is satisfactory to you.

The letter was signed by Boffey, who received a reply from Campbell dated July 22, 1960, acknowledging the price quoted by the league's silversmith, Petersen & Sons, and confirming his authorization to have Carl Petersen proceed with the manufacturing of the trophy. It would bear the following inscription:

HART
MEMORIAL TROPHY
Replacing the
DR. DAVID A. HART TROPHY
presented to the
NATIONAL HOCKEY LEAGUE
as its
MOST VALUABLE PLAYER
Award

In the minutes of the NHL's owners and governors meeting of September 8, 1960, it was recorded that President Campbell had presented an artist's drawing of the new Hart Memorial Trophy, which would be delivered before October 1. "Its theme is a 'torch' with the flame portion in gilt and the remainder in sterling silver. The meeting expressed general approval of the unique design."

The first name to be engraved on the new trophy was a fitting one, as Gordie Howe had been named the most valuable player for the 1959–60 season. His fifth (of six) MVP selection that season set a record for the most ever at the time, surpassing the four won by Eddie Shore in the 1930s. Only Wayne Gretzky, with nine, has won the Hart more times than Howe.

The Beginning of the Lady Byng

The story comes up every year on the NHL website at the time of the NHL Awards. It says the following about the annual award given to "the player adjudged

The original Lady Byng Trophy.

to have exhibited the best type of sportsmanship and gentlemanly conduct combined with a high standard of playing ability":

Lady Byng, wife of Canada's governor general at the time, presented the Lady Byng Trophy in 1925. She decided the first winner would be Frank Nighbor of the Ottawa Senators. Late in the season, Lady Byng invited Nighbor to Rideau Hall, showed him the trophy, and asked him if the NHL would accept it as an award for its most gentlemanly player. When Nighbor said he thought it would, Lady Byng, much to Nighbor's surprise, awarded him the trophy.

The first winner of the Lady Byng Trophy was definitely not selected in a poll of the Professional

Hockey Writers Association at the end of the regular season, as it is today. In a time long before the PHWA existed, it doesn't even seem as if there was a poll of sports writers that first year, as there was when Frank Nighbor won the Hart Trophy in its inaugural season of 1923–24, and again in 1925 when Hamilton's Billy Burch won the Hart. Even so, it would appear Lady Byng did go through the proper channels … even if it might have been her suggestion that Nighbor should win it that first year.

News that Lady Byng, the wife of Canada's Governor General, planned to offer a trophy to reward clean play was first released in a Canadian Press dispatch on March 8, 1925. It ran in various newspapers the next day. "Desiring to raise the standard of professional hockey," the story read, "Lady Byng of Vimy proposes to present a challenge cup to the National Hockey League to be held each year by the cleanest and most effective player in the league." That statement was followed by the content of a letter Lady Byng had sent to Frank Calder:

> Feeling a great desire to help your effort to "clean up hockey" and eliminate the needless rough play that at present is a threat to the national game, and also to leave a tangible record of the enjoyment I personally have had from the game during our sojourn in Canada, I am writing to ask if you will let me offer a challenge cup for the man on any team in the National Hockey League who, while being thoroughly effective, is also a thoroughly clean player.
>
> I am convinced that the public desires good sport, not the injuring of players, and if, by donating this challenge cup, I can in any way help towards this end, it will give me a great deal of pleasure.

According to the story, Calder met with Lady Byng on Saturday evening (March 7, 1925), and as a result of their "interview," Stanley Cup trustee William Foran and H.B. Given had been named trustees for the new "cup." The report also notes, "The same jury of sporting editors which selects the winner of the Hart Trophy will decide which player during the season has set the best example of clean and effective hockey in the NHL scheduled matches."

But that doesn't seem to have happened that first year.

In fact, it seems possible the Lady Byng Trophy wasn't intended to be awarded until the following season. After all, the 1924–25 regular season wrapped up on March 9, 1925 — the same day the announcement of the Lady Byng Trophy appeared in newspapers — and Billy Burch had already been named the winner of the Hart Trophy on March 7.

Consider further the following story from the *Toronto Star* on March 9:

> Last week Lady Byng donated a cup to be awarded annually to the cleanest and most effective player in the NHL. If that cup had been in existence in time one Wilfred Burch of Hamilton would now be holder of both the Hart and Lady Byng cups. Burch won the Hart cup as "the most useful player to his team" in the league by 19 points. [He outpolled Howie Morenz 79–60.] He would have won the Lady Byng Cup — had it been offered for this year — as far off as a jack rabbit would head a snail in a day's journey. Burch is the cleanest and most useful player in the NHL.

And yet, in a news bulletin datelined from Toronto on March 24, 1925, that appeared in papers the following day, Frank Calder announced Frank Nighbor as the first recipient of the "Lady Byng of Vimy cup." Indeed, the *Ottawa Journal* reported on March 25 that "the management of the Ottawa Hockey Association had been notified by Government House that both their excellencies the Governor-General and Lady Byng, with a party from Government House, will be present at the match between the Ottawas and the Ottawa Combines at the Auditorium tonight," and "before the start of the game Her Excellency Lady Byng will present the Lady Byng of Vimy Trophy to Frank Nighbor, the captain of the Ottawa team, who has been declared winner of the cup for the present season by President Calder of the NHL."

Lady Byng was there that night and came onto the ice before the game to present her new trophy to Nighbor. "She shook hands with each of the players," reported the *Ottawa Citizen* on March 26, "who combined to render three rousing cheers for the gracious donor."

But not everyone was impressed.

This again from the *Toronto Star*, this time from March 25, 1925:

> It would be interesting to know who awarded the Lady Byng of Vimy trophy to Frank Nighbor of the Ottawas. Nobody in this neck of the woods appears to know anything about it, and if the trophy is for the combination of effectiveness and good sportsmanship, few, if any, critics around here could see Nighbor's effectiveness during the past NHL season. What's the matter with Billy Burch of the Hamilton Tigers, or "Happy" Day of the St. Pat's. Either of those players is just as sportsmanlike as Nighbor, and a thousand times more effective. And do not forgot boys like John Ross Roach, Bert McCaffery, of St. Pats, or "Cucumber" Vezina of Canadiens. They are all both effective and sportsmanlike. It looks

like some Ottawa "pap" for the Pembroke Percolator. He did not win the Hart Trophy and it looked like he was handed this one on a silver platter.

Other NHL cities didn't seem impressed either, as a story in the Chicago-based sports weekly *Collyer's Eye* made clear in its April 4 edition:

> Montreal, April 3.—National hockey league officials and the press of the cities comprising the league are having a good laugh over the award of the Lady Byng trophy to Frank Nighbor, of Ottawa. The trophy was to be awarded to the cleanest and most effective player in the league, and it was announced at first that no award would be made this year. President Calder suddenly decided to award the trophy to Nighbor during an exhibition series in Ottawa, which in the first game had suffered sadly from lack of patronage. The word is around the circuit that Frank Ahearn, president of Ottawa, was anxious that Nighbor should be given the cup, and it is stated that Lady Byng, who is an ardent Ottawa fan, concurred in these sentiments, and when President Calder was apprised of her wish in the matter he anticipated the presentation for a year and gave the trophy to Nighbor.
>
> So far as it went all were agreed that the trophy should be presented if Her Excellency wished, but those who were to make the award could not see why Nighbor should be preferred. So far as consistency was concerned all season he was one of the most inconsistent players in the league. Based on the selection of the Hart trophy he didn't stand a chance except on the item of clean

play, and then his penalties were higher than several others, though of trifling nature. There was no doubt that the sports editors who were called on to the make a selection would have considered "Happy" Day, Billy Burch, or Georges Vezina before Nighbor. The foxy Ottawa president anticipated this, and as a result Nighbor got the cup, though hardly entitled to it.

For sure Nighbor's 1924–25 season was far from his best. In playing 26 of 30 games on the schedule, he managed only five goals and five assists — although his 10 points did place him in the top third among all

The First Byng Vote

Here are the total points earned in the first vote for the Lady Byng Trophy in its second season of 1925–26, along with the statistics of the players:

Player, Team	Votes	GP	G	A	PTS	PIM
Frank Nighbor, Ottawa	76	35	12	14	26	40
Billy Burch, Americans	63	36	21	3	24	33
Carson Cooper, Boston	60	36	28	8	36	10
Cy Denneny, Ottawa	44	36	24	12	36	18
Dunc Munro, Maroons	40	33	4	6	10	62
Howie Morenz, Canadiens	35	31	23	3	26	40
Hib Milks, Pittsburgh	28	36	14	5	19	17
Harold Darragh, Pittsburgh	27	35	10	7	17	2
Hooley Smith, Ottawa	26	28	16	9	25	58
Lionel Conacher, Pittsburgh	25	33	9	6	15	66
King Clancy, Ottawa	21	35	8	4	12	82
Pit Lépine, Canadiens	19	27	9	1	10	18
Jimmy Herbert, Boston	17	36	26	9	35	53
Nels Stewart, Maroons	16	36	34	8	42	121

scorers in the league. Many players had fewer penalty minutes than the 18 he recorded that season, though among those who did there probably weren't many who had as much ice time as he did, or were responsible for checking the league's top scorers.

Nighbor was the type of player who had to be seen to be truly appreciated. A prolific scorer in his pre-NHL career, his goal-scoring numbers in the NHL were less impressive than many of his contemporaries. Still, Nighbor led the league in assists three times, so he was a good playmaker. Also, with his mastery of the poke check and hook check, he was widely considered to be the best defensive forward — even the best defensive player — in the NHL in his day, and he played nearly a full 60 minutes each night even when that was ceasing to be the norm. Especially among forwards.

Another thing the Montreal-based staff correspondent to *Collyer's Eye* reported about Calder's unexpected selection of Nighbor as the first Lady Byng winner was, "It is likely that the sports editors will decline to make a nomination next year." Not only would that prove untrue, but when sports writers did vote for the award after the 1925–26 season, they voted for Nighbor! Once again, the trophy was presented to him on the ice by Lady Byng prior to an exhibition game in Ottawa, this time between the Senators and the Saskatoon Sheiks of the Western Hockey League.

The 1925–26 season was Nighbor's last truly great one. He led the NHL in assists, led Ottawa to a first-place finish in the league standings and finished third in voting for the Hart Trophy as well. Still, based solely on numbers, Carson Cooper of the Boston Bruins might have been a better selection for the Lady Byng Trophy that season.

Rideau Hall Rumor

The story of Lady Byng inviting Frank Nighbor to Rideau Hall, asking him about her trophy and then presenting it to him, seems to have started — or at least started taking on a life of its own — in February of 1963. In a short note about Nighbor, who had turned 70 on January 26 (he would die of cancer on April 13, 1966), in the *Ottawa Journal* on February 8, 1963, Bill Westwick wrote: "They didn't need a vote the first time the Lady Byng Trophy was donated. Lady Byng called Nighbor to Government House, told him she was donating a trophy for sportsmanship and gentlemanly play and made it apparent that it was expressly for him that year."

The story gained wider circulation later that month when a Canadian Press feature by Ben Ward appeared in newspapers across the country. The NHL archives has an advance copy of the article, mailed on February 12, 1963, which is a week before it first appeared in newspapers. Though it's not obvious in the advance copy, the full newspaper story makes it clear that Ward had spoken with Nighbor, and it appears as if Nighbor told the story himself about Lady Byng inviting him to Rideau Hall.

The Pembroke Peach

Frank Nighbor played pro hockey from 1911 until 1930, starring in three of the top leagues of his day — the Pacific Coast Hockey Association, the National Hockey Association and the NHL — mainly with the Ottawa Senators, but also with the Vancouver Millionaires, the Toronto Blueshirts and the Toronto Maple Leafs. In addition to his individual awards, Nighbor was a five-time Stanley Cup champion, winning first with the Millionaires in 1915 and later with Ottawa in 1920, 1921, 1923 and 1927. He was known by several nicknames during his hockey career, most commonly the Flying Dutchman and the Pembroke Peach.

Baseball Hall of Famer Honus Wagner, who starred from 1897 to 1917, mainly with the Pittsburgh Pirates, was also known as the Flying Dutchman. In both cases, the nickname comes from their German (Deutsch/Dutch) heritage and the legend of the ghost ship that was said to never be able to make port, and so was doomed to sail the seven seas forever.

Baseball's Ty Cobb, who starred from 1905 to 1928, mainly with the Detroit Tigers, was known as the Georgia Peach. The reference was to his Georgia heritage and the fruit famously grown there, but also to the slang usage of *peach*, meaning something very attractive or pleasing. For Nighbor, *Pembroke* paid homage to his hometown, where he was born on January 26, 1893, and lived much of his life. *Peach* was from the slang term and alliterated well with *Pembroke*.

There are no obvious stories about Nighbor earning the nickname, but his Pembroke heritage is often noted as early as his first season in Toronto in 1912–13. (Blueshirts teammate and childhood friend Harry Cameron — a fellow future Hockey Hall of Famer — was also from Pembroke, as was goalie Hugh Lehman, whom Nighbor would play with for three seasons in Vancouver.) References to Nighbor as the Pembroke Peach appear as early as the first season of the NHL in 1917–18.

Frank Nighbor suited up for Pembroke.

Alex Delvecchio of the Detroit Red Wings in a game during the 1969–70 National Hockey League season.

Quote ... Unquote

"Sure, it's nice to win it. But the name takes a lot away from it and what it's meant to be. Some of the comments [from heckling fans] aren't too easy to digest. I think if they changed the name of the trophy it would be much better."

— **Alex Delvecchio**, quoted in the *Detroit Free Press* on April 2, 1969, after winning the Lady Byng Trophy for the third time in his career

Who Was That Lady?

Regardless of the mocking her trophy has taken over the years, there is no doubt that Lady Byng was a hockey fan. She and Lord Byng attended many Ottawa Senators games when they were living in the Canadian capital while he was Governor General from 1921 to 1926.

"One thing I missed sorely in Canada was theater," Lady Byng would write in her 1945 autobiography *Up the Stream of Time*. "To me, the lack of good plays was a grievous loss…. But if plays were denied me, there was ice hockey, and woe betide any member of the staff who tried to make engagements for a Saturday night during the hockey season, when I went regularly to root for the Senators, with such fine players on the team as [Eddie] Gerard, [Frank] Nighbor, the Bouchers [mainly George, but also Frank], [King] Clancy, and [Cy] Denneny, to name but a few in those long-past days, who gave me many happy evenings during our five years at Rideau Hall."

Even when they were back in England, Lady Byng and her husband continued to follow the Senators on their way to the 1927 Stanley Cup. She even sent a telegram of congratulations on behalf of her and Lord Byng when Ottawa won that year:

Frank Ahearn, Ottawa:
Both of us are delighted at the splendid success of the Ottawa team. Please give them our warmest congratulations.

Evelyn Byng

Evelyn Byng, Viscountess Byng of Vimy, was born Marie Evelyn Moreton in London on January 11, 1870. She first came to Canada in November of 1878, when her father, Sir Richard Charles Reynolds-Moreton, served as the comptroller at Rideau Hall during the first year of the term of John Douglas Sutherland Campbell, the Marquis of Lorne, as Governor General. "It's strange how clearly I remember our one year out here when I was eight," wrote Lady Byng, noting that her mother hated the cold climate.

Hockey wasn't yet known in Ottawa during the winter of 1878–79, and wouldn't be until after the first Montreal Winter Carnival in 1883, but young Evelyn enjoyed tobogganing. She remembered not only the big wooden slide that was still standing (though derelict) when she returned to Ottawa in 1921 but also a steep hill that was forbidden to her and the children of other families who also lived on the grounds. "So, of course, we waited till the grown-ups were safely out of the way, and then flew down it on our small toboggans."

Evelyn Moreton married Julian Byng on April 30, 1902. (He was nearly 40; she was 32.) Lady Byng suffered two miscarriages in the early years of her marriage and was never able to have children. Her husband was well into his military career by the time of their marriage, and they lived mostly in India, where he was serving, until the outbreak of World War I. In late May of 1916, Byng was placed in command of the Canadian Corps. His greatest glory came when he led the Canadian victory at Vimy Ridge on April 9, 1917.

After the war, on October 7, 1919, Byng was elevated to the peerage as Baron Byng of Vimy. A month later, he retired from the army, and on June 3, 1921, it was announced that Byng had been appointed to serve as Governor General of Canada. He received his commission on August 2, and Lord and Lady Byng sailed for Canada aboard the *Empress of France* two days later. They arrived in Quebec City on the night of August 10 and reached Ottawa by train on the afternoon of August 12.

On December 15, 1921, the *Ottawa Journal* reported that the Governor General had accepted the honorary presidency of the Ottawa Hockey Club, and that he and Lady Byng, along with a party of guests from Government House, would attend all games that season. Two days later, the paper clarified somewhat, saying, "The Vice-Regal box, which is situated on the west side of the Arena and which was formally occupied by the Duke of Connaught and the Duke of Devonshire [the two previous Governors General] has been placed at the disposal of Lord Byng and the latter, with Lady Byng and a party of guests from Government House, will attend the National League games whenever able to."

The Byngs were in attendance for the home opener on December 21, 1921, when the Senators faced the Toronto St. Pats. Lord Byng handled a ceremonial faceoff to open the season, and Lady Byng was presented with a bouquet of American Beauty roses by Ottawa captain Eddie Gerard before the players from both teams — accompanied by the large crowd — offered three cheers to the couple. When the game was over, Toronto had upset the two-time defending Stanley Cup champs, winning 5–4.

"It was," said a report in the Montreal *Gazette*, "the first game of hockey that Their Excellencies had witnessed."

Despite the disappointing finish, it would not be their last.

The viceroyal couple even tried to learn to skate.

"Julian and I tried," Lady Byng would write, "with woeful results, for I never got beyond the state of pushing a chair around the rink, whilst enduring torment from aching shins." Lord Byng was somewhat better … for a little while. "He got far enough to plod around unsupported, but rather unhappily, till one day he sat down on the ice so violently that he jarred himself from head to foot." At nearly 60 years of age (Byng was born September 11, 1862), "he remarked sourly, 'You can't teach an old dog new tricks.'"

Lady Byng, 1921.

The couple gave away their skates … but they rarely gave away their hockey tickets!

Lady Byng mentions nothing of the trophy she donated in *Up the Stream of Time*, but her final remarks on hockey would seem to reflect some of the reason behind her decision to reward sportsmanship.

"The only blemish to that sport," she said, "was the childish mentality among a section of the crowd which would vent its annoyance, on umpires or players, by showering the rink with rubbish, stopping the game and also — when coins were thrown — endangering players."

Mr. Boucher and Mrs. Byng

It's often been written that Lady Byng was so impressed by Frank Boucher — a seven-time winner of the award she donated — that she decided to give him her trophy to keep. Boucher led the NHL in assists three times and was top 10 in points seven times in nine seasons from 1926–27 to 1934–35 while never accumulating more than 18 penalty minutes.

Boucher was from Ottawa and began his pro career with the Senators in 1921–22, the Byngs' first season in the capital city. But while his brother George starred with the Senators, Frank spent the rest of their term in Canada playing with the Vancouver Maroons. He didn't return to the NHL until the 1926–27 season, when he joined the New York Rangers. Though Lady Byng had met Frank, and knew his brother, it's pretty hard to believe she continued to follow the NHL closely enough from England for the next eight years to have been aware of Boucher's exploits.

That being said, it really is true she agreed to donate another trophy and let Boucher keep the original.

Here's how it happened.

Despite having already won the award six times, it was claimed that Frank Boucher had never actually seen the Lady Byng Trophy before winning it for the seventh time in 1935. Shortly after the 1934–35 NHL season, Boucher was back in his hometown of Ottawa for a charity game involving local pros from the NHL and the minors. (The original Senators had moved to St. Louis that year.) The game was played on April 16, 1935. NHL president Frank Calder was there that night and presented the trophy to Boucher as part of the evening's festivities.

It wasn't yet Boucher's to keep, but the wheels were in motion.

In the *Ottawa Journal* that same April 16, 1935, sports editor Walter Gilhooly wrote an open letter to Lady Byng. In what was really just his column for the day, Gilhooly recapped the history of the trophy since its donation. "Between 1925 and 1935 lie 11 full hockey seasons," he writes, "and … three players [Frank Nighbor twice, Billy Burch and Joe Primeau] held it through four of them. What disposition of the trophy was made through the other seven? Well, Lady Byng, it may be difficult for you to believe since you are so far away from the center of things — I mean the hockey center, of course — but one single player claimed it in those seven years, and that player is Frankie Boucher."

Gilhooly added, "The suggestion so often made, and that I would like to convey to you is this — that the cup be withdrawn from competition and your trustees be instructed to turn it over to Frank Boucher to become his permanent possession."

It's not clear if Gilhooly was aware of it or not, but Lady Byng was visiting Washington when his letter appeared in the *Ottawa Journal*. Upon the contents being communicated to her, she got in touch with officials at Rideau Hall and wrote that she would be pleased to see the original trophy given to Boucher and that she would replace it with a new one. Colonel Willis O'Connor of Government House then contacted Frank Ahearn, the former owner of the Senators, who was serving as a Member of Parliament in Ottawa. On April 24, 1935, Ahearn sent a telegraph to Calder, who made it happen.

Although Calder couldn't be there himself, Boucher was given the Lady Byng Trophy for his permanent possession on April 25, 1935, at a civic banquet honoring four Ottawa-born players who had won the Stanley Cup that season as members of the Montreal Maroons. In Calder's absence, Thomas Clancy — father of King Clancy — presented the trophy to Boucher. Frank Nighbor was there that night and spoke about the importance of pro hockey in Ottawa, and his belief that Ottawa could still support an NHL club. (The NHL wouldn't return to Ottawa until 1992.) He also spoke about the positive role models hockey players could be with "fighting heart, and not fighting fists," and his hope that Lady Byng would donate a substitute trophy in order that the ideals of clean play and ability would be carried on.

A day later, Colonel O'Connor sent a letter to Calder, and on May 14, Calder wrote to Lady Byng at the address in Essex, England, O'Connor had provided. From a copy of the letter preserved among the NHL archives, Calder wrote about the public presentation and assured Lady Byng that Boucher was "the very finest type of athlete and a sportsman in every sense of the word," adding that he "has become in no small way an idol to the boys of this country."

In his letter, Calder also thanked Lady Byng for agreeing to donate a new trophy, and by August 12, 1935, it had arrived from England at Calder's office in Montreal. Boucher may well have won that new trophy too during the 1935–36 season, except that in June of 1935, he had written to Calder saying he would like to withdraw from further competition for the honor.

The Ottawa Journal, *March 16, 1935.*

"It's just the sort of sporting thing that Frank would do," Calder told reporters.

Though there's no record of it, Lady Byng likely approved of that too.

Original Up in Flames

On February 23, 1965, the *Ottawa Journal* reported on a fire that swept through a farm home owned by Frank Boucher in Kemptville, Ontario, some 25 miles south of the Canadian capital. Boucher himself was living in Regina at the time, where he served as commissioner of junior hockey in Saskatchewan. The house was occupied by his son, Earl, Earl's wife and their five children. All escaped without injury. Earl's wife thought the fire may have been caused by mice chewing through electrical wires. She estimated the damage at $25,000. Among the items lost in the fire was the original Lady Byng Trophy and the seven small miniatures of it Boucher had been presented with over the years.

"You know, you just take them for granted until you lose them," Boucher said in a follow-up story the next day. "When you're out in the country and fire hits, the best you can hope for is a bucket brigade. And even that's not much good." Boucher said he lost all his hockey mementos in the fire, including a large painting of him with linemates Bill and Bun Cook, which he cherished.

"I am particularly sorry about losing the Lady Byng Trophy because I had promised I would leave it in my will to the Hockey Hall of Fame," he said. "I had been considering turning over the Lady Byng Trophy to Bobby Hewitson (curator of the Hockey Hall of Fame) sooner. But it's like I said. You take these things for granted. Then you lose them."

Frank Boucher.

Frank Boucher and Leo Durocher

From the *Ottawa Evening Journal*, December 3, 1949:

[Coach] Frank Boucher of the New York Rangers has taken a leaf from Leo Durocher's book. When [New York Giants manager] Durocher made his crack about "nice guys not winning pennants" there were protests from baseball followers. But in a recent interview with the *Detroit Times*, Boucher agrees.

"I can say the same thing in regard to the National [Hockey] League," says Frank, "and no one will raise an eyebrow."

He admits that some who look back to his seven Lady Byng Trophy victories might be a bit surprised at the statement, but Frank

The Rangers top line featuring Bill Cook, Frank Boucher and Bun Cook of the New York Rangers in 1927.

claims he has come to the conclusion that "clean hockey no longer pays."

"That's the modern trend and it must be recognized even by me.... It's become increasingly evident that aggressive hockey — the kind that invariably draws penalties — is winning hockey."

The Ranger official claims that the teams are now bringing the game to a point near "mayhem on ice," and maintains Rangers are going to do the same. He points to the failure of officials to check up closely on the Leafs' tactics while winning three titles in as many years and no one doing much about it. In future he claims Rangers will "hit them and let the penalties fall where they may."

It's Boucher's notion that the icing rule [where a shorthanded team is allowed to ice the puck] nullifies the effects of penalties to a great degree and doesn't make it worthwhile avoiding them.

The Lady Byng Memorial Trophy

After the end of his term as Governor General on August 5, 1926, Lord Byng and his wife left Canada on September 30. They returned to their home, Thorpe Hall, in Thorpe-le-Soken, Essex, England. They continued to travel together, visiting friends in South Africa, Jamaica, California and Canada, until Lord Byng's death in 1935.

With the outbreak of World War II in 1939, British Home Secretary Sir John Anderson urged the widowed Lady Byng to evacuate to Canada for the duration. She remained in Canada from 1940 until the end of the war in 1945, writing her memoir, *Up the Stream of Time*, while there. She would die on June 20, 1949, back home at Thorpe Hall in Essex, at the age of 79. Three days later, the *Ottawa Citizen* ran a story headlined "Hockey Star Pays Tribute to Lady Byng." In it, Frank Boucher recalled their encounters.

"I am very sorry to hear of her death," said Boucher. "Lady Byng was a great hockey enthusiast. I don't think she ever missed a professional game in Ottawa when she was in the city. She was a great admirer of sportsmanly players and she often talked to Frank Nighbor about his clean play."

Boucher, who had lived in the Ottawa neighborhood of New Edinburgh, near Rideau Hall, remembered Viscount and Lady Byng well. "There were times when they used to stroll in our back yard for a friendly chat about hockey. One time, I remember, [my brother] George and I were doing some work on our car when Their Excellencies came into the yard and we had quite the talk about sport. Viscount and Lady Byng often invited the hockey players and their wives to Government House and she took great delight in showing us the flowers in which she took keen interest,... [but] even during the summer time... we talked hockey. In fact, Lady Byng liked to talk about the game all year around.... Lady Byng was the most democratic and mixed with the crowd at all times. Viscount Byng looked stern but he, too, was very friendly when you met him."

Accounts of the Lady Byng Trophy generally state that after her death in 1949, the NHL presented a new trophy and changed the name to the Lady Byng Memorial Trophy. That's all true... although the new prize wasn't actually discussed until almost a year after her death and wasn't presented for the first time until after the 1950–51 season.

In the verbatim minutes from the NHL Board of Governors meeting on May 30, 1950, NHL president Clarence Campbell is reported as saying:

> I already mentioned earlier in the day the matter of the replacement of the Lady Byng Trophy, because it is hardly up to the standard of the other trophies which the League has. Seeing that Lady Byng passed away last winter [*sic*], this would be an appropriate time to make any change if it is going to be done.

A motion was carried to leave the matter up to Campbell, who said he would "consult her executors in order that this trophy be withdrawn and a memorial trophy substituted." At a league meeting on September 8, 1950, Campbell reported that the personal representative of the late Viscountess Byng of Vimy had approved the proposal, and it was unanimously agreed by the NHL governors that Campbell should secure a suitable Lady Byng Memorial Trophy.

Following the 1950–51 NHL season, the winner of the league's award for sportsmanship was announced on April 30, 1951. A press release for the following morning went out from NHL publicity director and statistician Ken McKenzie saying that the "first winner of the new Lady Byng Memorial Trophy is... Leonard Patrick (Red) Kelly, high scoring rearguard of the Detroit Red Wings." The release further states: "The Lady Byng Memorial Trophy is presented by the National Hockey League in memory of the late Countess Byng of Vimy.... The Lady Byng Memorial Trophy replaces the Lady Byng Trophy but the basis for selection remains exactly the same."

Lady Byng's memorial award would continue to be presented annually to "the player adjudged to have exhibited the best type of sportsmanship and gentlemanly conduct combined with a high standard

Edgar Laprade during the NHL All-Star Game on October 10, 1949 at Maple Leaf Gardens.

Quote ... Unquote

"I do not care to be high-sticked. I was provoked — not once, but twice. The first time I was in a face-off, and he came charging at me with his elbows. I never liked Kyle, even when he was a teammate. Who can think about the Lady Byng Trophy when there is a stick in your face?"

— **Edgar Laprade** of the New York Rangers, 1949–50 winner of the Lady Byng Trophy, quoted by the Associated Press on November 27, 1951, after getting into his first fight at Madison Square Garden against former Ranger Gus Kyle of the Boston Bruins in a game on November 21

of playing ability during the season." The new trophy was engraved with a plate commemorating all the previous winners, from Frank Nighbor in 1924–25 through Edgar Laprade in 1949–50.

Norris Memorial Trophy

Three years after winning the inaugural Lady Byng Memorial Trophy, Red Kelly would win it again for the 1953–54 season. He also became the first winner of the James Norris Memorial Trophy as the league's best defenseman that year.

Norris had bought the NHL franchise in Detroit in 1932 and changed its name from the Falcons to the Red Wings. After he died on December 4, 1952, his daughter Marguerite Norris, president of the Red Wings (and the first woman to have her name engraved on the Stanley Cup), and sons Bruce Norris (vice president of the Red Wings) and James D. "Jim" Norris, an executive with the Chicago Black Hawks,

The James Norris Memorial Trophy is awarded annually to the NHL's best defenceman.

and another daughter, Eleanor Kneibler, offered a trophy in his memory to the NHL. It was accepted by the club owners on September 24, 1953.

Rewarding the Rookies

For the 1932–33 season, sports editors who had been tasked by the Canadian Press with voting for NHL All-Star Teams since 1930–31 (selections of the First and Second All-Star Teams included a coach from 1930–31 through 1945–46) were given the additional task of selecting an outstanding rookie. This decision was completely independent from the NHL.

When the All-Star Teams were announced in March of 1933, there seems to be no mention in any newspaper of Carl Voss (who had begun the season with the New York Rangers but was sold to Detroit on December 11, 1932) being named as the rookie

selection. Still, his win was confirmed the following year in the stories about Russ Blinco of the Montreal Maroons being named top rookie for 1933–34.

"Like Carl Voss, who won this distinction a year ago," read the Canadian Press dispatch of March 17, 1934, "Blinco is a center." Sweeney Schriner of the New York Americans (1934–35) and Mike Karakas of the Black Hawks (1935–36) were the top rookies for the next two years, but there was a new prize awarded to the NHL's Rookie of the Year the following season.

As noted by Andy Lytle in the *Toronto Daily Star* on February 3, 1937: "Frank Calder, president of the NHL, will donate a trophy to be awarded to the best rookie of the 1936–37 season.... Mr. Calder plans an ornate bauble, one that will be awarded in perpetuity and serve to designate the best rookie year after year, as well as to commemorate the memory of the donor who has already enjoyed 24 years of official hockey life."

When Voss won the first rookie honor in 1933, there appears to have been no criteria for what defined a rookie. Before spending the 1932–33 season with the Rangers and Red Wings, Voss had already played 12 games with the Toronto Maple Leafs late in 1926–27 and two more in 1928–29. However, according to a document on the history of the Calder Trophy in the NHL archives, "Canadian Press, realizing that there was potential for great embarrassment without clearly defined criteria, decided for the 1933–34 season the players would only be eligible for [the outstanding rookie] award if they had not played in a regular-season game previously." Russ Blinco, Sweeney Schriner and Mike Karakas all met the criteria.

When news of Frank Calder's new rookie trophy was first reported, Calder said he would ask the governors in each NHL city to nominate two writers to make the selection, but when those NHL governors approved the donation of the trophy as part of a four-hour meeting in New York on February 24, 1937,

Carl Voss of the Ottawa Senators stands by the side boards prior to an NHL game during the 1933–34 season.

the NHL president announced the selection would continue to be based on the best rookie vote in the annual Canadian Press All-Star poll. There is no mention of eligibility criteria in the minutes of the NHL meeting, although newspaper accounts would later make it clear that the criteria would be the same as it had been in recent years and that those eligible for the new trophy would have to be "true rookies." When the results of the CP poll were released on March 22 and reported in newspapers the next day, Syl Apps of the Toronto Maple Leafs was named the first winner of the Calder Trophy.

Apps had played football at McMaster University in Hamilton, Ontario, and led the Ontario Hockey League Senior A division in scoring with the Hamilton Tigers during the 1935–36 season. Having won a gold medal in pole-vaulting at the 1934 British Commonwealth

Games, he competed in the pole vault at the 1936 Berlin Olympics and finished sixth. After the Olympics, Apps decided not to go out for the Hamilton Tigers football team of "the Big Four" Interprovincial Rugby Football Union (a forerunner of the Hamilton Tiger-Cats in the Canadian Football League), but had yet to determine if he would sign a pro contract to play hockey for the Maple Leafs.

"In our circle, professional athletes were not looked upon as the right sort," Apps told Stan Fischler for his book *Those Were the Days* (1976). "Molly [his girlfriend, Molly Marshall] told me the chance with the Leafs was a golden opportunity. I decided to sign although I was scared when I went to see [Conn] Smythe."

Black-haired, blue-eyed and handsome, the 6-foot, 185-pound Apps was the Jean Béliveau of his day and made instantly good in the NHL. His 29 assists during the 48-game 1936–37 season were tops in the league and, with 16 goals, his 45 points were just one back of league leader Sweeney Schriner. "That Syl Apps would be adjudged the best rookie of the National Hockey League season has been a foregone conclusion these past few weeks," wrote *Globe and Mail* sports editor Tommy Munn on March 23, 1937, "but official announcement of the award calls for congratulations to Sylvanus, by Jiminy."

Frank Calder certainly thought so, and when Apps was honored in his hometown of Paris, Ontario, at a dinner on June 11, 1937, as part of a three-day local Lions Club carnival, the NHL president rode the train from Montreal that day to be in Paris to present his namesake trophy to the first winner. When handing over the award that evening, Calder told Apps and the large audience assembled that, since Apps could not be a rookie twice, for that reason, he had decided to give him the trophy to keep outright. Andy Lytle of the *Toronto Star* had more about that in his Behind the Sports Cue column on June 14:

The First Calder Vote

The 28 writers voting for the best rookie in 1936–37 were asked to rank three players. In compiling the vote, three points were given for a first choice, two for second and one for third. The most points possible was 84. Here are the total points earned in the first vote for the Calder Trophy, along with the statistics of the players:

Player, Team	Votes	GP	G	A	PTS	PIM
			W-L-T		SO	GAA
Syl Apps, Toronto	79	48	16	29	45	17
Gordie Drillon, Toronto	25	41	16	17	33	2
Ray Getliffe, Boston*	17	48	16	15	31	28
Neil Colville, NY Rangers*	16	45	10	18	28	33
George Brown, Canadiens	13	27	4	6	10	10
Turk Broda, Toronto	8	45	22-19-4		3	2.29
Jimmy Fowler, Toronto	5	48	7	11	18	22

*Despite the ruling about "true rookies," Getliffe and Colville had each played one game with their teams in 1935–36.

[Maple Leafs boss Conn] Smythe said he had been up to Paris where he saw Frank Calder give away a beautiful trophy to Sylvanus Apps and actually enjoy telling "Apesy" it was his own for life.

Smythe and your correspondent have a slight though unofficial interest in that trophy for the best rookie in hockey during the 1936–37 season. We sold the idea to Mr. Calder one day in his Montreal office. At the time, none of us knew what form the behest would take. We had merely succeeded in selling the idea to the league president. His was to be the pain of purchase entirely.

Riding up from Montreal to Paris with the trophy, Mr. Calder, with plenty of time for reflection, decided it would be a shame to present Apps with anything short of absolute possession. It was something he could never win again. His rookie days were permanently over.

So that is what he did and to the devil with the initial cost, the upkeep, or anything else. "It must have cost him plenty, too," confided Smythe. "It's a large handsome cup with as much color and glint to it as Apps himself showed on the ice when he was really going to town last winter."

Be-"Fore!"

Before donating the Calder Trophy for Rookie of the Year in 1937, Frank Calder had previously awarded a Calder Trophy annually to winners at the NHL's summer golf tournament.

The Calder Memorial Trophy

Until his death on February 4, 1943, Frank Calder continued to purchase a keepsake every year for the annual winner of the rookie voting after giving Syl Apps his original trophy in 1937. (The next five winners were Cully Dahlstrom, Chicago; Frank Brimsek, Boston; Kilby MacDonald, Rangers; John Quilty, Montreal; Grant Warwick, Rangers.) After the 1942–43 season, at the NHL's annual meeting in New York, which concluded on May 8, newspapers on Monday, May 10, reported among other items of league business that the Calder Trophy would be perpetuated with the Frank Calder Memorial Trophy.

Red Dutton had taken over the job of heading up the NHL upon Calder's death and had sent a letter to the NHL governors in each city on February 9, 1943. "It has been brought to the notice of this office that the Calder Trophy which the late Frank Calder gave to the outstanding rookie voted by the Press, was a trophy he himself donated. I would appreciate it if the owners of the clubs in the National Hockey League would inform this office if it is their desire to continue this award."

Letters quickly came back to Dutton supporting the idea of a permanent rookie trophy to honor Calder's memory, and the minutes of the NHL's annual meeting on May 8 show that, on a motion of Lester Patrick of the Rangers, seconded by Senator Donat Raymond of the Canadiens, "it was resolved that the Calder Trophy for the best rookie of the year … be perpetuated under the name of the Calder Memorial Trophy."

Still, it would be another two years, at an NHL meeting in Montreal on June 14, 1945, before the governors approved a design for the new Calder Memorial Trophy. As the CP story the next day noted, "Previously, a smaller individual trophy was presented each year for the permanent possession of the winner." The *Gazette* in Montreal reported, "Replicas will be given to the prize rookie each year," while adding — somewhat sarcastically — "Up to now, they have been getting three cheers and a piece of plate." Official approval for the new trophy was given by the governors at an NHL meeting in Montreal on September 7, 1945.

In Between Trophies

On February 13, 1943, Red Dutton wrote a letter to Robert R. Duncan, a governor of the Boston Bruins, who had written to him in reply to Dutton's original letter regarding the Calder Trophy on February 9. "Previous to Mr. Calder's death," wrote Dutton in his follow-up letter, "he had contacted Mr. [Alex] Falle, who made up this trophy for him each year and I am now going ahead with Mr. Calder's plans for this year."

Two days later, on February 15, the *Montreal Star* noted, "One of Frank Calder's last official acts was to select the trophy [for this season] and pay for it, as was his custom, out of his own pocket." On March 18, 1943, Frank Selke of the Maple Leafs told Toronto reporters the Calder Trophy had arrived at Maple Leaf Gardens and would be presented to Rookie of the Year Gaye Stewart by acting NHL president Red Dutton before a playoff game with Detroit on March 25. It was presented just after the playing of the national anthem and before the opening faceoff.

In the spring of 1944, Red Dutton made another trophy presentation to 1943–44 Rookie of the Year Gus Bodnar of the Maple Leafs. Since the Calder Memorial Trophy was still more than a year away, it seems likely that Dutton had arranged for another individual award from Falle as Calder always had. Bodnar received his trophy before the second period of a playoff game against the visiting Montreal Canadiens on March 25, 1944. His Calder selection over the Canadiens' Vezina Trophy–winning rookie goalie Bill Durnan was a controversial one — especially in

Gus Bodnar and Frank McCool pose for a dressing room photo as members of the Toronto Maple Leafs during the 1944–45 NHL season.

Montreal. The *Montreal Star* of March 27, 1944, said fans at Maple Leaf Gardens "chided" Toronto native Durnan prior to the ceremony for Bodnar, "but Canadiens led in the applause by rapping the ice vigorously with their sticks."

In the Navy

With more and more players looking to do their part during World War II, Maple Leafs rookie and 1942–43

Calder Trophy winner Gaye Stewart sought a commission in the Royal Canadian Naval Volunteer Reserve at Prince Edward Island during the summer of 1943. Newspaper stories on July 26 report on him sending a letter home to his parents in Fort William, Ontario (now a part of Thunder Bay). "Gaye also sent a parcel containing all his 'civvies,'" the story said. "Tucked among the shirts and socks, momma and poppa found the Calder Trophy which Gaye won last year as the National Hockey League's outstanding rookie."

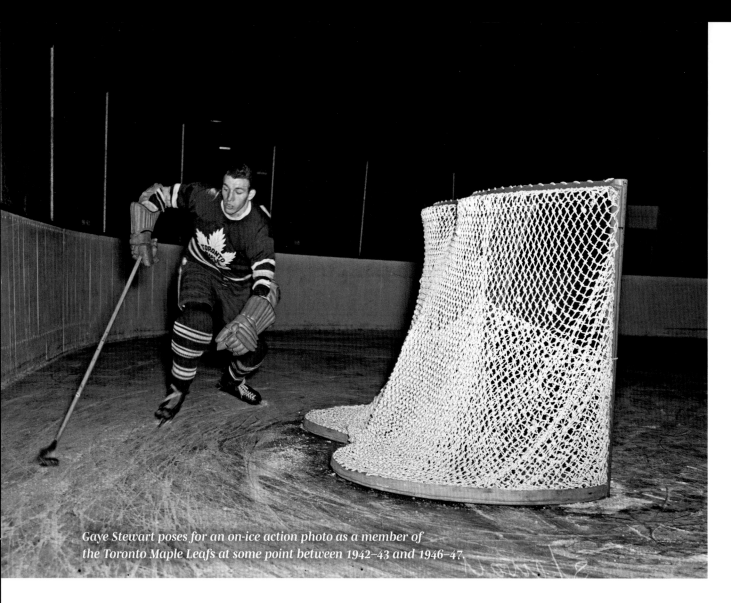

Gaye Stewart poses for an on-ice action photo as a member of the Toronto Maple Leafs at some point between 1942–43 and 1946–47.

Rookie Ruling

One of Frank Calder's last decisions regarding his trophy came in December 1942. At the time, there had been discussion as to whether or not Gaye Stewart would be eligible for the Calder Trophy after having played for the Toronto Maple Leafs during the Stanley Cup Final against Detroit the previous spring.

The then 18-year-old Stewart (he turned 19 on June 28, 1942) had made a meteoric rise through the Maple Leafs system in 1941–42, starting with the Toronto Marlboros junior team, moving up to the senior Marlboros and then going pro with the Hershey Bears. Stewart was called up to the Maple Leafs after the Bears lost the American Hockey League Calder Cup final (also named for Frank Calder) to the Indianapolis Capitals, the Red Wings' top farm club. When Toronto won Game 4 in the Stanley Cup Final against Detroit after falling behind

three games to nothing, Stewart was added to the lineup for Game 5 and helped the Leafs to a 3–0 victory. NHL records also show him in the lineup for Games 6 and 7 as Toronto completed its historic comeback.

On December 15, 1942, the *Globe and Mail* reported:

> The Canadian Press, which conducts the annual poll, has received from Frank Calder, NHL president and donor of the trophy, a ruling that participation in league playoffs is no disqualification in the voting as long as the player concerned did not take part in regular season play the previous season.

"Frankly," said Calder, "I think an injustice would be done the boy if he were barred because of his few minutes in the playoffs."

Stewart played 48 of 50 games for the Leafs as a rookie in 1942–43, collecting 24 goals and 23 assists for 47 points, and on March 12, 1943, he was named the winner of the Calder Trophy. Of the ballots cast by 27 sports writers in NHL cities, Stewart received 21 first-place votes and four seconds to easily outdistance Glen Harmon of the Montreal Canadiens and Don Gallinger of the Boston Bruins.

Gaye Stewart, a member of the Toronto Maple Leafs, accepts the Calder Trophy from NHL president Red Dutton after Stewart was named the league's best rookie for the 1942–43 NHL season.

Rookie Rules

At an NHL Board of Governors meeting in Toronto on January 21, 1944, a motion was made by Boston's Art Ross, and seconded by Detroit's Jack Adams, that the league's managing director (Red Dutton) and Toronto's Frank Selke "be asked to draw up conditions covering all trophies of the NHL." A year later, at a board meeting in Montreal on February 2, 1945, conditions of award with respect to the new Calder Memorial Trophy were discussed, and it was resolved that "any player that participates in three or more League or Stanley Cup [playoff] games shall be automatically barred from consideration."

Just two years later, at a governors meeting in New York on March 4, 1947, the restrictions on rookies changed. As of then, it would take up to 20 games in any previous season, or participation of any number of games in two previous seasons, to deem a player ineligible for rookie honors. Playoff games would not count at all.

These new regulations remained in place until a meeting in Toronto on September 24, 1968, when the rules for the Calder Trophy were amended to read: "To be eligible for this award, a player cannot have played in more than 25 games in any single season nor in six or more games in each of any two preceding seasons."

Prior to the 1979–80 season, when four former World Hockey Association franchises — and many former WHA players — were added to the NHL, the rules for the Calder Trophy were changed again. While the game counts remained the same (and have to this day), the line "in any major professional league" was added. This change, of course, would deny Wayne Gretzky the Calder Trophy that season … although Raymond Bourque, who won it instead, also went on to a Hall of Fame career. "I guess it's always nice to have individual awards," said Gretzky in a UPI story on

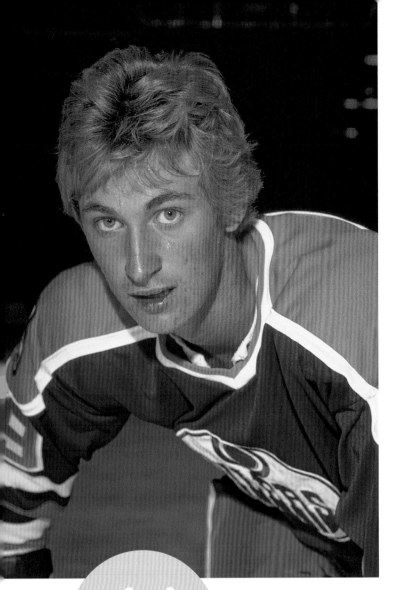

Quote ... Unquote

"Twenty years from now, Wayne Gretzky probably won't give a damn about the absence of silverware to remind him of his rookie NHL season. By 1999, it is likely he will have collected so many prizes that his trophy room will resemble the main salon of the Hockey Hall of Fame."

— **Jim Coleman**, syndicated columnist, writing about Gretzky's ineligibility for the Calder Trophy in the *Edmonton Journal*, April 7, 1980

April 1, 1980. "As far as the rookie award is concerned, I knew before I signed a WHA contract I would be ineligible, so I can't worry about that."

The rules were changed one final time before the 1990–91 season. After 31-year-old Sergei Makarov won the Calder in 1989–90 despite many seasons of elite-level (quasi-amateur) hockey in the Soviet Union, an amendment was made saying that to be eligible for this award, a player must not have attained his 26th birthday by September 15th of the season in which he is eligible.

Goalies and Point-Getters

At a semiannual meeting of the NHL in Montreal on Saturday, May 14, 1927, the league accepted the Montreal Canadiens' donation of a trophy to honor their late goalie Georges Vézina. Vézina had died of tuberculosis on Saturday, March 27, 1926, and throughout the 1926–27 NHL season, there had been talk that Canadiens management was planning some sort of lasting tribute to him. At a banquet for Canadiens superstar Howie Morenz in Montreal on March 12, 1927, and after delivering a toast to the man of honor, Léo Dandurand announced that the directors of the Canadiens had decided the conditions under which the Georges Vezina Trophy — Trophée Georges Vezina — would be awarded.

Newspapers reported the Vezina Trophy would go to the goalie with the best goals-against average. In truth, it would go to the goalie on the team that allowed the fewest goals. This would be the case until the introduction of a new trophy in memory of William Jennings, which was accepted at an NHL Board of Governors meeting in Palm Beach, Florida, on December 8, 1981.

Bill Jennings had been the president of the New York Rangers since 1962, and as a league governor

Charlie Conacher poses for an on-ice action portrait with the Toronto Maple Leafs no later than the 1934–35 NHL season.

he was a key figure in NHL expansion in 1967 and the league's growth from six to 21 teams by 1979. He died of cancer at the age of 60 on August 17, 1981. Starting with the 1981–82 season, the new William M. Jennings Trophy would be awarded to the goalie or goalies playing a minimum of 25 games on the team allowing the fewest goals each season. Since that time, the Vezina Trophy has been awarded by a vote of the NHL's general managers to the goalie adjudged to be the best in the league.

It's unclear why it took the NHL 20 years after the donation of the Vezina Trophy in 1927 to recognize

the league's best goaltender before someone finally chose to honor the league's best scorer. Charlie Conacher, a two-time NHL scoring champion (and five-time goal-scoring champion), certainly thought it was odd. In a daily column he wrote for Toronto's *Globe and Mail* during the 1936–37 season, Conacher, who had recently noted the intention of Frank Calder to donate a trophy for the top rookie, wrote on February 12, 1937, that until he won his first scoring title in 1933–34, "I was always under the impression that there was a trophy for realizing this ambition…. Then, the year I led the league I found that with the honour went no prize that I could keep for later years."

Conacher elaborated on his thoughts to honor the NHL's top scorer the next day:

> After considering the subject from every angle I am of the opinion that even a trophy for the scoring leader wouldn't be quite enough. If baseball can give cash prizes to the most valuable players why shouldn't hockey, which is certainly a major sport, do the same?
>
> …After all, while the hockey players may be well paid, they're not overpaid. The league places a salary limit of $7,000 in the rules. I'll admit that $7,000 a season is a lot of money, but any athlete's playing career is limited. Another thing that should be considered is that a man's income isn't limited in any ordinary business. Nobody ever told John D. Rockefeller that he had to quit taking money when his income reached a certain figure.
>
> I really think that this subject is entitled to serious consideration from Mr. Calder, and the National League Governors. They can secure a handsome trophy without trouble, and they can well afford a bonus for the leading scorer.

It would be another 10 seasons before the NHL introduced a policy of cash rewards to its players. When Clarence Campbell became the new league president at an NHL governors meeting on September 4, 1946, the league also announced that trophy winners and First-Team All-Stars would receive a bonus of $1,000. On March 4, 1947, President Campbell announced that the league governors had confirmed those cash rewards and had also introduced a pool of money for players (18 men per roster) based on where their teams finished in the regular-season standings — $1,000 for a first-place finish; $500 for second; $350 for third; $150 for fourth — as well as another $1,000 bonus to the players on each team for the playoff series they won, with $500 going to the losing team.

At another governors meeting on June 3, 1947, the NHL finally offered cash prizes to its top scorers, with the league leader to earn $1,000 and the runner-up to receive $500. (The league also offered $500 apiece to players chosen as Second-Team All-Stars.) Still, it would take another year before someone donated a trophy to the NHL for its leading scorer.

Art Ross Trophy: Take One

In the fall of 1910, when Cecil Hart expanded his Stars baseball empire onto the ice with the Stars of the Montreal City Hockey League, the Montreal *Gazette* of November 26, 1910, reported on a team meeting held two days before. The story noted that Art Ross, "the hockey star and slugging first baseman of the Stars Baseball Club of past seasons, was chosen as coach."

At the time, Ross was one of the National Hockey Association (NHA) players fighting league owners over the $5,000-per-team salary cap. He would eventually sign, and suit up, with the Montreal Wanderers, so it's unclear whether he ever did coach the Stars. (The database on the website of the Society for International Hockey Research lists Cecil Hart as both a player and coach with the Stars that year.) Still, Ross did referee some games in the city league that winter. A more important contribution to the league was his donation of the Art Ross Trophy.

Often referred to in that era as the Art Ross Cup, the silver jug was actually engraved with the name Art Ross Trophy. It was originally one of two championship trophies, along with the Jubilee Cup, competed for by the teams in the Montreal City Hockey League. Beyond donating it, Ross had little involvement with the Art Ross Trophy/Cup, as trustees Cecil Hart and

The original Art Ross Trophy, purchased by Art Ross in 1910 for competition in the Montreal City Hockey League.

Eddie St. Pierre oversaw its competition. Still, Ross would donate a similar trophy to the Quebec City Hockey League in December of 1913, which newspapers also referred to as the Art Ross Cup.

Earlier that year, in February of 1913, the Montreal city league moved its games from the Jubilee Rink to the Montreal Arena and dropped the Jubilee Cup from its competition. The Jubilee Cup had always been a challenge trophy, available to teams in other Montreal-based amateur leagues as well. Now the Art Ross Trophy/Cup would assume that role. It soon became available to teams all across the province of Quebec and was later recognized as emblematic of the amateur championship of Eastern Canada and the United States as well.

The last competition for the Art Ross Trophy took place in March of 1920, when Hochelaga of the Montreal City Hockey League defeated St. Regis of Sherbrooke in a two-game, total-goals series with a 13–2 victory in Montreal on March 8 and a 3–1 loss in Sherbrooke three nights later. There appears to be no record as to why competition for the Art Ross Trophy ceased after 1920. Art Ross was an all-around athlete who starred in many sports. During this time, there was also an Art Ross Trophy available for golf at the St. Lambert Country Club outside of Montreal, where Ross was a member, and also an Art Ross Trophy for marksmen at a Montreal hunting club.

Art Ross Trophy: Take Two

On November 16, 1920, the following story appeared on page 3 of the English-language newspaper the *Quebec Telegraph* of Quebec City:

TROPHY FOR QUEBEC CITY HOCKEY LEAGUE AGAIN

Cup Donated by Art Ross Some Years Ago Will Again Make Its Appearance in Local Hockey Circles · · · Was Won by Emmetts, Then Stowed Away in Telegraph Vault · · · Art Ross Appoints New Trustees

A few days ago I went scouting around the office, and in my travels discovered to my surprise a silver cup, well wrapped up as if it were to be kept in safety for years and years. Upon enquiry I was informed in rather a vague way that it was a hockey cup. That was about all that could be gathered.

Well, there was only one thing to do, and that was get down deeper into the matter and find out the why's and wherefore's etc. So I started to dive, and finally collected the following information from different sportsmen of the city who have been following hockey for several years.

About eight years ago [it was only seven] Mr. Art Ross, then one of the stars of the Wanderers Hockey Club of the National Hockey Association, had donated a silver trophy to the Quebec City Hockey League for competition. It was mentioned in the rules belonging to the cup that the trophy had to be held three years before the holders would become the permanent proprietors.

It seems that the first year that the cup was up for competition the championship of the Quebec City Hockey League was won by the Emmett Club and when they were presented with the silverware, the trustees of that time asked for a guarantee of $150, an amount exceeding the real value of the cup.

The Emmetts would not put up the amount so the cup was put away in the Telegraph vault for safe keeping and has been there from that date to this.

Not wishing to have a trophy lying useless in a vault I at once wrote to the donor, Mr. Art Ross, asking him in what manner he wished that I dispose of the cup. His answer, as received by me this morning, reads as follows:

Montreal, Nov. 15th, 1920
Art. Ross Sales Co., Ltd.
Sporting Editor, Quebec Telegraph,
Quebec City.

Dear Sir, – Replying to your favor of the 10th, I am glad you called my attention to the trophy which was donated to the Quebec Hockey League.

Might I suggest that you offer this cup for competition again in the present league and appoint as trustees the President of the League, whoever he may be this season, the Sporting Editor of Le Soleil and yourself.

I should imagine that the trustees mentioned, being connected with the press, generally would be able to take care of any difficulties arising.

Would suggest that you take this matter up with the other parties and would be glad to leave same entirely in your hands.

Yours very truly,
ART H. ROSS

As the above letter explains itself, I would be glad to get the cup in condition, and together with the other trustees of the cup, put it up for competition once more in the

City League, which really has no other trophy to compete for. Further information regarding the Quebec City League Cup will be published at a later date.

The writer of this article was likely Roy Halpin, who it would seem worked for the *Telegraph* and was later the coach and general manager of the Quebec Castors (Beavers). Quebec City directories from the era note an R. Halpin as a clerk, but an article in the French-language newspaper *Le Soleil* from Monday, March 7, 1921, mentions "Roy Halpin du Telegraph" in a story about the presentation of the Coupe Art Ross to the city league champion Royal Rifles at a luncheon the day before. The Royal Rifles won the championship of the city league by beating the Voltigeurs 2–1 on February 25, but later lost the Quebec Hockey Association title in an Allan Cup playoff when they were defeated 4–2 by McGill University on March 1.

It appears the 1921 victory by the Royal Rifles was the last hurrah for the Quebec City version of the Art Ross Trophy. Research by Marc Durand, a Quebec journalist and sports reporter, found a story in *Le Soleil* from February 11, 1922, reporting that a "magnifique" new trophy for the Quebec City league had been donated by a locally renowned merchant and sportsman, Napoleon Jacques (he owned a men's and boys' clothing business), for the 1921–22 season.

And a final note on the Emmetts, who had refused their city's Art Ross Trophy in its inaugural season of 1913–14. Interestingly, after winning the Quebec City Hockey League title in 1914, the Emmetts challenged the Montreal Victorias, city league champions of Montreal, for the first Art Ross Trophy, which the *Gazette* referred to on March 21, 1914 (the day of the game), as the Art Ross Challenge Cup. The Victorias won the game 11–0. The referees that night were former Montreal Wanderers goalie and future Hockey Hall

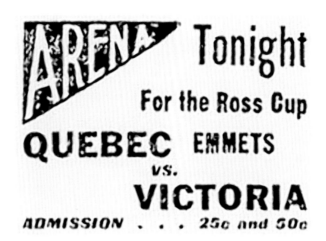

of Famer Riley Hern (a former teammate of Art Ross) and Léo Dandurand.

Art Ross Trophy: Take Three

At an NHL governors meeting in Boston on May 16, 1941, the governors accepted a new trophy offered by Art Ross. "The new trophy," wrote Herb Ralby in the *Boston Globe*, "which will bear the name of the Bruins vice president and general manager, will be awarded annually to the player voted the most outstanding performer of the season by other players in the league. No player may vote for a teammate. The trophy will be a perpetual one with the winner gaining possession of it for a period of one year as well as receiving a small replica for himself."

Ralby wrote that Ross had announced he was planning to donate such a trophy at the Bruins' Stanley Cup dinner upon returning to Boston after sweeping Detroit in the final in April. "He offered the trophy to the league yesterday and they accepted it with gratitude. It will be up for competition for the first time next winter."

Except it never went up for competition.

According to the History/Rules section of the Records page on the NHL's website, "due to wartime restrictions, the trophy was never awarded."

Milt Schmidt, Manager and Coach Art Ross who signals "V" for "Victory" and Frank Mario of the Boston Bruins in the dressing room on November 8, 1941.

It's hard to imagine what those restrictions might have been, although it's possible the United States entering World War II following the bombing of Pearl Harbor might have something to do with it. The NHL still had the Hart Trophy for its MVP, but 30 years later, in 1971, the NHL Players' Association created its own award so that the league's players could vote for the most outstanding player. The award was named after former Canadian prime minister Lester B. Pearson, who'd been appointed chairman of the NHLPA's sportsmen's mutual fund in 1970. It was renamed the Ted Lindsay Award in 2010 to honor the Detroit Red Wings star who'd led the fight to unionize the NHL's players in the late 1950s.

The Art Ross Trophy

In newspapers on June 3, 1948, in reporting on the NHL governors meeting in Montreal the previous day, it was announced that the governors had accepted a new trophy. The Art Ross Trophy, presented by Art Ross, vice president and managing director of the Boston Bruins, would be presented annually to the NHL's leading point-scorer.

More about the newest NHL award would appear in papers on June 29. Herb Ralby of the *Boston Globe* reported the trophy would be donated not just by the Bruins general manager but also by his two sons, Art Jr. and John, who had both served as pilots with the Royal Canadian Air Force during World War II. "The trophy," reported Ralby, "now being designed, will be held by the winning player's club the following year with a replica or suitable piece of silverware going to the player plus a $1,000 award from the league." When it was ready, the elaborate punch bowl of a trophy was inscribed as follows:

THE "ART" ROSS TROPHY
PRESENTED TO
THE NATIONAL HOCKEY LEAGUE
BY
ARTHUR H. ROSS
F/LT ARTHUR S. ROSS, D.F.C.
F/LT JOHN K. ROSS
TO BE AWARDED EACH YEAR TO THE LEAD-
ING SCORER

The Art Ross Trophy would go to the player whose total goals and assists combined to give him the greatest number of points. But it would appear that Ross had a fondness for players who could put the puck in the net, as the following conditions were outlined regarding who the trophy should be awarded to if two or more players had the same number of points.

▶ In case of a tie in points, to the player who has scored the greatest number of goals
▶ In case of a tie in points and goals, to the player who has participated in the fewest games
▶ In case of a continuing tie, to the player whose first goal came earliest in the season

Lester Patrick, Elmer Lach, Art Ross and NHL President Clarence Campbell.

Bobby Hull makes his way to the ice during the 1962–63 NHL season.

The Art Ross Trophy was awarded for the first time, retroactively, to 1947–48 scoring champion Elmer Lach of the Canadiens. It was presented to him partway through the 1948–49 season in a ceremony before a Boston Bruins game in Montreal on December 23, 1948.

Trophy Ties

Since the donation of the Art Ross Trophy, the race for the NHL scoring lead has ended in a tie three times. On all three occasions, only the first tie-breaking criterion was necessary.

In 1961–62, Bobby Hull of the Black Hawks and Andy Bathgate of the Rangers each had 84 points. Hull won the Art Ross Trophy because he had 50 goals to Bathgate's 28. Neither player won the Hart Trophy as MVP that year. It was awarded to Canadiens goalie Jacques Plante. Hull was third in the Hart vote, behind Plante and New York defenseman Doug Harvey. Bathgate was fifth, behind Gordie Howe in fourth.

In Wayne Gretzky's rookie season with the Edmonton Oilers in 1979–80, he made a late push in the scoring race to finish the schedule with 51 goals and 86 assists for 137 points. Marcel Dionne of the Kings also had 137 points, but with 53 goals and 84 assists, the Art Ross Trophy went to him. Gretzky was also denied the Calder Trophy that season but would win the Hart and the Lady Byng at the NHL Awards in 1980. (Dionne was second in both votes.) Gretzky went on to win the Art Ross Trophy a record 10 times.

The final tie to date came in 1994–95, when Pittsburgh's Jaromir Jagr and Philadelphia's Eric Lindros finished a lockout-shortened 48-game season (Lindros played only 46 games) with 70 points apiece. Jagr won the Art Ross with 32 goals to Lindros' 29. It was the first of five Art Ross Trophy wins for Jagr, but Lindros won the Hart that year with 10 first-place ballots and 63 voting points to Jagr's two and 27.

CHAPTER 2

Stanley Cup Rivals

The Stanley Cup is 25 years older than the NHL itself, so it's
obvious that other leagues used to play for hockey's top prize
too. For 10 seasons after the NHL was formed in 1917–18, its
league champions faced the champions of rival leagues,
which led to some pretty unusual playoff formats.

In the Early Days

NHL teams have played for the Stanley Cup since the formation of the league in 1917–18, but it wasn't until the league's 10th season that NHL teams started playing for it exclusively. The Stanley Cup is 25 years older than the NHL, so (obviously!) there were other teams in other leagues competing for the Cup in its early days. And even after the formation of the NHL, prior to that 10th season of 1926–27, the league champions had to face the champions of other rival professional leagues in order to claim hockey's top prize.

At its beginning in 1893 the Stanley Cup was a challenge trophy. The champions of the Amateur Hockey Association of Canada — which was considered a Quebec league despite the presence of an Ottawa team — were to play off against the champions of the Ontario Hockey Association. By 1896, the champions of Manitoba, playing in what was then known as the Manitoba and Northwest Hockey Association, were competing too. Soon the Cup competition was considered open to the senior champions of any officially recognized provincial hockey league. Stanley Cup games at this time might be played at any time

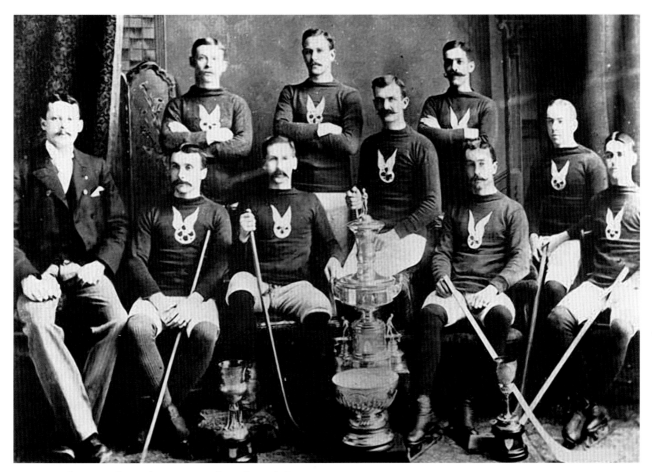

1893 Stanley Cup champion Montreal Hockey Club.

of the winter — before the hockey season, after the regular season, or even right in the middle of the schedule. The victor might be decided by a one-game winner takes all or a best of three but most often by a two-game, total-goals series.

What Was It Worth?

Though it's long been known the Stanley Cup was purchased for 10 guineas in 1893, the actual Canadian dollar equivalent of that amount has usually been recorded incorrectly as $48.67. That figure uses the longtime exchange value of the British pound and so has translated the value of 10 pounds instead of 10 guineas.

There were no guinea coins minted after 1814, and in 1816 the guinea was replaced by the pound as the major unit of British currency. But even as the coins ceased to circulate, the guinea still had a monetary function and a market value. That value was 21 shillings, as opposed to a pound, which was worth 20 shillings. In the modern decimalized currency — *decimalised* in Britain! — that's £1.05. Guineas became a form of aristocratic currency, often used to pay for luxury goods … such as fancy silver bowls.

So if the exchange rate in 1893 was 1 pound to 4.867 U.S. dollars (Canadian and U.S. currency was virtually at par in those days), then 10 guineas — which was the equivalent of 10.50 pounds — would equal $51.10 US/CDN based on 10.5 x 4.867.

As a comparison, a salary of $50 per month in 1893 would have been a decent living wage for the average working man. Today the original Stanley Cup might be worth about $3,000 or $4,000 Canadian. In fact, similar British antique bowls can often be found priced in that range.

The Game Goes Pro

Hockey in Canada was strictly amateur in the early days of the Stanley Cup. All sports in Canada were. Baseball players in the United States had been paid to play since 1869, and a football player first got paid in 1892. Even in England, players had been paid to play soccer (football) as early as 1885. Still, many Canadian sports administrators clung to the British amateur ideal of sports for sports' sake.

At the end of the 1890s and into the early 1900s, some Canadian hockey players were being paid to play in the United States. The Western Pennsylvania Hockey League in Pittsburgh generally disguised their payments by hiring players for cushy off-ice jobs. Some Canadian leagues and teams were soon thought to be acting similarly. The first openly professional hockey league — the International Hockey League — operated for three seasons from 1904 to 1907 with teams in Pittsburgh, in the Michigan cities of Calumet, Houghton and Sault Ste. Marie, and across the Canadian border in Sault Ste. Marie, Ontario.

By the fall of 1906, two of the top leagues in Canada — the Eastern Canada Amateur Hockey Association (ECAHA) and the Manitoba Hockey League — were considering the possibility of paying their players too. One of the key considerations at the time was what the Stanley Cup trustees would do if they did.

Would they allow the Stanley Cup to go pro?

People mostly thought not, but when the ECAHA (which included the Stanley Cup–champion Montreal Wanderers) announced their intention that November to allow professionals to play, trustee Philip Dansken Ross allowed the Wanderers to retain the Cup and take on challengers. In December, the Manitoba Hockey League, whose champion Kenora Thistles had already challenged the Wanderers (and would defeat them in January of 1907), also went pro.

P.D. Ross saw his main duty in regard to the Stanley Cup as ensuring that the former Governor General's gift to the game remain the top trophy in hockey, so if the top teams were going pro, the Cup would become a professional prize. The decision might seem like an obvious

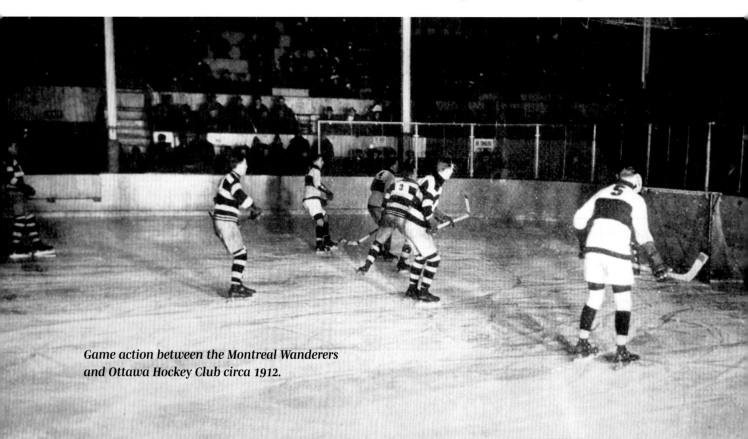

Game action between the Montreal Wanderers and Ottawa Hockey Club circa 1912.

Quote ... Unquote

"During a period of four years my own salary as a professional hockey player has varied from $1,000 to $2,700, the amount I got from Haileybury last season. But I would gladly give back all I have made as a professional player to regain my amateur standing and there are a good many other professionals who feel the same way I do. But once a man has become a professional, he naturally places the highest value he can on his skill. The pros of today who are standing out against the salary limit aren't asking for any princely salaries, but merely what their skill is worth as revenue producers."

> – **Art Ross**, speaking out against the NHA's proposed salary cap of $5,000 per team in a letter to the sports editor of the *Montreal Herald*, November 25, 1910

one — and obviously the right one — by today's standards, but it was quite controversial at the time.

In an era when most athletes played multiple sports, any player who signed a professional contract in hockey would need to relinquish his status not just as an amateur hockey player but as an amateur athlete altogether. Many hockey players also played football or rowed competitively. As pro hockey players, they would no longer be allowed to compete in those amateur sports. And it wasn't just the players who signed contracts who would be considered professional. According to the amateur rules of the day, any athlete would lose their amateur status merely by playing against a professional.

Once the decision was made, there would be no turning back. Though many sources still say the Stanley Cup didn't become a professional trophy until the formation of the National Hockey *Association* (forerunner to the NHL) in 1909–10, the Cup actually went pro as soon as the team holding it — the Montreal Wanderers — decided to pay some of its players before the 1906–07 season. By 1908, Sir Hugh Montagu Allan agreed to donate the Allan Cup to reward Canada's top senior amateur team. For many years, the Allan Cup playoffs were a big part of the annual hockey scene. It was a true Canadian championship. But since NHL expansion in 1967, the Allan Cup, and amateur hockey, has found its status significantly dwarfed by the Stanley Cup to the point where it has almost become irrelevant. So history has indeed proved the choice to let the Stanley Cup go pro was the right one.

Although there were many professional hockey leagues in Canada over the next few years, the ECHA (which dropped the word *Amateur* from its name in 1908–09) and then the NHA dominated the Stanley Cup scene, with the Wanderers, the Ottawa Senators and the Quebec Bulldogs winning league honors and defeating all comers. Challenges came from professional provincial leagues in Ontario, Manitoba, Alberta and the Maritimes. Those organizations would all fall by the wayside, but in 1911–12 a new professional league was formed in British Columbia that would give the NHA a run for its money.

The World Series of Hockey

The Pacific Coast Hockey Association (PCHA) was the brainchild of brothers Lester and Frank Patrick. Formerly top stars in the east — especially Lester, who won the Stanley Cup with the Wanderers in 1906 and

1907 — the Patrick brothers moved to Nelson, British Columbia, when their father relocated his Quebec lumber business to the Kootenay region of Canada's westernmost province.

Using funds from the sale of the family business in 1911, Lester and Frank built Canada's first artificial ice rinks in Vancouver and Victoria, raided NHA rosters for hockey talent and set up for business. Lester would own, operate and star for the PCHA team in Victoria.

Lester Patrick in 1912, with the Victoria Aristocrats.

Frank would do the same in Vancouver, while a third franchise was placed in New Westminster. The PCHA planned to challenge the NHA for the Stanley Cup at the end of the 1911–12 season, but the schedule wrapped up too late to accommodate more games.

In October 1912, while in the east hunting for more players for the second season of the PCHA, Lester Patrick spoke of his desire to do away with the Stanley Cup. He was fed up with trustee William Foran and the two-game format he and P.D. Ross seemed to favor. Patrick was known to be a baseball fan and a pretty good player in that sport too. No doubt inspired by the thrilling championship recently won by the Boston Red Sox over the New York Giants, Lester was quoted on October 18, 1912, by the *Globe* newspaper in Toronto as saying, "My idea is to have a series of games, such as the World Series, to decide the championship — not a series of two games, but one of seven or more, which would decide beyond all question which is the better team."

The second annual meeting of the PCHA was held at the Hotel Vancouver on November 15, 1912. Though the main item of business was the decision to continue raiding NHA rosters for talent, the Stanley Cup was also discussed. Asked about an attempt that season after the trustees had refused to let a late-season bid by the PCHA go forward on artificial ice in Boston in the spring of 1912, Frank Patrick told the *Vancouver Sun*: "Of course we intended to challenge for the Stanley Cup. We have made proposals to the National Hockey Association to form a commission, the winners of the two leagues playing a post-season series, the same as the world's baseball series, but so far they have not made any definite answer." In the *Vancouver Province* he said, "After we get the Cup we will talk about changing the conditions so that a series similar to the world's baseball series may be played annually instead of just two games."

The 1913 Sydney Millionaires team photo.

The 1912–13 PCHA season got under way on December 10, and with Cyclone Taylor newly added to Frank Patrick's roster, many predicted a championship for his Vancouver Millionaires. But as the season reached its midway point on January 31, it was Lester's Victoria team that was comfortably in front. (They were officially known that season as the Capitals, and sometimes the Senators, but they are usually referred to as the Aristocrats, although that wouldn't become the team name until the following year.) Lester announced that his team would challenge for the Stanley Cup if they won the PCHA championship, but with Quebec pulling away in the NHA, Lester quickly realized he would not be able to cover expenses if he took his team nearly 3,000 miles to play a two-game series in the tiny, old arena in Quebec City.

The Stanley Cup trustees would have allowed Quebec to play for the trophy on neutral ice in Toronto or out west in Victoria, but the Bulldogs would only defend the Stanley Cup at home — which was their right as champions. When Quebec did agree to travel to Victoria to face the Aristocrats, many newspapers reported the Stanley Cup would be at stake, but the *Victoria Colonist* of March 2, 1913, had been quite clear it wouldn't be: "As for putting [up] the Stanley Cup as the stake, [Bulldogs manager Mike Quinn] said that was absurd. Quebec will only defend the Stanley Cup at the Ancient Capital."

Victoria defeated Quebec two games to one amid widespread speculation that this "World's Professional Series" would mark the end of the Stanley Cup as hockey's top trophy. Whether or not anyone really intended to do away with the Stanley Cup in 1913, the most important aspect of the three-game series between Victoria and Quebec was that it paved the way for improved relations between the PCHA and the NHA.

Until then, bad blood caused by contract jumping had dominated any talks between the two leagues and had pushed to the back burner any discussion of creating a national hockey commission to oversee the professional game. However, with the PCHA winning games on the ice and at the box office (every NHA team lost money in 1912–13), a hockey commission was back in the headlines by the late summer of 1913.

The paper trail begins in the *Ottawa Citizen* on August 11, 1913, when it was reported that Frank Patrick was the guest of Bob Meldrum in Montreal. Patrick was reportedly in town to recover from a recent operation in New York, "but the chances are that he will take a few of the Eastern hockey players with him for next season." Patrick himself is quoted as saying that "the chances of a hockey commission are as far away as ever." However, just two days later, the *Citizen* reported that Lester Patrick would be in Montreal by the end of the month, and that the pair of Patrick brothers would "then be in a position to make or break any hockey commission that is broached by the Eastern magnates."

On August 23, a *Citizen* headline said, "Commission Assured." On September 3, "Peace in Sight." Then on September 5, 1913, numerous newspapers all across Canada reported that an agreement on a hockey commission had been reached. Most of the 15 terms drawn up concerned the transfer of players and the respecting of each other's contracts, but two terms would have a direct impact on the future of the Stanley Cup. Term 10 of the agreement stated: "A post-series of not less than three games out of five must be played annually between the champions of each league at the close of the season alternating [yearly] between the east and the west." Term 13 read: "Arrangements for post-series and exhibition games between both leagues to be left in the hands of the presidents of both associations."

Nothing about the "post-series" mentions the Stanley Cup, but the first specific reference to the trophy in regard to the NHA-PCHA treaty seems to appear in the *Victoria Times* on November 12, 1913:

> There is a movement in the East to have the Stanley Cup rules modified as to make this trophy emblematic of the world's hockey championship. Under the present rules, there are various clauses which prohibit any inter-league struggles between the coast and the East for this trophy. With the national commission in force, the Quebec Club is taking a leading part in having the rules changed so that [the Cup] may be played for on a different basis from that which has existed in the past.

Three days later, the *Times* reported:

> Stating that he had no objections to the national hockey commission taking over the Stanley Cup now that the pro leagues have got together in a business-like manner, [trustee] William Foran is willing to have that trophy remain as the emblem of the world's hockey championship. The trustees will continue to hold office, but the hockey commission will look after the details of all matches and challenges for the trophy. This means that if the coast champions in their Eastern invasion next spring can win the series, they will bring [the Stanley Cup] back with them.

Team photo of the Portland Rosebuds from the 1914–15 season.

On February 28, 1914, Lester Patrick and his champion Victoria Aristocrats departed for the east along with PCHA president Frank Patrick and his Vancouver Millionaires (who would play a series of exhibition games). On March 3 the *Victoria Colonist* reported the following:

According to word received yesterday, it is practically certain that Victoria and the NHA champions will play for the Stanley Cup in the world's hockey series this month. A message from Ottawa reads: "Trustees Foran and Ross, for the Stanley Cup, will leave everything regarding arrangements for the Stanley Cup games in the hands of the NHA."

When Frank Patrick arrived in Montreal on March 6, he met almost immediately with NHA president Emmett Quinn to work out the details of the championship series. So it came as a great surprise to Lester Patrick after Game 2 of the series against the NHA-champion Toronto Blueshirts to learn that the trustees had ruled the Cup would not go to Victoria if the Aristocrats won because the PCHA had failed to submit a formal challenge for the trophy.

It has long been reported in many hockey sources — and still continues to be — that the trustees did not recognize the Toronto-Victoria series as a Stanley Cup series. It was certainly reported that way at the time, but a closer look reveals that story just isn't true. Even as word of the Victoria snub was reported in newspapers across Canada on March 18, 1914, a contradictory piece appeared that day in P.D. Ross' *Ottawa Evening Journal*:

STANLEY CUP IS AT STAKE FOR THE SERIES ALL RIGHT
Mr. Wm. Foran, trustee for the Stanley Cup, denies that the famous old mug is not up for competition at Toronto. "Mr. Emmett Quinn made all arrangements to have the Stanley Cup put up for the world's hockey series and both leagues agreed to all the conditions set by the trustees," said Mr. Foran. "There is absolutely nothing to the story from Toronto claiming that the trophy would not be handed over to Victoria if they win. If the western challengers win the world's series they will take the Cup west with the full sanction of the trustees."

Several newspapers printed retractions of their original story on March 19, though most claimed only that the trustees had changed their minds. However, on March 21, both the *Toronto News* and the *Evening Telegram* quoted Foran as saying, "There is nothing to all this talk about a disagreement over the Stanley Cup." The final word on the subject was printed in many newspapers across Canada on March 25, 1914:

There will be no more wrangling in connection with the Stanley Cup. The trustees, Messrs. Foran and Ross, are evidently glad to have at least some of the responsibility for the famous trophy lifted off their shoulders and have written President Emmett Quinn of the NHA stating that as the Cup has been accepted as the emblem of the professional championship of Canada, they will in future leave everything in the hands of the National

Commission. All they request is that they be kept in touch with the condition of affairs in order that there may be no failure on the part of the winning club to provide the usual bond for the safekeeping of the silverware. Only in cases of dispute … will the Board of Trustees be called upon to readjust matters.

Further complicating the situation in March of 1914 had been the Sydney Millionaires of the Maritime Professional Hockey League. The NHA had signed a similar agreement about contracts with the Maritime league, bringing it into the hockey commission as well. Though there was nothing in that agreement about a "post-series," the trustees had accepted a Stanley Cup challenge from the Maritimes before the Toronto-Victoria series even got started. However, Sydney decided not to follow up, and when the Maritime league went out of business after the season, the NHA and the PCHA were left undisputed as the top professional leagues in hockey.

The "challenge era" in Stanley Cup history had come to a close.

The NHA and the PCHA would now be the only ones to compete for the trophy.

There would still be problems between the two leagues — mainly over player status and continued contract jumping — but the champions of the NHA and the PCHA would continue to meet yearly for the Stanley Cup. Because the new arrangement was similar to the annual championship meeting of the National League and American League in baseball — as the Patrick brothers had both said it should be — the Stanley Cup Final of this era was often referred to as the World Series of Hockey. Although unlike baseball's World Series, which was a best of seven, and occasionally even a best of nine, the so-called World Series of Hockey would always be a best of five.

After Toronto defeated Victoria in 1914, the Vancouver Millionaires became the first PCHA team to win the Stanley Cup the following year with a lopsided three-game sweep of the Ottawa Senators in Vancouver. In 1916, the Portland Rosebuds won the PCHA title and became the first American-based team to play for the Stanley Cup. They went east to face the NHA champions, but Portland lost to the Montreal Canadiens, who won the first of a franchise-record 24 titles. After the two leagues formally renewed their commitment to each other with a new five-year agreement later in 1916, the Seattle Metropolitans became the first American-based team to win the Stanley Cup by defeating the Canadiens in Seattle in March 1917.

When the NHA disbanded in November of 1917 and reformed as the NHL, the new league stuck by the old agreement, and now it was the NHL champions and PCHA champions who met for the Stanley Cup. The Toronto Arenas — historians dispute whether the team should be called the Blueshirts that season, as it was in the NHA, and as many newspapers still labeled the club — became the first NHL team to win the Cup by defeating the Vancouver Millionaires in 1918.

A year later, the 1919 Stanley Cup Final between the Canadiens and the Metropolitans in Seattle was canceled before the final game because of the Spanish flu. Seattle won the PCHA title again in 1920 but lost the Stanley Cup to the Senators in a series played in Ottawa and Toronto. In 1921, the Senators became the first NHL team to win the Stanley Cup in back-to-back seasons, and the first team during the World Series era to claim the title while playing on the road, when they beat the Millionaires in five tight games at Vancouver.

Name Game: Part One

As per the second term of Lord Stanley's deed of gift upon donating the Stanley Cup in 1893, early winners

Lord Stanley of Preston.

engraved the name of their team, and the year they won it, onto a silver ring mounted on the base beneath the original Stanley Cup bowl. When the ring was filled, teams began engraving their name on the bowl too. When Ottawa dominated all comers from 1903 until 1906, they also engraved the name of the teams they had defeated.

The first team to formally engrave the names of its players onto the Stanley Cup was the Montreal Wanderers when they defeated the Kenora Thistles in a rematch in March of 1907 after the Thistles' victory in January. Twenty names were engraved inside the Cup, in the bottom of the bowl, including Wanderers players and club executives. Among the player names are L. Patrick.

Lester Patrick.

The Wanderers engraving is clearly visible inside the original Stanley Cup bowl that resides permanently in the old bank vault at the Hockey Hall of Fame in Toronto, as well as inside the bowl of both the Presentation Cup that is given out to teams every year and the replica Cup that goes on display at the Hall when the Presentation Cup is away. Less clearly visible — but also there inside the bowl on all three versions of the Stanley Cup — are nine names from the next team to engrave their players into the trophy. That team was the 1915 Vancouver Millionaires.

Among the names for that year is Frank Patrick.

Though there's nothing official to confirm the theory, it's easy to believe that as the team owner and a star player, Frank was inspired to engrave the names of his Vancouver champions after seeing Lester's name in the bottom of the bowl — perhaps even as he was drinking champagne from it.

Three-Cornered Cup

On Monday evening, May 9, 1921, five weeks after his Millionaires lost the Stanley Cup to the Ottawa Senators, Frank Patrick boarded a train for the east from his home in Vancouver. With him were his wife and his parents. They were bound for Scotland, and an international Rotary Club convention in Edinburgh in June. In all, the Patricks would be gone for nearly six months, traveling 20,000 miles round-trip, including — according to an account in the *Victoria Daily Times*

on October 19, 1921 — 5,000 miles through England, Scotland, Belgium, Holland, France, Switzerland and Italy, mostly in a Dodge automobile they purchased in London. But first, the Patricks would visit Ottawa, then Montreal and finally Quebec City, from which they would sail for Liverpool aboard the Canadian Pacific steamer *Empress of France* on May 24.

Though his playing days were essentially over, Frank Patrick's role in running the Vancouver Millionaires and as president of the PCHA meant he was still a major Canadian sports celebrity. While in the Canadian capital, the *Ottawa Journal* noted in its Social and Personal column on May 18, 1921, that "Mr. and Mrs. Joseph Patrick, Victoria, and Mr. and Mrs. Frank A. Patrick, Vancouver, B.C., are staying at the Chateau Laurier." That day's *Ottawa Citizen* was more interested in talking to him about hockey:

> Frank seems to have recovered from the shock of losing the World's Hockey Series to Ottawa, and yesterday he looked up officers of the local club, just to show that there were no hard feelings.

"The World's Series of 1921 was the greatest ever played," said the famous Pacific Coast

Stanley Cup Games—The Arena

1—FRIDAY, MARCH 17.   2—TUESDAY, MARCH 21.
3—THURSDAY, MARCH 23.

Usual professional prices.   Plan on sale Wednesday only at Arena, for patrons wishing to purchase the 3-games at one time.   Plan on sale for single game Thursday.   Those purchasing seats for the 3-games on Wednesday will be assured of seats for the 4th and 6th games, if played. Watch the papers for further ads.   x

Marlene Geoffrion, wife of Bernie Geoffrion, and Lucille Richard, wife of Maurice Richard, hold an artifact concerning the Stanley Cup win by the Montreal Canadiens in 1924.

hockey magnate. "It was fought to a finish on its merits and though there was very little difference between the teams, I think Ottawa had the edge.... I consider their team one of the greatest I have ever seen. They are a well-balanced, clever aggregation, and a credit to the city."

The differences in rules between the PCHA and the NHL (which were alternated from game to game during the Stanley Cup Final each year) were discussed, with Patrick saying he still preferred the PCHA's seven-man game and their wider neutral zone, which encouraged more forward passing. (At this point in hockey history, forward passing was allowed only between the blue lines.) The Patrick party left for Montreal that same afternoon, and Frank spoke more about the rules in a story that appeared in the *Gazette* on May 20:

All our patrons like the seven man hockey better than the six man game, and even easterners who have been in the west for not more than a year favor the western game to the eastern. Our seven man rules are better than the six in my opinion. The play is faster and with playing the three man defence and the elimination of the old time "rover" it leaves only three forwards to play on the offensive.

It was said while he was in Ottawa that Frank Patrick would confer with NHL president Frank Calder in Montreal with a view toward arranging a new five-year agreement between the two leagues. The two men probably met briefly, but Patrick told the *Gazette* he "was going to forget about business until his return from the old country in September." Still, there would be plenty of hockey talk among others before then. Frank Patrick may have been kept apprised of the doings in August via telegraph, but whether he was or not, his brother Lester was front and center as a new professional league prepared to join the NHL and the PCHA.

The Big Four had been a high-level amateur league set up in Alberta in 1919 with two teams in Calgary and two in Edmonton. The intention had been to challenge for the Allan Cup, but the league was dogged by allegations of professionalism — most prominently by Frank Patrick — during its two seasons. Then, in what some newspapers referred to as "a secret session of hockey moguls" in Calgary on August 9, 1921, the decision was made to disband the Big Four and operate an out-and-out professional organization to be called the Alberta Hockey Association. The teams were to be the Edmonton Eskimos, Edmonton Dominions, Calgary Canadians and Calgary Tigers. Plans were being made for another meeting in Edmonton within two weeks, where the new league would discuss aligning itself with the PCHA and with a possible new pro league to be established in Saskatchewan.

With Frank Patrick still in Europe, an invitation was extended to Lester to attend the second meeting, which was held in Calgary on August 20. On behalf of the PCHA, Lester signed agreements relating to player rights within and between his association and the new Alberta league, and also regarding how players could be bought, sold or traded. Some — but not all — newspapers reported that the winner of the new Alberta league would be included in the Stanley Cup

playoffs. But official word on that would have to wait until the NHL met … and signed off on its new agreement with the PCHA.

That wouldn't happen until Frank Patrick returned from Europe.

At 6:30 on the morning of September 21, 1921, with Captain E. Cook in command, the *Empress of France* docked at the breakwater in Quebec City. The ocean liner left Liverpool on September 15, and newspapers reported on "a fine and fast crossing of the Atlantic with 1,028 passengers on board." They also noted that "among the passengers were Frank Patrick, president of the Pacific Coast Hockey League [*sic*], accompanied by his wife and mother." (No mention of Frank's father, Joseph Patrick, but he was there too.) By that same evening, Frank was in Montreal. He held a conference with Frank Calder and Eddie Poulin of the Calgary Tigers at the NHL office on Friday, September 23, and then met with them again, along with delegates from all the NHL teams, in a more formal meeting at the Windsor Hotel the next day.

The main order of business at the meeting on September 24, 1921, was to renew the five-year agreement between the NHL and the PCHA. Poulin wasn't considered an official delegate, so the inclusion of the new Alberta league into Stanley Cup competition wasn't finalized, but everyone believed it would happen. "It is practically certain that there will be a three-cornered playoff in the Stanley Cup series," reported the *Morning Bulletin* of Edmonton on September 26 in a story from Montreal. "President Frank Patrick, of the Pacific Coast league was authorized by the meeting to negotiate with the Alberta Hockey league for inclusion in the series. Mr. Patrick will represent both the Pacific Coast and the National Hockey league at the negotiations."

The meeting with Frank Patrick, Alberta Hockey Association president E.L. (Ernest Lamont "Ernie") Richardson and representatives of the four clubs took place in Calgary on October 5, 1921. Little was promised, though Patrick did make it clear the new Alberta league would be included in the competition for the Stanley Cup in some way. But Patrick seemed a bit patronizing too in explaining how all three leagues were going to have to cooperate when it came to signing players. Newspapers had been speculating since the September meeting that the Edmonton Eskimos were after Sprague Cleghorn, and Patrick informed those gathered that the Ottawa Senators did not take kindly to the attempt to sign one of their stars.

Ken McKenzie of the Eskimos explained that Cleghorn had come to him, sending a telegram saying he wished to play in Edmonton and that he was "a free lance" (free agent).

"You offered him $2,000 to play for the season," said Patrick, as quoted by the *Edmonton Journal*.

"I certainly did not," replied McKenzie.

But then Patrick produced a telegram, signed by McKenzie, stating he would go as high as $2,000 for Cleghorn.

"I just want to convince you that this procedure is all wrong," said Patrick. "We must work in harmony, and not approach players that belong to other clubs. Cleghorn is property of the Ottawa club, and it would be well before dickering with any player to first find out from the club he played for last winter if he is still their property." (Admittedly, Cleghorn's contract status at this time is difficult to ascertain. The Hamilton Tigers of the NHL would later claim him from Ottawa, but Cleghorn said he had no intention of joining them. Léo Dandurand would work out a deal to bring him to Montreal, and Cleghorn remained with the Canadiens through the 1924–25 season.)

Patrick's point had been that the NHL and the PCHA had managed to keep the peace since the second NHA-PCHA treaty of 1916, and now all three leagues would have to work together. As such, it appears that by October 18, 1921, the three leagues had signed an agreement, and the result, reported in that day's *Ottawa Citizen*, "means there will be much greater interest each year in the World's Series." (That tag would persist even during this three-league era.)

A few days before these reports, on October 12, 1921, the Saskatoon Crescents had been admitted to the Alberta Hockey Association along with the two Edmonton and two Calgary teams, and the league name was changed to the Big Five. As had been speculated since the meetings with Lester Patrick in August, it was now official that the champions of the Big Five would face the champions of the PCHA in a postseason series, "after which the survivors will come East to play the National League winners for the Stanley Cup and World's Championship." But before the season even started, the Big Five became the Western Canada Hockey League (WCHL).

The new name came about at a meeting in Edmonton on November 9, 1921, when the league fell back to four teams again after the amalgamation of the Calgary Canadians and the Calgary Tigers, who would play under the Tigers name. But the newly named league would be up to five teams again when it was announced on November 18 that Regina had been admitted. There was also talk of further expansion, with a sixth team added in Moose Jaw, Saskatchewan (the Saskatoon team would actually relocate its home games to Moose Jaw during the season), but at a league meeting in Calgary on December 3, the Edmonton Dominions dropped from the WCHL, leaving only the Edmonton Eskimos, Calgary Tigers, Saskatoon Crescents and Regina Capitals.

For the next three springs, in 1922, 1923 and 1924, the champions of the NHL, the PCHA and the WCHL would all take part in a three-cornered World Series for the Stanley Cup, although the format would change slightly in each year.

The First WCHL Season

The first season of the Western Canada Hockey League was a star-studded affair. Among the 50 skaters on the rosters of the four teams, nine would one day be inducted into the Hockey Hall of Fame. On the green-and-white-clad Edmonton Eskimos, Duke Keats and Bullet Joe Simpson were the future Hall of Famers. The black-and-yellow Calgary Tigers had Barney Stanley, Red Dutton, Harry Oliver and Herb Gardiner. The Regina Capitals, dressed in red, white and blue, boasted Dick Irvin and George Hay, while Rusty Crawford — who had already been playing pro hockey since 1909, and would remain in the game until 1930 — led the Saskatoon/Moose Jaw team, whose sweaters were maroon and white. Like the NHL, the WCHL played with six men a side.

The new league faced off its first season in Edmonton on December 16, 1921, with the Eskimos hosting the Regina Capitals at 8:30 that evening. Edmonton's Duke Keats scored the first goal in league history on a setup from Joe Simpson midway through the first period, and the Eskimos led 2–0 after one. Regina scored in the second and third, and the game was 2–2 at the end of regulation time. Overtime was supposed to be played until a winner was decided, but league rules also called for the referee to end play 30 minutes before the last train, so after four 10-minute overtime periods settled nothing, the game was halted at midnight with the score still 2–2.

The tie game on opening night set the tone for a remarkably tight race that inaugural 1921–22 campaign. When the season ended on February 27, Edmonton and Regina had both finished with records of 14-9-1. Calgary was just behind them at 14-10, while Saskatoon/Moose Jaw was well off the pace at 5-19. But since the playoffs in all three leagues called for the second-place team to meet the first-place team in a two-game, total-goals series for the league championship, the WCHL needed some playoffs just to get to the playoffs!

The schedule would be unforgiving.

First, Edmonton and Regina replayed their tie game from opening night to determine who would be the first-place team. The game was played on March 1 with Edmonton at home, as they had been in the opener. The result was a surprising 11–2 romp for the Eskimos, who took top spot with a record now standing at 15-9. Regina, having fallen to 14-10, was tied for second with Calgary, so those teams would play a two-game series to determine who would face Edmonton for the championship.

Barney Stanley.

Regina won the opener 1–0 in Calgary on March 2. In Regina for Game 2 the next night, Calgary got a goal from Harry Oliver just 1:22 into the first period to give the Tigers a 1–0 lead and tie the series at one goal apiece. Dick Irvin scored later in the first frame to make it 1–1, and when neither team scored again, Regina secured a 2–1 total-goals victory.

The Capitals would now host the Eskimos to open the WCHL championship series in their fourth game in four nights. As Regina had lost the replay with Edmonton so decisively, and since the Eskimos had the benefit of two days of rest while the Capitals had played two more games, the first-place team may have been overconfident. Dick Irvin scored early for Regina, and the Capitals hung on until late in the third, when Joe Simpson scored for Edmonton. There was no need to play overtime to break the 1–1 tie, since the second game would decide the winner.

Regina finally got a day off before having to play again in front of a full house of 6,000 Eskimos fans in Edmonton on March 6 … and the Capitals won. After a scoreless first period, Amby Moran and Dick Irvin scored for Regina in the second. Edmonton scored late in the third but couldn't score again, and Regina claimed a 2–1 victory and a 3–2 series win.

Now it was off to Vancouver, where the WCHL champions would take on the Millionaires, who had finished second to Seattle in a tight race but had beaten the Metropolitans for the PCHA title with a pair of 1–0 playoff wins. This Vancouver-Regina series would determine who would go east to face the NHL champs for the Stanley Cup.

Game 1, on March 8, would be played under PCHA rules using seven men a side. Regina dressed 10 skaters for the game and moved players in and out freely. "They made 32 substitutions," reported the *Vancouver Sun*, "regulars subbing for the subs that had substituted for the regulars, that had substituted for

the subs." As a result, Regina set a blistering pace and outskated Vancouver for a 2–1 victory.

The Capitals now got two full days off before hosting the Millionaires in the series finale on March 11. Still, it wasn't enough. On slow, sticky ice, and despite a crowd of 7,000 fans cheering them on, Regina was outplayed in every department as Vancouver scored a 4–0 victory to take the series 5–2. So it would be the PCHA's Millionaires moving on to face the NHL champions, who had yet to be determined.

It had been a tight race in the NHL as well that season. Ottawa finished on top at 14-8-2 to Toronto's 13-10-1 (Montreal was 12-11-1, while Hamilton lagged behind at 7-17-0), but the St. Pats opened the playoffs with a 5–4 win at home on March 11. They stalled the Senators with defensive tactics on slushy ice in Ottawa two nights later, and the result was a scoreless tie that gave Toronto the series and the right to host Vancouver.

The best-of-five Stanley Cup Final between the St. Pats and the Millionaires went the distance, but in the end, Toronto won handily with 6–0 and 5–1 victories in Games 4 and 5. Babe Dye's four goals in the fifth game would mark the last hat trick in a Stanley Cup–clinching game for 101 years until Mark Stone's three-goal effort in the Vegas Golden Knights' 9–3 victory over the Florida Panthers in 2023.

A New Format …

On Thursday, August 17, 1922, the two sports pages of the *Vancouver Daily World* were filled with news of baseball, boxing, horse racing, track and field, golf and tennis. Even cricket and polo. There was hockey news too, with a story on an upcoming meeting on Monday between delegates from the teams in the PCHA and the WCHL.

"The matters to come up will include a new working agreement between the coast and prairie leagues

The 1923 Stanley Cup champion Ottawa Hockey Club.

to replace the temporary arrangement made last year when Lester Patrick visited the inland loop and helped the directors with their plans for launching the league. Player trades will also be discussed and matters of a general character affecting the hockey situation will receive attention. New playing rules, to be adopted uniformly both here and on the prairies, may also come up at the meeting."

The day-long session at the Hotel Vancouver on August 21, 1922, changed the look of hockey in the west. The two leagues agreed to play an interlocking schedule, with their seasons expanded from 24 to 30 games. Each of the four WCHL teams would make one road trip to each of the three PCHA cities throughout the season, while each of the coast teams

would make a similar trip to the prairies. Still, the two leagues would maintain separate standings and hold their own playoffs. Even so, rules would be standardized, with the WCHL accepting all PCHA rules (including the penalty shot, which Frank Patrick had introduced to the PCHA the previous season) — except one.

The PCHA finally agreed to switch to six-man hockey.

The big news to come out of the second day of meetings on Tuesday, August 22, was a change to the format of the Stanley Cup playoffs. With the final to be played in the west that year, the WCHL insisted that their champions meet the winners of a series between the NHL and the PCHA. Given that the games would be played so late into March, the WCHL was happy to have them take place in Vancouver, where the artificial ice surface would guarantee good conditions. The NHL and PCHA champs would meet first, in a best of five as they always had, even though the series would, in fact, be a semifinal. The WCHL champs would then meet the winner in a best of three. NHL president Frank Calder, though admitting he had not yet given the new format any consideration when he arrived in Calgary to meet with the other leagues on September 7, agreed to the change.

Once again in 1922–23, Edmonton (19-10-1) and Regina (16-14-0) proved to be the top teams in the WCHL. The Eskimos won the playoff opener 1–0 at Regina on March 14, 1923, but when the Capitals won 3–2 in Edmonton two nights later, the total-goals series was tied 3–3. Twenty minutes of overtime settled nothing, and then at 10:25 of the second extra session, Regina defenseman Percy "Puss" Traub tripped Ty Arbour when he was on a breakaway. Edmonton was awarded a penalty shot, which was taken by Duke Keats, who fired the puck past goalie Bill Laird to put the Eskimos through to the Stanley Cup Final.

In the PCHA, Vancouver, whose team name was changed from Millionaires to Maroons that season, finished first with a 17-12-1 record and then knocked off the second-place Victoria Cougars (16-14-0) in the playoffs. In a tight race in the NHL, Ottawa topped the standings at 14-9-1, while the battle for second place went down to the final night before the Canadiens (13-9-2) clinched a playoff spot at the expense of the defending Stanley Cup–champion St. Pats (13-10-1).

Having concluded the regular season at an early date in order for the NHL champion to get out west, Ottawa opened the playoffs in Montreal on March 7 and scored a 2–0 victory despite the vicious play of Canadiens defensemen Sprague Cleghorn and Billy Coutu. Montreal manager Léo Dandurand was so

Eddie Gerrard.

appalled by their conduct he suspended both his players from the second game before the NHL took any action. Even so, the Canadiens had a 2–0 lead in Game 2 before Cy Denneny (who played sparingly with his head swathed in bandages) scored early in the third period to give Ottawa a 3–2 total-goals victory.

After wrapping up the NHL title on March 9, the Senators arrived in Vancouver on the morning of March 16, just in time to face the Maroons that evening. Ottawa was banged up from the series with Montreal and was without veteran Jack Darragh, who couldn't make the trip west. Another Ottawa veteran, Punch Broadbent, played the hero, scoring the only goal of Game 1 with just five minutes remaining. After a 4–1 Vancouver victory in Game 2, Broadbent scored twice more in two other Ottawa victories to help the Senators take the best-of-five series in four games. "That's the greatest hockey team I ever saw in action," said Frank Patrick after the final game. Still, the

Senators had suffered two more injuries in beating Vancouver, and neither star defenseman Eddie Gerard nor right winger Harry Helman were sure to play against Edmonton for the Stanley Cup.

The well-rested Eskimos were confident.

"You can tell the people of Edmonton that we have an excellent chance to win," said Ken McKenzie in a story that appeared in the *Edmonton Morning Bulletin* on March 29, the day of Game 1 in the best-of-three final. (McKenzie was noted as the Eskimos manager but would be recognized as the team's coach and general manager today.) "All the boys are in excellent shape, have been keeping good hours, and taking the best care of themselves since arriving here." The team had held three practices on the large artificial ice surface in Vancouver and had been able to see the Senators play in the last two games of the series against the Maroons. Most importantly, they had a healthy 11-man roster.

Ottawa played Game 1 with King Clancy filling in on defense for Eddie Gerard and with Lionel Hitchman as their only substitute. Despite the depleted roster, Clint Benedict played brilliantly in goal for Ottawa and Frank Nighbor kept Duke Keats under wraps. The Senators got an overtime goal from Cy Denneny just 2:08 into the first extra session and won Game 1 by a score of 2–1. Gerard was back for Game 2 on March 31, and while his injured shoulder was still a problem, he played almost the entire game. But Gerard's defense partner, George Boucher, had hurt his ankle and didn't play. Clancy and Hitchman filled in for Boucher, while Harry Helman returned to action to support the forward line. Benedict was again said to be brilliant in the Ottawa net, and Punch Broadbent scored the only goal of the game midway through the first period as the Senators scored a 1–0 victory to sweep the short series and win the Stanley Cup.

... and a New Hero

King Clancy had completed just his second season in the NHL in what would be a 16-year Hall of Fame career. Modern hockey records generally show Clancy to have been born on February 25, 1903, although genealogical records — and early Ottawa newspapers — show he was born on February 25, 1902.

Clancy had only recently turned 21, but newspapers largely considered him to have been the best man for Ottawa against Edmonton in the 1923 Stanley Cup Final. He is reputed to have played all six positions for the Senators during the Cup-winning game against the Eskimos, but that doesn't appear to have been the case.

Clancy definitely took over in goal for Clint Benedict during the finale with Edmonton. Game summaries generally show Benedict being penalized in the second period, but game stories report the penalty as occurring in the first period. The *Victoria Daily Times* of April 2, 1923, has the best account:

> The Eskimos took charge of the proceedings during the first ten minutes of play and Benedict was in brilliant form. Ottawa did nearly all of their shooting from centre ice or the blue line, rushing back to repel the forthcoming attack. Then came a break for the Eskimos which looked good. Benedict brought his [stick] down across Joe Simpson's legs as the latter was circling the Ottawa goal. [Referee Mickey] Ion ruled him off. Clancy took up the burden between the posts. For two minutes the Eskimos fought frantically for possession of the rubber, but the Ottawa forwards were here, there, and everywhere and Clancy never so much as touched the disc before Benedict was back again. The winning goal came shortly afterwards when Broadbent scored

from the blue line after Nighbor had slipped the rubber over to him.

Obviously, Clancy did play in the net that night. Basil O'Meara, writing in the *Ottawa Journal* on Monday, April 2, 1923, after the final Stanley Cup game on Saturday night, March 31, had this to say: "Frank Clancy made hockey history.... The kid with the tousled thatch went in and played goal and tried his hand at every other position on the team." Yet the game report on the previous page in that day's *Journal* only describes Clancy and Lionel Hitchman taking turns on defense, with Harry Helman taking a few shifts to relieve the forwards.

In the *Ottawa Citizen* that same day, a headline on the sports page read, "'King' Clancy Sets Unique Record of Playing Every Position on Team, Taking Benedict's Job When Goaler Is Ruled Off." The text of the article written by *Citizen* sports editor Ed Baker notes: "Clint Benedict ran afoul of Referee Ion at one stage and was banished for two minutes for chopping at the puck too close to Joe Simpson's feet. 'King' Clancy then went into the net, and that gave the youngster [the] unprecedented distinction of having played every position on the lineup during the present tour. He had previously subbed in both defense positions, center, and on right and left wing." In the Vancouver papers, the *Vancouver Sun* similarly noted after Benedict's penalty that "Clancy, completing his utility performance of the series, replaced him."

It would seem, then, that Clancy had played all six positions during Ottawa's playoff trip to the West Coast, but likely not in the same game. Confirming this, Clancy himself, in his autobiography written with Brian McFarlane and originally published in 1968, admits the story of his goaltending in the Stanley Cup Final "was given a twist here and there." He writes that his appearance in goal that night was the first time he

Portrait of Francis "King" Clancy as a member of the Ottawa Senators no later than 1929–30.

had ever played that position, but that he had played all five positions other than goaltender during the third game of the semifinal series with Vancouver.

The *Ottawa Citizen* of March 24, 1923, bears this out:

> The Ottawas went through the entire sixty minutes of gruelling hockey with only seven players, King Clancy, the youngest member of the team, being the only substitute used and he was compelled to play every position on the ice except in the nets.

Similarly, a headline in the *Vancouver Daily Province* on that same day noted, "Clancy Only Substitute Used,

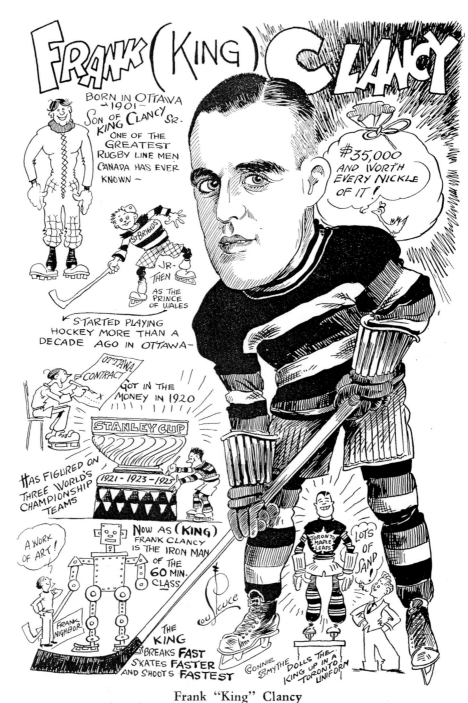

Frank "King" Clancy

All Star Defence, Toronto Maple Leafs

Chosen by popular vote of hockey writers of America as the year's best Defence

but He Is Brilliant." In the game story, it appears that Clancy first came off the bench early in the second period when Eddie Gerard hurt his knee. "Young Mr. Clancy got into the limelight, decided he liked it, and kept right on playing a star role. Hitchman was not used all evening. Clancy filled in on the forward line, and on defence and was good all the time."

So King Clancy did, indeed, play every position on the ice for the Senators, as the stories have long suggested … just not all on the same night. It actually happened in two different games, in two different series, during Ottawa's 1923 Stanley Cup trip to Vancouver.

King of the Heelers

King Clancy certainly made a name for himself during the three-team Stanley Cup competition in 1923. While Frank Patrick would walk back his early praise for the Ottawa Senators somewhat in a story that appeared in the *Vancouver Province* on April 2, 1923, he had nothing but admiration for Clancy:

> Ottawa has a wonderful club, although hardly, I think, quite up to the standard of the 1921 team, which I regard as the greatest aggregation the game has ever seen. Certainly they are to be congratulated for going through two hard series in the manner they did and with a crippled aggregation. . . . In Clancy I figure the Senators have one of the coming stars of the game. In the last two matches he was the individual star. He is a true son of his father, "King" Clancy, the greatest football player of his day and generation.

This was the second time in just a few days the *Province* had referred to Clancy and his famous father. After his multiposition effort against Vancouver, the paper noted that the "dashing Irishman was going in the form which made his father the most famous rugby player of his time." Indeed, Francis Michael Clancy the hockey star (genealogical records sometimes note his given names as Michael Francis) inherited his famous nickname from his father, Thomas Francis Clancy.

The original King Clancy starred in football with Ottawa College in the 1890s and then had a long career as a coach and executive with the Ottawa Rough Riders. Clancy Sr. was known as the King of the Heelers, from the days when Canadian football was more like rugby and there was no center snapping the ball to the quarterback. The ball was heeled back, much in the way a hooker in rugby might use his feet to clear the ball from a scrum to one of his teammates. King of the Heelers was shortened to King, and the nickname was passed down from father to son.

The Bye Series

As in 1922–23, the PCHA and the WCHL played an interlocking schedule in 1923–24. The WCHL dominated to such an extent that when the season ended on March 3, none of the three teams in the PCHA had a winning record. Seattle finished first at 14-16-0. Vancouver was second at 13-16-1, with Victoria last at 11-18-1. On the prairies, Calgary was 18-11-1, Regina 17-11-2, Saskatoon 15-12-3 and Edmonton 11-15-4.

Unlike in 1922–23, no Stanley Cup playoff had been arranged prior to the start of the season except that the final series would be hosted by the NHL. Though the PCHA season began on November 12, WCHL teams launched their home schedules on December 6, and the NHL faced off on December 15, it wasn't until early February that speculation as to a new Stanley Cup format began. It would soon appear that NHL teams expected the WCHL and PCHA to play off and send one team east, as they had in 1922, but the *Vancouver Sun* of February 6, 1924, noted that the "Prairie moguls" were inclined to insist on "three-sided finishes in the East." Nothing had been decided yet, but "what actually will be done will be the subject of conferences shortly between coast, mid-western, and eastern loops."

STICKHANDLING the PUCK
IN THE ARENA

Patrick gave his detailed version of the events leading up to the 1924 Stanley Cup Final to the *Boston Sunday Globe* on March 17, 1935, in the final instalment of an eight-part series about his life that appeared in the paper while he was the coach of the Boston Bruins. "I decided that both teams should come East to play Les Canadiens," said Patrick. "It was my idea that the Eastern fans would like to see both Vancouver and Calgary in action against the famous Canadiens."

Instead of each team playing three games against Montreal, as the original idea called for, Patrick decided that the winner of the Vancouver-Calgary series should get a bye directly into the final, with the losing team playing Montreal for the second spot. "At

Frank Calder.

first," Patrick explained, "I thought we could toss a coin to decide which club would oppose Les Canadiens first. Then the thought occurred to me to play off for the 'bye' berth."

That doesn't seem to be in keeping with anything that had been discussed in February of 1924. Clearly, Patrick had talked with WCHL president Richardson, but in Boston in 1935 he claimed to have gotten in touch with Tigers manager Lloyd Turner directly to make the arrangements. And as the Maroons and Tigers played in front of big crowds in Vancouver, Calgary and Winnipeg, "the National Hockey League in general, and Les Canadiens in particular, were burning up. It was getting late in the season, it was a natural ice rink in Montreal with the danger of poor ice for the series, and Les Canadiens didn't want to play two clubs anyway."

Having lost to Calgary, Patrick now expected his Vancouver team to play Montreal in a semifinal series while Calgary got a bye into the final. But NHL president Frank Calder and Canadiens co-owner, coach and general manager Léo Dandurand were decidedly unhappy with the western arrangement. They wondered, among other things, what right Vancouver would have (having already lost to the Tigers) to play Calgary for the Stanley Cup if they beat Montreal. They also worried about who would show up for the final if the hometown Canadiens weren't in it.

The two western teams arrived in Montreal on the morning of March 18. Both "will get a crack at the Stanley Cup and the world title," the *Montreal Star* had reported the previous day, while admitting "there was a lot of controversy over the two teams coming down, but it was finally decided to allow both to make the trip, provided the expenses of one team only was to be collected here." As Dandurand put it: "We might just as well have agreed to that or there might have been no world series at all. Then again, they could have left

Quote . . . Unquote

"At the end of the game in Ottawa, Charlie Reid, the Calgary goalie, skated up to Art [Ross] and said: 'As long as you're refereeing the Stanley Cup will stay in the East.' Quick as a flash Art came back: 'Well, as long as you're goal-tending, the Stanley Cup certainly won't go West.'"

— **Frank Patrick**, speaking about his long-time friend (and current boss in Boston) Art Ross in the *Boston Sunday Globe*, March 17, 1935

their playoff undecided and challenged individually, and we would have had to accept both challenges. It would probably have amounted to the same thing in the end."

Frank Patrick explained himself, as reported in the *Star* on March 18: "The sentiment, both in the far and middle west, was so strong for both teams coming down east to play for the Stanley Cup, that it was either bring them or cease operating hockey leagues there." As to the expenses, Patrick claimed the western teams were getting more than the $4,500 being reported. Dandurand admitted they were getting $5,000 but added: "He shouldn't feel elated over an extra five hundred dollars. It's nothing to boast about."

In Patrick's telling in the *Boston Sunday Globe*, Dandurand was still angry after Vancouver and Calgary got to Montreal. "[He] wouldn't even speak to me," Patrick wrote. "He staged a party for the Western clubs and invited everybody but me. Finally, after a couple of days, Leo weakened and asked me what we had played the bye series for. 'For $20,000,' I calmly replied. Then he laughed. He knew what I meant."

What Patrick meant, of course, was the western teams' profits from the gate receipts of those three playoff games!

Having already swept Ottawa in two games to win the NHL title, the Canadiens beat Vancouver in two and then took two in a row from Calgary to win the Stanley Cup. The warm spring weather during the last week in March meant the final game on March 25, 1924, was moved from the natural ice surface of Montreal's Mount Royal Arena to the artificial ice of the Ottawa Auditorium. Even so, a respectably large crowd for the era of 7,000 fans showed up.

Name Game: Part Two

In 1909 a new silver band was attached beneath the original base of the Stanley Cup to record the names of winning teams. But after that band was filled in 1918, nothing more was engraved on the Stanley Cup for five years. Then, in 1924, the Canadiens added a brand new band, completely filling in the space between the earlier two. On it was engraved, "Canadiens of Montreal / World's Champions / 1924" along with the teams the Canadiens had defeated, "Ottawa Vancouver Calgary Two Straight Games Each." The Canadiens also engraved the names of the 11 players who had taken part in the playoffs, as well as those of the club executives. Names had only been engraved previously in 1907 and 1915, but they have continued to be added to the Stanley Cup every year since 1924.

The End of the PCHA

The Pacific Coast Hockey Association officially came into being on December 7, 1911. Though two of its teams would live on for another two seasons, the PCHA ceased to be on August 26, 1924. In its nearly 13 years of existence, the Patrick brothers had revolutionized hockey.

It's long been said that Frank Patrick was responsible for some 20 regulations that became part of the NHL rule book. Whether that number is accurate or not — and whether or not some of those rules were borrowed from smaller, less known leagues — Patrick and the PCHA definitely spearheaded many major changes to the game.

While they were late to embrace six-man hockey, the Patricks were the first to divide the rink into zones by painting blue lines on the ice. Within the neutral zone created by those blue lines (and later everywhere on the ice), the PCHA introduced forward passing to the game. It was the first league to tabulate assists, and also the first major league to allow goalies to fall to the ice to stop the puck. The PCHA introduced the concept of delayed penalties and added the penalty shot to hockey. It also created the modern playoffs and established an early version of a farm system. And when the league was abandoned, it wasn't for hockey reasons: it was because the Arena in Seattle had been converted into a parking garage.

In his 2012 book, *Empire of Ice: The Rise and Fall of the Pacific Coast Hockey Association, 1911–1926*, author Craig Bowlsby writes that in February of 1924, the University of Washington informed the Seattle Metropolitans it would soon demolish the Seattle Arena. That isn't quite true. The building wasn't demolished, but repurposed in order to house 450 cars, mainly for the guests of the brand new Olympic Hotel, which would have its grand opening across the street from the arena on December 6, 1924. That same day, on the front page of its Automobile Section, the *Seattle Star* ran a lengthy article on the new garage, which featured seven floors of parking spaces and an automotive store with a complete line of accessories and fixtures. Garage manager Bruce A. Griggs explained

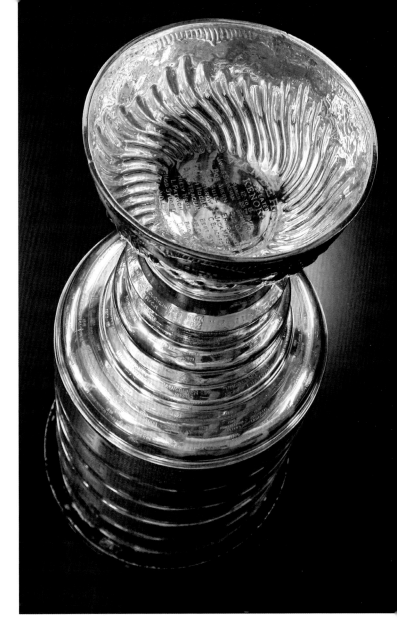

A view of the inside of the Stanley Cup.

it had cost $500,000 to remodel the old arena, which was more than it would have cost to build a parking garage from scratch, "but not more than it would have cost to tear down the Arena, cart away the debris, then build a new garage."

Bowlsby points out that — though they hadn't made the fact widely known — the Patrick family owned the Seattle Arena. So how could the University of Washington kick them out? Because the university owned the land the arena was built on, and they had received a better offer for it from the owners of the Olympic Hotel. Pete Muldoon, who operated the Metropolitans, hoped to find backers to build a new arena for his hockey team, so the death knell for the PCHA hadn't sounded immediately upon the conclusion of the 1923–24 season.

As late as Monday, August 25, 1924, a headline in the *Vancouver Sun* quoted Frank Patrick as saying "Inter-League Hockey This Year as Usual." Patrick was on the eve of departure for a WCHL meeting in Calgary on Tuesday when Andy Lytle received the word, and so the *Sun* sports writer presumed: "When it is a certainty there will be inter-league games, it naturally follows there will be major hockey here. Talk of merging the Coast and Prairie Leagues or to include Vancouver and Victoria in the prairie circuit is thus given the ambient too, for with inter-league hockey assured there must be two major leagues functioning more or less as usual."

The next day, Tuesday, August 26, the *Sun* picked up a report from Calgary on the 25th noting that Frank and his brother Lester were in the city "regarding interclub games for the 1924–25 season and also to arrange for the Stanley Cup series which will be played in the west next spring." The story reminded its readers, "There was considerable confusion last [season] and plans that will be made will do away with any future trouble." And yet, after the meetings in Calgary on August 26 — as reported the following day — the real news was announced:

> Amalgamation of the Pacific Coast and Western Canada Hockey Leagues was effected at the afternoon session of the Western Canada League meeting here today, and henceforth Western professional hockey will be conducted under the direction of the Western Canda League. After 13 years of successful operation, the Patricks' famous hockey loop on the Pacific Coast has ceased to exist, and Vancouver and Victoria will line up with

Frank Foyston.

> Calgary, Edmonton, Saskatoon, and Regina, comprising a six-club group and wiping out the three-legged combination that's operated for three seasons.

Frank Patrick addressed the changes, including the fact that players from the now defunct Seattle franchise would prop up the Maroons and Cougars:

> It is certain to create tremendous enthusiasm all through Western Canada, instead of dividing the interest between the prairies and the coast. It will simplify the world's series between East and West. A series best of five games will comprise the Stanley Cup playoffs with the champion club having the games at home and alternating each season between

East and West. I am delighted with the new arrangements and I feel satisfied that the fans at the coast will feel the same way toward it.... While I regret the passing of the Pacific Coast League, which has run 13 successful seasons, I believe that this amalgamation is being carried out in the best interests of the game. Matters will be greatly simplified under one organization. With the Seattle players to bolster up Victoria and Vancouver, I believe that two super-teams will be produced and coast crowds are certain of better hockey than ever before in the annals of the winter pastime in the West.

There would be changes in the NHL that season too, with the league expanding from four to six teams. A second Montreal franchise (which would become known as the Maroons the following season of 1925–26) would be added, along with the NHL's first American-based team, the Boston Bruins. With two more teams in both the NHL and the WCHL, the playoffs would be expanded too. Three teams would now qualify, with the first-place team being given a bye into the league final to await the winner of a series between the second- and third-place teams. Both rounds would continue to be two-game, total-goals series.

The race among the playoff teams was very close in the NHL and in the WCHL. Victoria had certainly picked up the cream of the crop from Seattle, adding future Hall of Famers in goalie Hap Holmes and forwards Jack Walker and Frank Foyston, to go along with their own star center, Frank Fredrickson. Still, at 16-12-0 on the season, Victoria was third behind Calgary (17-11-0) and Saskatoon (16-11-1). In the playoffs, Walker and Fredrickson starred on home ice in Game 1 on March 6, 1925, as the Cougars beat the Crescents 3–1. They starred again in a 3–3 tie in Saskatoon four

nights later that gave Victoria the series by a total score of 6–4. Opening the WCHL final in Calgary on March 14, Walker scored for the third straight game in a 1–1 tie and then scored again, along with Fredrickson, on home ice on March 18 as Holmes earned a shutout in a 2–0 win for a 3–1 series victory.

The Montreal Canadiens were the defending Stanley Cup champions but could finish no better than third in the NHL that season with a record of 17-11-2. The four established teams waged a tight battle that saw only four points separate first from fourth, while the two new expansion teams struggled. The Hamilton Tigers, who'd placed last in each of the previous four seasons, went 19-10-1 that year to finish one point ahead of the Toronto St. Pats (19-11-0) for first place, but the Hamilton players were upset that the season had been lengthened by 25 percent (from 24 to 30 games) without a comparable increase to their salaries. They refused to take part in the playoffs unless they received an extra $200 each. After Montreal beat Toronto by scores of 3–2 on March 11 and 2–0 on March 13, NHL president Frank Calder suspended the Hamilton players and declared the Canadiens to be league champions. The decision was made on Saturday morning, March 14, when Calder was assured the Hamilton players wouldn't back down, and on Sunday evening the Canadiens boarded the Canadian Pacific Railway's *Imperial Limited* for the trip west. They arrived in Vancouver on the morning of March 20.

"The eastern champions looked very fit as they stepped off the train," reported the *Vancouver Sun*. "There were the two Cleghorns, Odie and Sprague, the former a sartorial vision from spats to chapeau; Howie Morenz ... Aurel Joliat, Billy Boucher, Billy Couture, whose foot is bothering him; [Georges] Vezina, daddy of the goalies, [Sylvio] Mantha, [Fern] Headley, Johnny Matz, formerly of Saskatoon, Mr. and Mrs. Dandurand, Mrs. Cleghorn and [Eddie] Dufour, the club trainer."

The team checked in to the Hotel Vancouver prior to an hour's practice at the Vancouver Arena at 1 p.m., and would leave at midnight on a ferry to Victoria. The next morning Canadiens boss Léo Dandurand spoke to reporters, denying he had said his team would beat the Cougars easily:

I wish to make it plain that I did not at any time during the trip across Canada make any statement to the effect that Canadiens expected to win the world's series in three straight games. It was unfortunate that such a statement was sent out as it looks as though we looked with contempt upon Victoria. Let me say right now we are looking for a spirited series with every game a battle. Of course we are confident, as any team should be when entering upon a series. But I know Lester Patrick, I have heard of your Fredrickson and your defense which has been so hard to score upon, and I do not need to be introduced to Foyston, Walker, and Holmes, so I would not be surprised if we needed five games to settle the series.

The series went only four games.

But it was Victoria that came out on top.

The Cougars won the opener 5–2 at home and took the second game 3–1 in Vancouver, where the arena was much larger and the gate receipts bigger. Howie Morenz scored a hat trick in a 4–2 Montreal victory back in Victoria, but the Cougars wrapped things up with a decisive 6–1 victory on March 30. The Cougars used a better-balanced attack to beat the Canadiens. Montreal relied heavily on its big line of Morenz, Aurèle Joliat and Billy Boucher, while Victoria made much more liberal use of its spare players. "Lester Patrick substituted his line every five minutes so as to

give the Frenchmen no chance to catch their breath," read the report of the fourth and final game.

No one knew it yet, but the WCHL-champion Victoria Cougars had become the last non-NHL team to ever win the Stanley Cup.

Name Game: Part Three

The story has long been told of Lester Patrick's sons, Lynn and Muzz (his real name was Murray), scratching their names into the Stanley Cup with a nail when they were children. There are two versions as to when this happened. The more common one says it was when the Cup was being stored in the basement of the Patrick family home in Victoria following the Cougars' victory in 1925. Other stories say it happened three years later, after Lester had moved on to the New York Rangers in the NHL. However, there is little evidence that Patrick got to bring the Cup home to Victoria following the Rangers' victory in 1928.

There appears to be no evidence, either, of the homestyle engraving on the original Stanley Cup bowl or on the early collars on display at the Hockey Hall of Fame. Still, it does appear the story is true — though it may have been only Muzz who did the deed — and that it happened in 1925.

Lynn Patrick (born February 3, 1912) joined his father's New York Rangers in 1934–35 and became a high-scoring center. Younger brother Muzz (June 28, 1915) was a defenseman who played one game for the Rangers in 1937–38 before becoming a regular the following season. The two Patrick brothers and their father, who was coach and general manager, all became Stanley Cup champions together on April 13, 1940, when the Rangers defeated the Toronto Maple Leafs 3–2 in overtime to win the series in six games. A few days later, the following story ran in newspapers across Canada:

Colonel John Kilpatrick, Clint Smith, Lynn Patrick, NHL President Frank Calder, Manager Lester Patrick, Babe Pratt, Bryan Hextall and others celebrating their Stanley Cup Final victory on April 13, 1940 at the Royal York Hotel in Toronto.

New York Rangers' victory over Toronto Maple Leafs in the Stanley Cup playoffs meant just a little bit more to Murray (Muzz) Patrick perhaps than to the other Blueshirts. It was the realization of a wish made 15 years ago.

Muzz, son of Lester Patrick, the Rangers' manager, came across the historic trophy in the basement of his home in Victoria after his father's Cougars won it in the spring of 1925. The husky defenseman said that, as a 10-year-old boy, he looked at it and wondered if his name would ever be inscribed on it. To make sure, he scratched it on.

"When we won it Saturday night I took a look to see if my name was still there," he

continued. "And it was. Now, however, it will be engraved in a place where it can be seen by everyone."

End of an Era

There were changes again in western hockey for the 1925–26 season. But there were plenty of rumors first.

At a special session of the WCHL brass in Calgary on May 1, 1925, an application was made for a new franchise in Seattle. A few days later, on May 6, came reports that Lloyd Turner, who had run the Tigers and the arena in Calgary, was leaving for Minneapolis, Minnesota, to manage the huge new rink there. "Many weeks back," the story said, it had been rumored that

Turner would be leaving, but it was thought then that his destination would be Portland, Oregon. "With Seattle coming back into pro hockey, Portland would also revive interest in the game and ask for a berth in the WCHL or a rejuvenated coast league."

A month later, on June 9, the *Morning Leader* in Regina reported that Regina Capitals owner Wes Champ had left the day before on an extended trip to the east. "Combining business with pleasure … he will scout around for talent for the local hockey club." Yet by June 19 there was a report that Champ had sold the franchise to interests in Detroit. "Locally," said the *Leader*, "the report is causing quite the flurry. While the Caps finished ingloriously last season, failing to get in the running at all, and trailing all other five entries at the end, Regina would be lost without professional hockey. Since the western circuit organized the Stadium Rink here has held an average crowd of about

4,000 people each hockey night, and many times taxed to its capacity of 6,000. That's an indication of interest and it's not to be expected that such a popular item in the city's affairs is to be allowed to slip out without a struggle." In fact, "Several local sportsmen, it is reported, are already pulling every string to have the club taken over by other interests if Wes Champ is determined to dispose of his property."

But the truth all came out on September 2.

The Capitals had indeed been sold. But they were moving to Portland.

According to the *Morning Leader*, Frank Patrick had first broached the possibility of a sale to Portland "at a mid-summer conference in Detroit, and there made a deposit to bind the bargain if the Regina owner failed to sell his franchise locally." Even at that, the Vancouver hockey magnate had some difficulty selling the plan to Portland interests, but in response

Front Row: Gordon Fraser, Cully Wilson, Charles McVeigh, Ken Doraty, Babe Dye, Mickey MacKay.   CHICAGO BLACK HAWKS 1926-27   Back Row: Pete Muldoon (coach),Red McCusker,Duke Dutkowski George Hay,Dick Irvin(capt.)Frederick McLaughlin(Pres) Bob Trapp, Percy Traub, Art Townsend, Hugh Lehman.

CHICAGO BLACK HAWKS

Team photo of the 1926–27 Chicago Black Hawks.

to a message from Champ on the evening of Tuesday, September 1, Patrick told him he had "just returned from the south" and "everything [is] set here. Story will be released from there for Wednesday papers. Am mailing cheque today."

A Canadian Press dispatch from Portland made the announcement:

PORTLAND, Ore., Sept 1.—Portland will have a professional hockey team this fall and will be a member of the Western Canada Hockey Association. The team will be known as the Rosebuds. It is understood that the price of the team and the franchise was $25,000.

After the sale was announced, Champ told his side of the story:

Like many Regina citizens, I sincerely regret the removal of the Capital Hockey Club to Portland, and I do not know of anyone that will be affected either financially or personally, as myself, but owing to business and personal reasons I had no alternative but to dispose of my interests in same. Early in June I was offered $25,000 for my club, but would not accept the offer at that time, as I wished to dispose of it in the city if at all possible. Since that time, however, my efforts to interest any Regina citizens or organizations have been futile, even though I offered it at the same price and on almost any kind of terms; and my only alternative was to dispose of it to outside parties.

While I realize that my action in this matter will be a distinct disappointment to the Regina fans who have so loyally supported the team during the past four years,

and that it is a considerable loss to the city in general, there are times when we are placed in the unfortunate position of being unable to carry out our personal wishes.

The sale wouldn't become official until it was ratified at a league meeting in Calgary on September 15. "Regina is out and Portland is in in the Western Hockey League, the new name under which the Western Canada circuit will function in future," the *Calgary Daily Herald* noted in its report of the meeting on September 16. Though team officials in Saskatoon threatened to oppose the sale — or to drop out of the league themselves — and despite a belated appeal from Regina fans to save their franchise, the move was approved unanimously after several hours of discussion.

"It is three months since Mr. Champ sought to interest Regina fans," said league president E.L. Richardson, "and he has satisfied the league that he made every reasonable effort to dispose of the club at home." The Portland Rosebuds would be owned by the Coliseum Amusement Company and run by Pete Muldoon, who had run both the previous PCHA team in Portland and the Seattle Metropolitans. As for a new team in Seattle, the *Herald* reported Richardson as saying: "No mention was made of a franchise for Seattle. The city is not ready to take a hockey club, and in fact the matter was not taken up in any way during the conference."

Meanwhile, changes were afoot in the NHL as well.

After expanding to Boston for the 1924–25 season, the league added the New York Americans and the Pittsburgh Pirates for 1925–26. The long-told story is that New York interests (Madison Square Garden impresario Tex Rickard or bootlegger Bill Dwyer or both) bought the Hamilton Tigers franchise for $75,000. In actual fact, the *New York Times* reported as early as February 6, 1925, that a deal had been

Jack Walker as a member of the Detroit Cougars during the 1927–28 NHL season at Northwestern High School in Detroit, Michigan.

reached to bring a team to the city. That was long before there was any trouble with the players in Hamilton. And even as reports of the sale picked up steam in September of 1925, directors of the Tigers continued to deny it. Indeed, the New York Americans were already purchasing players by September 18, when the team bought Bullet Joe Simpson, John "Crutchy" Morrison and Roy Rickey from the Edmonton Eskimos, but it wasn't until four days later, at an NHL meeting in Toronto, that any issue of the suspended Hamilton players appears to have been cleared up.

Newspapers reported the sale of the Hamilton franchise to New York, but it appears that only the players were sold. After a series of follow-up meetings in New York, it seems the actual Hamilton franchise had been taken over by the league. The *Ottawa Citizen* speculated on September 28 that there would still be

a team in Hamilton for the 1925–26 season, still run by Percy Thompson but no longer owned by Abso-Pure Ice Company. It did admit the possibility that the franchise might be sold to interests in Chicago or Cleveland. In the *Gazette* in Montreal, Thompson was questioned flat out about what he planned to do. "It's far too early to make promises," he said, and pointed out that if a Hamilton team was to be operated by him this season, he would probably go on the open market for material.

The saga would continue, and on Friday, October 2, 1925, Lou Marsh wrote in the *Toronto Star* about Frank Calder being in town. "I am making out six schedules," he quoted Calder as saying. "Three for a seven-club league and three for an eight-club league." Marsh noted that this "was the rather significant remark of the prexy," adding: "Seven clubs means Hamilton is out. Eight clubs takes care of Hamilton."

It wasn't until the weekend of November 7–8, 1925, at a league meeting in Montreal, that plans were finalized. "The reported desire of Percy Thompson, of Hamilton, to once again have his city included in the league this year came to nothing," reported the *Montreal Daily Star* on November 9. The sale of the Hamilton players to New York was also discussed:

> Mr. Thompson was in the city, but did not attend the meeting as a delegate. He was called in to the league conference following the general meeting, but all he did was to settle up his affairs with the New York people who'd taken over his old club. Mr. Thompson wanted to be sure that the money he was to receive from New York was deposited with the league, and it was finally decided that the first instalment would be paid to the league for Thompson as soon as the players that New York had purchased were all reinstated. Some of them have been placed in good standing already, but there are others who have yet to receive the smile of President Calder. Every one of them sent a letter to the league for the meeting apologizing for their former actions and asking for reinstatement. The matter now rests with the league president to deal with.

Thompson did make statements about his ability to put together a new team in Hamilton, but nothing was done. To this day, there has not been another NHL team in the city. Pittsburgh was admitted to the league that day, despite opposition from Ottawa, while requests from two Chicago syndicates were set aside for further consideration. As the *Chicago Sunday Tribune* explained it, "National Hockey League governors at the annual meeting here today discussed the possibility of admitting Chicago into the league this year,

but decided it was too late in the year to take action."

Still, the NHL now had teams in Boston, New York and Pittsburgh, and since Montreal and Toronto were already much larger than the markets of any of the WHL teams, the writing was on the wall for western hockey. Increased salaries were starting to dominate the conversation. Numbers weren't published the way they are today — "Frank Patrick is one owner who believes that all contracts between players and owners should be regarded as confidential," noted the *Vancouver Sun* on November 5, 1925 — but that wasn't stopping people from gossiping.

"It would be very nice indeed if recent reports in Eastern Canadian newspapers regarding salaries allegedly paid professional hockey players were true," opined Andy Lytle in his Ye Editor's Column for the *Sun* on November 5. "Unfortunately for the players concerned, however, they're anything else but."

> There isn't a hockey mogul west of Toronto who doesn't know that Joe Simpson is not drawing anything like $6,000 for a season in New York. There isn't one out of five thousand interested in the great ice sport who doesn't mentally twiddle thumb to nose when he reads that others are getting $7,000 and $7,500 from one club or another.
>
> Hockey owners know that these munificent wages just can't be earned by even the super-stars. If the money doesn't flow through the gateways, who is going to be philanthropic enough to dig down in the well pressed balloon bottoms for the deficit? Certainly not the average owner.
>
> As now constituted, the NHL groups seven active clubs, roughly 75 players. Of this small army, there isn't half a dozen in the $3000 class or over.

Yet a few days later, in the same paper on November 16, Lytle wrote of Joe Simpson making $10,000, "described by one well-known newspaper which syndicates its output, as the highest priced player in the game." Still, in Lytle's earlier column of November 5, Frank Patrick had certainly backed up his claims of lower salaries. "I am in a position to know," said Patrick, "that the average hockey salary paid in the West is higher than in the East. These tales of $6,000 and $7,000 salaries are untrue and therefore to be deplored. Why broadcast incorrect information?"

But the wealthy owners of the newly christened Montreal Maroons were certainly throwing their money around. Despite the presence of future Hall of Famers Clint Benedict, Punch Broadbent and Reg Noble in the lineup in their inaugural season, as well as 1924 Olympic gold medalist Dunc Munro, the new Montreal team had finished 9-19-2 in 1924–25. They were spared last place only by their expansion cousin Boston Bruins, who were 6-24-0. For their second season, the Maroons held on to that talented foursome but went in search of new recruits. "With George Horne of Grimsby, Hobie Kitchen and Babe Seibert of Niagara Falls, and Nels Stewart of Cleveland already signed up for next year," reported the *Sault Daily Star* of Sault Ste. Marie, Ontario, on July 28, 1925, "the Montreal millionaires seem to be setting the pace."

Stewart and Siebert — two more future Hall of Famers — were the main difference makers, particularly Stewart, who led the NHL with 34 goals and 42 points in the newly expanded 36-game season and won the Hart Trophy as well. The Maroons finished second with a record of 20-11-5, defeated the third-place Pittsburgh Pirates (19-16-1) in the semifinals and then knocked off first-place Ottawa (24-8-4) to earn the right to host the western champions for the Stanley Cup. That team would be Lester Patrick's defending champion Victoria Cougars, who once again finished third in the league standings (15-11-4), but after going on a 10-2-2 run to close out the schedule knocked off second-place Saskatoon (18-11-1) and first-place Edmonton (19-11-0) to win the WHL title.

Victoria's hot streak ended there. With Nels Stewart scoring six goals and Clint Benedict earning shutouts in all three victories, the Maroons beat the Cougars in four games to win the Stanley Cup in their second season.

But losing on the ice wasn't what bothered the Patrick brothers most about the series.

It was the realization they were going to lose at the box office.

Frank Patrick was definitely singing another tune about salaries now.

"I'll never forget talking with Lester in the Victoria dressing room in the Forum after he had played [the] final game of the Stanley Cup series in 1926," wrote Frank in the *Boston Sunday Globe* in the seventh of his eight-part series on March 10, 1935. "'Whew,' he exclaimed, 'we can't keep pace with these babies, Frank. Why look at the Maroons. One of their players has a good night and one of those millionaires walks into the dressing room and slips the player a thousand bucks. Some of the Maroons are making 10, 12, 15 thousand a year.'"

During the 1926 Stanley Cup series, Art Ross had been asking about purchasing WHL players for the Bruins, but Frank Patrick had a bigger plan in mind:

There was open to us the course of selling our superstars into the Eastern fold and repairing our losses that way. We had been offered from $10,000 to $15,000 for odd players. But I was firmly set against this plan because it would reduce the Western League to a minor outfit and still we wouldn't get enough money from individual sales to keep our heads above

The Stanley Cup trophy featuring the original bowl and collars as during the 1926–27 NHL season.

water financially. As far as I was concerned, it was going to be sell all or none.

With the agreement of five of the six Western Hockey League owners (the Saskatoon Crescents made their own arrangements), Frank Patrick's idea was to form three strong rosters and sell them intact for $100,000 apiece to the new NHL teams planned for New York, Detroit and Chicago in 1926–27. Things didn't go as smoothly as he'd hoped, but interests in Detroit and Chicago each agreed to pay him $100,000.

Essentially, the Black Hawks (who wouldn't officially become the Blackhawks until 1985–86) bought the roster of the Portland Rosebuds, while Detroit purchased the Victoria Cougars. (The team would be known as the Cougars for four seasons before becoming the Falcons in 1930–31 and, finally, the Red Wings in 1932–33.) When the Rangers refused to buy in bulk, and after the Canadiens selected three men they wanted, Bruins owner Charles Adams paid $50,000 for the rest of Patrick's players, a few of whom he later sold himself.

In the end, a process that began in May wasn't fully resolved until October, but when it was done, the NHL stood alone as the last remaining major professional league in hockey.

The NHL Takes Control

By the 1926–27 season, the NHL had grown to 10 teams. The league split into two divisions of five teams each, and at the end of the season, the Ottawa Senators, winners of the Canadian Division, and the Boston Bruins of the American Division met in the first all-NHL Stanley Cup Final. It was won by the Senators.

Before the start of the 1926–27 season, there had been talk of the newly formed American Hockey Association (AHA) taking the place of the Western Hockey League as a Stanley Cup rival for the NHL. However, the NHL quickly came to see the AHA as a minor league and an outlaw organization, so no agreement was made. Still, the Montreal *Gazette* reported on April 8, 1927, that the AHA-champion Duluth Hornets had challenged for the Stanley Cup.

But Ottawa wasn't called upon to defend its title.

Over the next few years, the AHA champions would again challenge for the Cup. On April 11, 1931, the Tulsa Oilers issued a challenge, but trustee William Foran ruled it was too late in the season to order the Montreal Canadiens to play more games. Hoping to get an earlier start the following season, AHA president William F. Grant issued a new challenge at the beginning of February in 1932. The Stanley Cup trustees accepted the challenge on February 3, but there were immediate protests from NHL president Frank Calder.

"As far as I am personally concerned," said Calder on February 4, 1932, in a statement widely reported in newspapers the next day, "there will be no truck or trade with any outlaw league for the Stanley Cup or any other trophy. The sponsors of the outlaw league are fully aware of that. They are also aware of the requirements necessary to enter organized professional hockey. Any attempt to chisel their way in by means of a challenge for the Stanley Cup is nothing but an attempt to evade those requirements."

Calder went further four days later when he claimed he would forfeit the trophy rather than play against the AHA champs, adding "a prominent sportsman" had already offered another cup "valued at over $1,000" to replace the Stanley Cup. Calder also expressed his doubts that trustee William Foran would hand over the trophy to the AHA when the NHL champs refused to play, believing it was more likely the Stanley Cup would be withdrawn from competition and donated to the Dominion Archives in Ottawa.

With the AHA dispute lasting well into March, other leagues were showing an interest too. The owners and directors of the new Canadian-American Hockey League had issued a challenge back on January 30, but president James E. Dooley advised league officials at a meeting in Boston on March 22 that Foran had refused to consider it. Still, the AHA wasn't backing down, as an Associated Press report soon made clear:

> CHICAGO, Ill., March 24.—The American Hockey League has no intention of letting the Stanley Cup, emblem of world hockey supremacy, go to the NHL.
>
> Tom Shaughnessy, president of the Chicago Shamrocks, who led the American League and were favorites to win the intra-league playoffs, today said that his team would issue a formal challenge to the National League winners with every expectation of playing for the Cup as would any other club in his league.
>
> William Foran, prominent Ottawa sportsman, who is one of the trustees of the Stanley

Philip Dansken Ross.

will be no series for the Stanley Cup with the American Hockey League. There will be no interference with the present Stanley Cup series."

Questioned for further details that evening, Foran said the following:

> The challenge of the American Hockey
> League for the Stanley Cup has been accepted
> but as the National Hockey League has
> refused to meet the champions of the Amer-
> ican league, there will be no series between
> the two leagues this year.
>
> The present National Hockey League
> playoff series will continue and its ultimate
> winners will receive the Stanley Cup. The
> future of the Cup after this season is a matter
> which we (the trustees) will have to decide.
>
> There is nothing further we can say.

No non-NHL team has ever played for the Stanley Cup since the Victoria Cougars of 1926, but the matter wouldn't truly be resolved until 15 years after William Foran's statement of 1932.

On June 30, 1947, original Stanley Cup trustee P.D. Ross, who was 89 years old at the time (he would die at 91 on July 5, 1949) and J. Cooper Smeaton (who succeeded Foran as the second trustee upon Foran's death in 1945) signed a formal document with the NHL and league president Clarence Campbell. Among the seven terms in their agreement, the trustees delegated full authority to the NHL to determine and amend from time to time the conditions of the competition for the Stanley Cup, and agreed not to accept any challenges unless they conformed with the NHL's wishes. The agreement states it will remain in force "as long as the League continues to be the world's leading professional hockey league as determined by its playing calibre," although the NHL is allowed to

Cup, stated this afternoon that if the National Hockey League refuses to see the American League challengers there will be no Stanley Cup games.

"I am going to Montreal tomorrow to meet Frank Calder, president of the National League," said Mr. Foran. "We have accepted the challenge of the American League and will settle the whole matter tomorrow."

The two men did meet in Montreal on the morning of March 25, and that afternoon, Foran announced his decision in a short speech at a luncheon hosted by the Canadiens for Montreal and New York reporters covering the Canadiens-Rangers playoff series. "There return the Cup to the trustees any time it wishes. The Cup will also revert to the trustees in the event of the dissolution or other termination of the NHL.

Final Challenges

In 1953, the NHL would turn down a challenge from the AHL-champion Cleveland Barons, after having turned down Cleveland's efforts to enter the NHL in the summer of 1952. Twenty years later, on May 6, 1973, the New England Whalers defeated the Winnipeg Jets 9–6 for a four-games-to-one victory to claim the Avco Cup as the first champions of the World Hockey Association (WHA). Immediately after the game, Whalers president Howard Baldwin issued a challenge for the Stanley Cup. He suggested a one-game playoff, on neutral ice, with the proceeds going to charity. "This challenge is meant in no disrespect to either of those two fine teams (Montreal or Chicago, who were playing in the Stanley Cup Final) or the National Hockey League," said Baldwin. "This is a challenge intended only to restore the people their right

Ray Ceresino as a member of the Cleveland Barons at some point between the 1949–50 and 1953–54 AHL seasons.

to see a true champion decided in this, the world's fastest sport."

Brian O'Neill, who was then the NHL's executive director and would become a Stanley Cup trustee himself in 1988, said the decision to face the WHA champions would be up to NHL president Clarence Campbell, but "I can't imagine we are going to be accepting the challenge."

The NHL did not.

Two weeks later came word of a proposed new European professional hockey league with teams in Sweden, Finland, England and Germany. Organizers hoped their champion might face teams from the Soviet Union and Czechoslovakia for the right to challenge the NHL's Stanley Cup champions. To this, Campbell said there would be "time enough to consider" any challenge series when the proposed league got into action, adding that while he knew of no reason any "legitimate professional league" should not challenge the top NHL club in an international series, such a challenge would not likely involve the Stanley Cup.

Finally, during the NHL lockout of 2004–05 — and particularly after the season was canceled — the Hockey Hall of Fame received countless calls from fans offering ways to ensure the Stanley Cup might still be presented that year. Adrienne Clarkson, Canada's Governor General at the time (the same job Lord Stanley held when he donated the trophy) suggested the Cup be awarded to the top women's hockey team. She would later donate the Clarkson Cup to women's hockey.

In Toronto, a couple of pickup hockey players took the NHL to court and actually won concessions that may allow other teams to play for the Stanley Cup if a season ever again gets canceled. (They also won a $100,000 donation from the NHL to grassroots hockey organizations in Canada.) However, despite

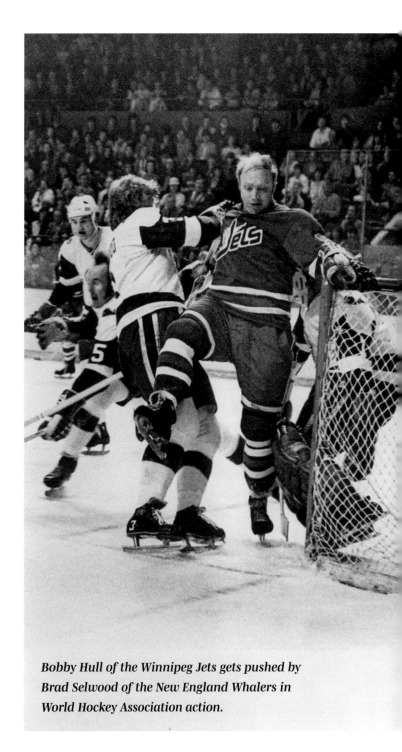

Bobby Hull of the Winnipeg Jets gets pushed by Brad Selwood of the New England Whalers in World Hockey Association action.

all the hoopla, Stanley Cup trustees Brian O'Neill and Scotty Morrison announced there would be no outside competition for the trophy in the spring of 2005, and the Stanley Cup remains exclusively the top prize of the NHL.

Hockey Rules

The game of hockey looked very different in the early days. Two halves instead of three periods; small rosters, but an extra player (the rover); and no forward passing. New rules — and new lines on the ice — would change the game immensely.

▼

Three Periods

Other sports are played in two halves or four quarters, so why is hockey played in three periods? Google it and you're likely to find a couple of explanations. Some answers will say having two intermissions instead of one halftime improves the quality of the ice by allowing the Zamboni or other ice-resurfacing machines to flood the rink twice.

Makes sense … but the change from two halves to three periods was made long before there were mechanical ice machines. (Though it would have given rink attendants two opportunities to shovel off any built-up snow.) Other stories will credit the innovation of three periods instead of two halves to Frank and Lester Patrick, who did create many modern hockey rules after launching the Pacific Coast Hockey Association (PCHA) in 1911–12. But the change from two halves of 30 minutes to three periods of 20 minutes was made the season before the PCHA started, in 1910–11, by the National Hockey Association (NHA).

The NHA began play in 1909–10. The league was formed after a dispute with the reigning top league of the day, which had changed its name that season from the Eastern Canada Hockey Association to the

Canadian Hockey Association (CHA). In reorganizing itself, the CHA had kicked out the Montreal Wanderers, who had promised to support the team from the tiny town of Renfrew, Ontario, in its bid to enter the top echelons of hockey. Ambrose O'Brien, who was heading up the Renfrew bid, and Jimmy Gardner of the Wanderers, then took the lead in establishing the NHA, which went head to head with the CHA in a battle to sign the top stars of the day.

The son of wealthy mining and railroad magnate M.J. O'Brien, Ambrose O'Brien used the family fortune to bring many top stars to Renfrew, whose team people began to call the Millionaires. The Renfrew signings included Lester Patrick, his brother Frank, and the star they would later lure to the PCHA: Cyclone Taylor.

It's long been said that Renfrew paid Lester Patrick $3,000 for the 1909–10 season and gave Frank (who had yet to play hockey at the highest level) $2,000. Cyclone's salary has been recorded as $5,250 for the 10-game season, though it's possible none of those three were paid quite so much. Regardless, the NHA was clearly outbidding the CHA for players, and early in 1910, the Ottawa Senators and Montreal Shamrocks abandoned the CHA (which went out of business) to join the NHA, which became the game's top professional league.

After the reckless spending of the 1909–10 season, and with no viable rival for 1910–11, the NHA sought to cut costs and put the game on a more businesslike footing during its annual meeting in Montreal on Saturday, November 12, 1910. News of what was being proposed first seemed to appear in the *Montreal Star* (perhaps other papers as well) on October 28. "It has been agreed that professional sport in Canada had been carried on under very loose methods, hence the officers of the National Hockey Association have taken up the matter of contracts, salaries, and changes in rules."

The biggest news to come out of the November 12 meeting would be the implementation of a salary cap that meant NHA teams could spend just $5,000 on their entire rosters. The proposed salary limit would dominate hockey talk for the better part of a month, with most players saying they would refuse to sign for such drastically lower amounts. There was talk of forming their own players league, but in the end, most players re-signed with their teams at the reduced rates.

The salary squabble overshadowed all the other changes introduced by the NHA for the 1910–11 season, including how the 60-minute game would be divided. (Another important change was the decision to allow teams to substitute players at any time, not just in the case of injuries.) As the *Montreal Star* had reported about the length of games in its October 28 story: "It has often been stated that play lags in the last ten minutes of each half. In order to maintain an even speed throughout it is proposed that the present two halves of thirty minutes each be changed and that three periods, each of twenty minutes be played instead of two half-hour sessions."

The first game in hockey history to feature three 20-minute periods was played in Montreal between

Cyclone Taylor on the Vancouver Millionaires of the PCHA.

the Canadiens and the Ottawa Senators on New Year's Eve, 1910. The Canadiens led 2–1 after the first and 3–2 after the second, but in the third period the Senators got goals from future Hall of Famers Jack Darragh (who was playing his first professional game) and Marty Walsh, plus another from Bruce Ridpath, to pull out a 5–3 victory.

In the game story in the *Gazette* on January 2, 1911, the paper noted: "For the first time the three twenty-minute period system of play was used instead of the two thirty-minute halves. It proved a success, the players getting more rest and consequently being able to play a faster game, while the spectators did not seem to find the extra delay irksome." However, the paper also reported that "at the conclusion of the second period many people unfamiliar with the new ruling as to playing time started to leave the rink under the impression that the game was over, but were recalled by Eddie St. Pierre, who announced through a megaphone that there was still twenty minutes of play to be seen."

In its Gossip of the Game feature, the *Gazette* related the following:

> Opinion seems to be that the change from two thirty-minutes periods to three of twenty minutes was a success. The play was faster and the possibilities of the final outcome of the match more interesting.

Others also approved. This is from the *Ottawa Journal* on January 3, 1911:

> The National Association innovations regarding the changing of the two thirty minute halves to three periods of twenty minutes each, though strange at first, resulted in faster hockey all the way, the men being benefitted by the two rests that enabled them to stand the pace much better.

Poor Scouting . . .

In addition to Jack Darragh for the Senators, another future Hall of Famer made his pro debut on the night of December 31, 1910. Along with fellow rookies Henri Dallaire and Eugène Payan, Georges Vézina played his first game for the Canadiens. The papers mainly raved about the Senators' new star, and the *Ottawa Journal* didn't seem impressed by the new Montreal goalie. In its story of the game on January 3, 1911, the paper

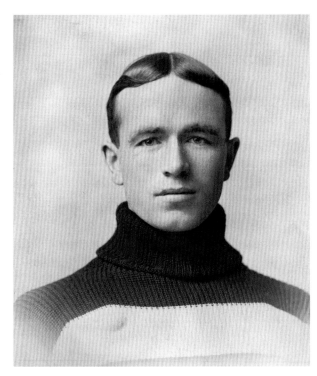

A portrait of Jack Darragh.

reported that "Vezina, Dellaire [*sic*] and Payan are newcomers to the National, and the latter is by far the best of the trio."

The Rover Is Over

An even bigger innovation than changing the number of periods in the game was changing the number of hockey players on the ice for those periods. The decision to eliminate the rover, taking away the seventh player on the ice and turning hockey into a six-man game, was introduced by the NHA for the 1911–12 season. While many other leagues quickly followed suit, the otherwise innovative PCHA would wait on this change until the 1922–23 season before finally adopting it.

William Northey is credited with the idea of eliminating the rover. Elected to the Hockey Hall of Fame as a builder in 1947, his biography (and other sources) also credit him with the idea of going from two halves to three periods. Northey had been involved in hockey since moving to Montreal in 1893 and becoming associated with the Montreal Amateur Athletic Association. During the winter of 1897–98, Northey and Montreal AAA president Ed Sheppard built the Westmount/Montreal Arena, which is considered the first rink designed specifically for hockey. Northey would manage the arena until it was destroyed by fire in January of 1918. Mainly involved with amateur sports, Northey played a key role in the formation of the Canadian Amateur Hockey Association in 1914 and would help to build the Montreal Forum in 1924. Born in 1872, he remained a regular attendant of games at the Forum until he was nearly 90 years old; he passed away on August 9, 1963.

The NHA moved to accept Northey's suggestion to drop the rover at its October 11, 1911, meeting at Kastel's hotel and restaurant on Ste-Catherine Street West in Montreal. Delegates were present from the Ottawa Senators, Montreal Canadiens, Montreal Wanderers, Quebec Bulldogs and Renfrew Millionaires, although Renfrew's team would soon withdraw from the league. Toronto representatives attended as well, although the entry of the Tecumsehs and the Toronto Hockey Club (usually known as the Blueshirts) would be put off for a year because of delays in construction of the Arena Gardens on Mutual Street.

Of the decision to end seven-man hockey during the NHA's four-hour meeting, the *Ottawa Citizen* remarked the next day: "The national winter game will, for the coming winter at least, be played with six men a side instead of with the old septet, the position of rover being abolished. Such is the decision reached, in their inscrutable wisdom, by the National Hockey Association magnates ... although all reasons for the change were scrupulously withheld."

But the *Montreal Star* either knew the reason behind the move or was willing to speculate:

Percy LeSueur playing for Ottawa.

The idea of limiting the players to six a side, which will abolish the old position of rover, is accepted for the purpose of making the game more open and interesting to the spectators. The impression is that six-man teams will do away with a lot of the close play in centre ice, and make for more of the spectacular runs which make the game what it is. If the change does not have that effect, the old order can easily be renewed.

The PCHA wouldn't officially hold its formational meeting until December 7, 1911, but the Patricks had been talking about raiding the east for players since August, and the *Ottawa Journal* suspected those plans also had something to do with the NHA's decision to eliminate the seventh man:

> It is expected that [dropping the rover] will make the game faster and at the same time relieve the management of the expense. There is no doubt that it will tend to make the game faster. The rover has always been more or less in the way and his place could easily be filled by the cover point. [Defensemen in this era generally played one in front of the other and were known as point and cover point.] The scarcity of players may have been the reason for the change, for it is likely that the Western League will take many of the Eastern hockey stars.

In its report on the meeting, the *Ottawa Citizen* related that members of the press had been excluded from the proceedings, but a statement from NHA president Emmett Quinn said all decisions reached had been unanimous. The Ottawa paper also claimed the Senators had been represented by N.C. Sparks and Martin Rosenthal, but the next day a *Citizen* story had team secretary Rosenthal saying he'd not been able to make his train connection in Cornwall and was therefore absent from the meeting. Rosenthal said that had he been there, he would have voted against the new rules.

"In my opinion," Rosenthal said, "the changes are very poor indeed. I do not see how it is possible to produce with but six men as fast hockey as we have had with seven. It appears to me as though the Montreal teams are weak again. They know, apparently, that they cannot muster seven men good enough to win the championship from Ottawa, and are endeavoring to weaken our chances."

Elsewhere on the same sports page, another unnamed officer of the Senators seemed to like the change, saying: "We have often noticed that games become much faster when one or two men are off the ice. It is also a fact that with seven men there has been a great deal of unnecessary crowding. We believe the reduction of teams to six men will make the game much faster and that it will do away with a lot of loafing." But he did add that if eliminating the rover didn't actually improve the play, "we will immediately rescind the motion and go back to our seven-man team."

As for the Ottawa players, reaction was definitely mixed. Star center and future Hockey Hall of Famer Marty Walsh, along with left winger Albert "Dubbie" Kerr, was said to be against the change. They believed a six-man team would spoil combination work (passing) and quickly tire the forwards. But goalie and team captain Percy LeSueur, another future Hall of Famer, was all for it.

"I agree that the game will be made much faster," he said. He didn't agree with others who thought the change would make individual play more predominant than team play. "It will certainly make the forwards work harder," he thought, "but for the spectators the game will be greatly improved." As to the criticism that teams playing six-man hockey would be hurt worse if a player or two took a penalty, LeSueur's response was simple: "A man who is continually going to the penalty bench is of no value to his team. His place is on the ice." LeSueur believed having one less player on the ice would encourage cleaner hockey. "Personally," he said, "I am delighted with the changes."

Opinions among players, executives, fans and sports writers were still split even after the season got underway. Some loved the change while others didn't, and by the end of January, the Senators and the Wanderers were both pushing for a return to seven-man hockey. Nothing came of it that season, but before the start of the 1912–13 campaign, the decision was made to start the season with six players a side but reinstate the rover on February 1. Eight of the next nine games on the schedule were played using a seventh man through February 8, but the switch back proved unpopular.

Six-man hockey was restored before the next games on February 12, 1913, and the rover would never return to the NHA or the NHL.

Western Six-Shooters

PCHA teams did play six-man hockey before the league finally adopted the rule in 1922–23. In exhibition games over the years, and in Stanley Cup games from 1914 through 1922, the rules of the NHA and

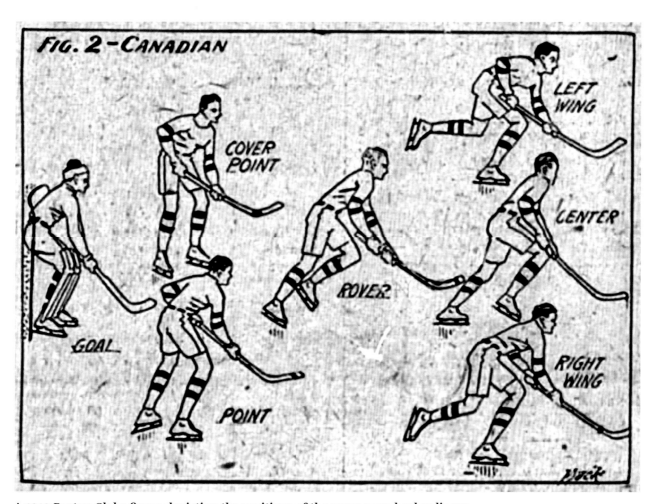

A 1912 Boston Globe figure depicting the positions of the seven-man hockey lineup.

Quote ... Unquote

"You might as well do away with the shortstop in baseball."

— **Marty Walsh** of the Ottawa Senators, quoted in the *Ottawa Citizen* on October 13, 1911, on his thoughts about the elimination of the rover

the PCHA would alternate from match to match, with Games 1, 3 and 5 being played under the rules of the host city (be it in the east or the west) and Games 2 and 4 under the rules of the visiting team. (NHA teams would play under PCHA rules, including

forward passing, under those same circumstances.) But the PCHA did at least play one of its own league games without a rover.

In February of 1913 there was talk of the PCHA playing out the rest of its season under six-man rules in order to be ready for a Stanley Cup challenge. On Saturday, February 15, 1913, New Westminster beat Vancouver 5–3 without rovers. The *Victoria Daily Times* reported on February 17 that both Lester and Frank Patrick liked the six-man game "and will advocate its adoption by the Coast League next season." The rest of the current campaign would continue with seven men per side, and by the time the peace treaty was agreed between the two leagues in September of 1913, it was decided that the seven-man game would stick in the PCHA even with the six-man game prevailing in the NHA.

The Life and Times of Marty Walsh

After the NHA's decision to abandon the rover, hockey leagues everywhere — except the PCHA — quickly followed suit. The transition, it seems, was more or less seamless, although it did appear to be a setback for the Ottawa Senators. The elimination of the rover might also have caused Senators star center and future Hockey Hall of Famer Marty Walsh to lose his job.

Although he's little known today, Marty Walsh was one of the biggest names in hockey in 1911. A native of Kingston, Ontario, Walsh had starred for the hockey team at Queen's University from 1903 to 1906. He was also a top football player for Queen's and would coach the Ottawa Rough Riders in 1911.

Walsh joined the Ottawa Senators in 1907–08, a year after the Eastern Canada Amateur Hockey Association (ECAHA) first allowed professional players to suit up with unpaid players. Cyclone Taylor also arrived in the Canadian capital that year. Taylor had

The 1911 Ottawa Senators.

mostly played as a forward until then, but he became a defenseman in Ottawa and would serve as the Bobby Orr to Walsh's Phil Esposito.

Like Orr, Taylor could do it all, while Walsh was a center who scored goals like few others in his day. In what was essentially Walsh's first season as a pro in 1907–08, he scored 27 goals in just nine games and placed second in the ECAHA behind Russell Bowie, who scored 31 times in 10 games. (Bowie was the greatest scorer in hockey in the early 1900s, when players routinely played all 60 minutes.) The next season, in 1908–09, Walsh led the league with 42 goals in 12 games as he and Taylor helped bring the Stanley Cup to Ottawa.

Two years later, in 1910–11, Walsh led the NHA in scoring. Sources vary, but he scored either 35 goals or 37 in a 16-game season. What is undisputed is that in a single-game Stanley Cup challenge on March 13, 1911, he scored three goals to provide the margin of victory in a 7–4 win over the Galt Professionals. Three days later, in another one-game Stanley Cup challenge on March 16, Walsh scored 10 times in a 13–4 win over Port Arthur. That's a performance topped only at the highest level of hockey by Frank McGee's legendary 14 goals for Ottawa against Dawson City in a Stanley Cup challenge in 1905.

Senators players had seemed particularly vocal in their displeasure with the NHA's salary for the 1910–11 season. During preseason salary negotiations, when Walsh returned to Ottawa from his home in Kingston, he was reported in the *Citizen* on November 16, 1910, as having said he was looking forward to the coming winter, but that a $500 salary "wouldn't pay his beef steak bill at Benny Bowers' [a cafe popular among Ottawa sportsmen] during the hockey season."

The salary dispute in 1910 briefly led to the sport's first player strike, although no league games were lost.

It's unclear how effectively NHA owners held the line on salaries that year, but the Senators were said to have signed only eight players and paid them all $625 apiece. (The decision to change the structure of the game from two 30-minute halves to three 20-minute periods may have made it slightly easier for Ottawa to get by with just seven regulars.) It's also been said that, as a championship bonus, management allowed the Ottawa players to split all the gate receipts from their two Stanley Cup games and from a postseason tour of New York and Boston.

Despite any lingering resentment over the reduced salaries in 1910–11, the Senators had no real competition that year. They started the 16-game schedule with 10 straight wins and finished the five-team regular season with a 13-3 record, well ahead of Renfrew and the Montreal Canadiens, who both finished 8-8. The Montreal Wanderers were 7-9, while the Quebec Bulldogs went 4-12.

With essentially the same lineup as in 1910–11 but now playing six-man hockey in 1911–12, the Senators fell to 9-9 in the expanded 18-game season and dropped into second place. A tight four-team race saw Quebec top the NHA with a 10-8 record to claim the league title and the Stanley Cup.

The loss of the rover had definitely hurt the Senators. "When the rules were changed," explained goalie and team captain Percy LeSueur in the *Ottawa Journal* on November 13, 1912, "we were completely at sea and it took half the season to get any system in our play. … In the seven-man game we used to play [a] three-man combination…. [Now] when a combination was broken up, there was no one there to check the man; the rover had been done away with and there was no trailer to the three-man rush." As for offense, "in previous seasons we had depended a lot upon the center man being able to hang around the nets and get the rebounds, at which Marty Walsh shone."

Indeed, a description of Walsh's style in the *Citizen* a few years later, on February 11, 1916, noted that he often liked to flip a soft shot at the net and then — in an era when goalies didn't have specialized gloves, carried their sticks with two hands like other players and were not allowed to drop to the ice to smother shots — "take an extra swing if the first [shot] did not ring the bell." But as LeSueur explained in 1912: "With the six-man game the center man had no chance to do that; he had to be back on the job [defending]. That threw us off a lot."

Walsh basically lost his job as Ottawa's main man at center during the 1911–12 season. He took part in only 12 of 18 scheduled games and dropped from 30+ goals to 11. He never played again. After just five seasons, and at only 27 years of age, Walsh walked away. He moved west, briefly to Winnipeg and then to Edmonton. There were rumors he would sign on with a team in the PCHA, but Walsh stayed in Edmonton, where he would coach the Eskimos hockey team during the 1912–13 and 1913–14 seasons.

During the fall of 1914, Walsh left Edmonton. Around September, he relocated to a ranch outside of Cochrane, Alberta. He may have moved on the advice of his doctors. Sometime early in 1915, he moved again, this time to Gravenhurst in the Muskoka region of Ontario. Gravenhurst was the first site in Canada, and only the third in North America, with a sanitorium to treat patients with tuberculosis.

By the end of February 1915, Walsh was reported as being gravely ill with the deadly lung disease. Friends in his hometown of Kingston established a fund, which would be supported as well by the hockey community in Ottawa. (Frank Patrick of the PCHA is known to have made a donation, and one would have to think the Edmonton hockey community also contributed.)

Marty Walsh died of tuberculosis on March 27, 1915. His funeral was held four days later, on March 31,

Dallas Stars' Jamie Benn celebrates scoring a goal.

at St. Mary's Cemetery in Kingston. He was survived only by a sister, Mrs. Loretta Keaney of Sudbury. Frank McGee, then in training with the Canadian Army in Kingston, represented the Ottawa hockey club at the funeral. The fund for Walsh had raised sufficient money to cover all of his medical and funeral expenses, with enough left over to erect a commemorative monument at his grave that stands there to this day. Largely through the work of his nephew Martin Keaney (who was only about four years old when his uncle died), Marty Walsh was elected to the Hockey Hall of Fame in 1962 and inducted in 1963.

7–6–5–4–3

With the PCHA finally doing away with the rover in 1922–23, the era of seven-man hockey was finally over. Six-man hockey — five skaters and a goalie — has been in vogue now for more than 100 years. But for the 1999–2000 season, the NHL introduced 4-on-4 hockey (four skaters and a goalie) for overtime. The idea, of course, was to open up the ice so that more goals would be scored and fewer games would end in ties. Ties were eliminated altogether with the advent of the shootout for the 2005–06 season, but even after that, the NHL introduced 3-on-3 overtime in 2015–16.

The 2014–15 season had seen Jamie Benn of the Dallas Stars lead the NHL in scoring with just 87 points. That was the lowest total to win the Art Ross Trophy in a nonstrike season since Gordie Howe led the league with 86 points in 1962–63. But the NHL season was just 70 games long back then. There was talk throughout the 2014–15 season of the impending move to 3-on-3 overtime, but no one was really thinking seriously about a permanent move to 4-on-4 hockey — even though that idea had been discussed by at least one old-time Hockey Hall of Famer as early as 1946.

Newsy Lalonde had suited up in no fewer than nine leagues that were eligible for (or attempted to challenge for) the Stanley Cup in 23 years from 1904 to 1927. During that time, while Joe Malone was the only other player to top 300 goals, Lalonde played in 341 league games and scored 449 goals. (Or close to that. Exact totals are difficult to determine.)

He won scoring titles (either goals or points or both) in the Ontario Professional Hockey League, the National Hockey Association (twice), the Pacific Coast Hockey Association, the NHL (twice) and the Western Canada Hockey League. He played for, literally, a dozen teams in his career but is most closely associated with the Montreal Canadiens.

Lalonde had starred in the seven-man game and continued to thrive in 6-on-6 hockey after the elimination of the rover. On December 18, 1946, in a story by Canadian Press staff writer Ian MacNeil that appeared in newspapers across the country, Lalonde predicted the game would move to five-man hockey someday.

"Hockey as it is played today is much speedier and more interesting to watch than the game 25 years ago," the 59-year-old hockey great said. "The game is kept moving at a faster pace because of frequent player changes and ample reserve strength." Lalonde also noted there was less bodychecking in the game than there used to be, but more of what we'd later call obstruction penalties. "I predict because of the increased interference and holding … we'll be seeing five-man hockey in a few years. When you get ten players and a goaler inside the blueline there isn't much room to move around. I think five-man hockey will make the game even faster and more wide open than it is now."

Passing Thoughts

The introduction of the forward pass in hockey for the 1913–14 season revolutionized the game. It sped up play and cut down on stoppages. Still, traditionalists opposed it and would slow down the advances — it would take until the 1929–30 season before the game truly opened up. The mastermind behind the forward pass in hockey was Frank Patrick of the PCHA, but he certainly had to fight for it. Even with his brother Lester.

In the early days of hockey, the only safe way to advance the puck was by skating with it. Passing the puck, as we think of it today, was against the rules, but most hockey historians have probably been guilty of oversimplifying hockey's early passing rules by comparing them to rugby and saying the puck could only be passed laterally or behind.

The first official rules of hockey written in Canada are known as the Montreal, or McGill, Rules. The rules are generally agreed to have been written by James George Aylwin Creighton, who had grown up playing an early version of hockey in his hometown of Halifax. Creighton introduced the sport to fellow athletes in Montreal after moving to the city in 1872, and he captained one of the two teams that gave the first demonstration of hockey indoors at Montreal's Victoria Rink on March 3, 1875. The rules Creighton is said to have written were heavily based on the rules of field hockey, which had been written and published around 1876. The Montreal/McGill Rules appeared in the Montreal *Gazette* on February 27, 1877. There were

Canada's Royal Winter Game book (1899), the first book written about hockey played on ice.

seven rules in all, but the second one is key in terms of onside, offside and passing:

> When a player hits the ball, any one of the same side who at such moment of hitting is nearer to the opponents' goal line is out of play, and may not touch the ball himself, or in any way whatever prevent any other player from doing so, until the ball has been played. A player must always be on his own side of the ball.

But as the game advanced and players got more skilled, it became permissible to pass the puck forward. Sort of.

Arthur Farrell was a star with the Montreal Shamrocks from 1896 to 1901. The Shamrocks were Stanley Cup champions in 1899 and 1900. A future Hall of Famer, Farrell published *Hockey: Canada's Royal Winter Game* in 1899. It is considered the first book written solely about the sport. In it, Farrell claims the best strategy for passing the puck — even if the player who received the puck needed to be behind the passer when the pass was made — is to pass the puck forward:

> A scientific player rushing down the ice with a partner will give the puck to the latter, not in a direct line with him, unless they are close together, but to a point somewhat in advance, so that he will have to skate up to get it. The advantage in this style of passing is that the man who is to receive the rubber will not have to wait for it, but may skate on at the same rate of speed at which he was going before the puck was [passed], and proceed in his course without loss of time.

And by the 1901–02 season, the Ontario Hockey Association had introduced a rule saying that a player passing the puck ahead to one of his own team could put that player onside by skating ahead of him. As explained in the *Montreal Star* on April 12, 1902:

> The rule governing offsides in the Ontario Hockey Association is as follows: The player shall always be on his side of the puck. A player is offside when he is in front of the puck, or when the puck has been hit, touched, or is being run with, by any of his own side behind him…. A player being offside is put on side when the puck has been hit by, or has touched the dress, or person of any player

of the opposite side, or when one of his own side has run in front of him, either with the puck, or having played it when behind him.

This was known as "skating a player onside."

Still, these rules and tactics were a long way from what would be introduced in the Pacific Coast Hockey Association in the fall of 1913.

Passing Fancy

Referees were always halting play or disallowing goals. The constant stoppages were because of offside calls every time someone would pick up the puck after breaking ahead of the play. According to Eric White-head in *The Patricks: Hockey's Royal Family*, this was becoming a point of concern for the Patrick brothers: "Seated in the stands to check the situation during a 1913 World Series game between Victoria and Quebec, Lester [who actually played in all three games of this non–Stanley Cup series and so couldn't have been in the seats] counted fifteen stoppages in the first five minutes of the first game…. After that game, Lester and Frank got together to devise a rule to cut down on those dreary stoppages."

Whitehead explains that the result of their get-to-gether "was the installation of blue lines that divided the rink into three equal parts, with unrestricted passing allowed in the center zone." Though generally referred to at the time as the new offside rule, this was the birth of the forward pass in hockey.

It may have happened almost exactly as Whitehead tells it.

Or maybe not.

Talk of forward passing definitely seemed to be in the air in 1913. The postseason series of games in which the NHA champions from Quebec visited the PCHA champions from Victoria took place on March

24, 27 and 29 in 1913, so the Patrick brothers might have been discussing it as early as then. They certainly must have been talking about it by the time they met with NHA executives in September to hammer out their peace treaty, because by September 13, 1913, Vancouver's *Daily News Advertiser*, in a story datelined from Montreal on September 11, referred to the two leagues being hard at work trying to make improvements to the rules. "While the officials of the National Hockey Association refuse to discuss the question as yet," the paper said, "it is stated on the best authority that a new plan will be tried out this winter both in the West as well as in the East. This new plan will be in the form of marking a line across the ice sixty feet from each of the goals. Between these two lines offsides will not be called."

Two days later, the *Victoria Daily Times* noted Lester Patrick's return to the city from the meetings in Montreal, saying that the agreement reached with the NHA would be ratified at a PCHA meeting in October and that "several changes in the present rules of the PCHA, including the offside rule, will come up for consideration." That same September 15, the *Vancouver Province* reported that eastern hockey executives "expressed themselves as delighted with the proposals which emanated from Frank Patrick," and that since the artificial ice rinks in the PCHA would allow games to be played well in advance of the natural rinks in the east, "the NHA magnates decided to take the verdict of the coast league on the new offside rule," which would be tested out in November before the season got underway.

Forward passing — while new to hockey — was certainly not a foreign concept in other sports. Lacrosse had long allowed the ball to be passed forward, and shortly after these early articles about the "new offside rule" in hockey appeared in newspapers, the *Toronto Star* reported on September 24, 1913, that executives of the Intercollegiate Rugby Union had recently been discussing changing the rules of university football … although forward passing wouldn't be introduced into the Canadian game until 1929.

American football had adopted the forward pass in 1906. The new rule was introduced after a 1905 U.S. season in which about 19 players had been killed and more than 100 seriously injured. President Theodore Roosevelt demanded the rules be changed. Forward passing helped open up the game, although its usage would be rare until the 1920s. Still, the team from Pennsylvania's Carlisle Indian Industrial School, coached by Pop Warner and featuring Jim Thorpe, had made the forward pass a key part of its strategy as early as 1907. Even so — perhaps for racist reasons — credit for popularizing the forward pass in American football has long been given to a Notre Dame–Army game, which was played on November 1, 1913.

As the story goes, Notre Dame quarterback Gus Dorais and end Knute Rockne had been practicing passing plays at the request of their new football coach, Jesse Harper, in the twilight of a late summer day in 1913 on Cedar Point Beach, after finishing their shifts as lifeguards at the Sandusky Resort in Ohio where they both worked. Once the football season started on October 4, Notre Dame tuned up its passing attack in three lopsided wins over lesser opponents before unleashing their aerial assault on Army.

With Dorais completing 14 of 17 passes for 243 yards — numbers virtually unheard of at the time — Notre Dame scored a 35–13 upset victory. As Michael K. Bohn would write in the *Indianapolis Star* on the eve of the 100th anniversary of the historic encounter, "The game didn't introduce the forward pass to college football, but it gained enough attention to permanently influence the modern game." (Though there were other professional football leagues dating back to the 1890s, the NFL wouldn't be formed until

1920, and forward passing didn't become a big part of the NFL until the 1930s.)

A few days before the Notre Dame–Army game, the PCHA held its annual meeting on October 27, 1913. (It had been delayed from its original date of October 23.) Though newspapers don't seem to report on it, the new offside/forward passing rule must have been discussed at the meeting. The following story, discussing the pros and cons of the PCHA's decision and whether or not the NHA might follow suit, appeared in the *Toronto Star* on October 30. While it purported to give a balanced opinion, it summed up pretty clearly the opposition to the rule change that would seem to be the main view among hockey people in the east:

> At the forthcoming meeting of the National Hockey Association in Montreal, the advisability of the adoption of the rule permitting offside play in the centre third of the ice, as will be used in the Pacific Coast Pro League this winter, will be discussed and it promises a lively battle.
>
> The arguments pro and con regarding this style of play are many and varied. Those in favor of the rule contend that it will make the game faster by causing fewer delays for offsides in mid-ice, which they think do not materially affect the play to any extent….
>
> From the standpoint of … those who oppose this style of play, there is certain to be a strong protest. It is certain to encourage loafing … which was too much in evidence in the NHA games last winter. Last year it was very noticeable that the players loafed offside so persistently as to make the game drag listlessly along, while one player went after the puck and brought it back to centre ice, when the other would again either join in the

play or 'soldier' while the lone rush was being made on the opposing goal.

If this new rule were adopted most of the players would camp in centre ice on the edge of their opponent's third line, waiting for the forward pass and the short dash to the opposing goal. It is plain that the game under these conditions would develop into burlesque, as arguments with the officials would constantly arise as to whether the players making or taking the pass were within the charmed lines, and therefore free from penalties.

While the NHA continued to dither about whether or not to accept the new rule at a series of league meetings throughout November, the PCHA was moving forward. On November 14, 1913, it was reported that an exhibition game would be played on November 28 at the Victoria Arena between the home Aristocrats and the visiting Vancouver Millionaires. "In this contest," said the *Victoria Times*, "the new rules will be given a thorough tryout before a committee composed of the sporting writers of Vancouver, New Westminster, and Victoria [the three PCHA cities]."

In Victoria, the players had begun practice on November 11. In Vancouver, the *World* reported on November 21 about "the first real practice of the season yesterday" for the players of the hometown Millionaires and the New Westminster Royals. "The ice was marked for the new off-side rule … and the players were coached in the new system."

Two days later, at a meeting in Toronto, the NHA owners voted against making the rule change. "It being decided," reported the *Ottawa Citizen* the next day, "to wait and see how the new style of play worked in the Pacific Coast League."

Whose Idea Was It?

Did Frank Patrick "invent" forward passing in hockey? On February 18, 1913, the following story appeared in the *Vancouver Province*. (It had already appeared in other newspapers across Canada, and would continue to appear in a few more.) Vancouver had several daily papers at the time. There's no proof that Patrick would have seen the story, but it's hard to believe someone didn't at least bring it to his attention.

Frank Patrick, playing for Vancouver of the PCHA.

NEW OFFSIDE RULE PROPOSED IN EAST
Port Arthur Man Would Abolish Offsides
in Mid-Ice to Speed up the Play.

Port Arthur, Ont., Feb. 18.—Believing that the interpretation of the existing hockey rules makes the refereeing a far too prominent feature of the games, and very often stop play at its most exciting moments, rob it of many of its spectacular features, and tend to discourage team work, Hugh Gawley, a prominent hockey enthusiast of Port Arthur, is out with a brand new suggestion for their revision.

Gawley would practically eliminate the offside rule as far as it affects play in mid ice. His plan is to have dark lines made across the ice, twenty, twenty-five, or thirty feet in front of each goal net, and remove the application of the offside rule between those two lines.

"The intention of the offside rule," said Gawley, in explaining his plan, "is to prevent loafing offside and to keep players from standing in front of their opponents' net for a chance or intentional forward pass so that they could slap the puck into the net. The enforcement of the rule for offside passes immediately in front of the goals may be all right, but I see no reason why it should be so strict for mid ice play. Not a game is played but very many fine passes and spectacular rushes are broken up by the referee's bell, when the spectators would be much more delighted to see the players continue their dashes down the ice....

"If we could cut out from fifty to seventy-five percent of the amount of refereeing that goes on in the hockey games of today the game would be more pleasing to the spectators, more spectacular, and show more team work. It would be fifty or seventy-five percent better all round. The people want to see more hockey and less refereeing."

Whether or not Frank Patrick's idea to paint blue lines on the ice and allow forward passing in the neutral zone was completely original, he was the one who put it to practical use for the first time in the PCHA. And he continued to stand by the rule in the face of criticism from most other hockey bodies.

Quote ... Unquote

"Frank in particular had an amazing grasp of the science of hockey, and [he and Lester] were both already dreaming about changes that would improve the game. . . . At dinner, the talk always got around to hockey. Frank was always there with his ideas and views, Lester embellished them, and the rest of us would just sit and listen with the greatest respect. Of course, none of us dreamed then that Frank and Lester between them would eventually change so much of the game, but if anyone had suggested it to us that this might happen, we certainly would have believed it."

— **Cyclone Taylor** on sharing a boarding house in Renfrew with the Patrick brothers during the 1909–10 season in Eric Whitehead's *Cyclone Taylor: A Hockey Legend*

No Passing Fad

In *The Patricks: Hockey's Royal Family*, author Eric Whitehead quotes Frank Patrick on how the decisions about rule changes worked in the PCHA. "In all new suggestions for bettering the game, I always consulted Lester and had his valuable support, and vice versa. We'd argue about every suggestion from all angles, and if we then thought it might be good for hockey we tried it out."

The new offside/forward passing rule got its tryout on November 28, 1913. Frank Patrick was in the lineup for his Vancouver Millionaires that night, while Lester played for the Victoria Aristocrats. The crowd filled only about half the seats in the arena in Victoria, which had a capacity of 4,000 (the Denman Arena in Vancouver held 10,500), but the hometown fans saw the Aristocrats rally after falling behind 3–0 early in the third period to score a 4–3 win after 50 seconds of overtime. "The game was an excellent exhibition for a season's opener," reported the *Victoria Daily Times*, "and the teams staged a mid-season clash that had the fans on their feet from the start."

As to the main point of the evening, Barney Goss in the *Vancouver World* believed it was the almost unanimous belief of the fans at the Victoria Arena that "the new rules to govern the game of hockey, as devised by Frank Patrick for the coming season, will do with such slight alterations as experience may dictate in future." Goss later added, "The new rules were devised by Manager Patrick with the object of speeding up the game: giving the spectators action all the time, and that object was accomplished."

The game was definitely faster. Even so, "the opinion of the Patricks that it would speed up the play seemed to be vindicated for there was certainly fewer stoppages for offside than is usual," reported Vancouver's *Daily News Advertiser*. "But the test was hardly a fair one for as the players were plainly unaccustomed

to it they did not make the best use of its advantages and more than one of them were assuredly of the opinion that it was a fine excuse for loafing."

The Aristocrats seemed to have more trouble than the Millionaires, according to the *Daily Times*: "Victoria appeared mystified by the new offside rule, and the locals gave a very poor account of themselves in the opening periods.... The offside rule confused the men for part of the time, but they were slumbering, and it took Vancouver's third goal to rouse them from this sleep."

Perhaps Victoria's problem with the new rule was that Lester Patrick wasn't as enamored with the change as his brother Frank. "I am not greatly in favor of the new offside rule and will have to be shown

Frank Patrick.

where this rule will benefit the game before I lend my support to the move to have this clause inserted into the PCHA constitution," was the reply of the Victoria boss when asked his opinion by the *Daily Times* reporter after the game.

Hugh Lehman, the New Westminster goalie who refereed the game, wasn't thrilled either. Nor was his assistant, judge of play Frank Kavanagh. They felt the forward passes broke up the usual combination passing, made it harder to follow the puck and created more interference. "The game is faster and there are fewer occasions to blow the whistle," the *Daily Times* noted, "but there was too much looseness in the play to suit either Lehman or Kavanagh."

But Frank Patrick was happy. He believed the mere fact that the game was finished inside of two hours from the advertised start time was proof enough the new rule was an improvement. "I am sure that the spectators were satisfied with the fewer stops in the play and as for myself, I am sure that the new rule accomplished all that was looked for in the matter of speeding up play."

Vancouver star Cyclone Taylor agreed with his boss and friend, but teammate and fellow future Hockey Hall of Famer Si Griffis said the new offside rule was an impossibility in hockey as the game was currently played. "Too much bunching of the players," he thought. "Less teamwork and a greater tendency to loaf offside."

A few days later, on December 2, 1913, the *Ottawa Journal* offered thoughts that show the increasingly snarky opinion of hockey people in the east:

The "freak" offside rule introduced into the PCHA for a trial turned out to be about what was expected — a farce. The forwards loafed off-side, waiting for the off-side pass all through the game, and usually kept a couple

of men well past centre ice to take a chance of getting a forward pass and scoring. It also broke up any attempt to check back, one of the bad features of six-man hockey.

Allowing a forward pass in certain sections of the ice would tend to break up a defence or, rather, make it necessary for too much of a defensive game. Both teams would have to play three or four men well back in order to watch for an opponent getting clean away by the use of the offside pass.

The forwards could hardly be expected to check back when an opponent had received a forward pass a dozen yards beyond them towards their own goal. Checking back is hard enough in the six-man game without the "freak" off-side rule when the players must go at top speed for a full sixty minutes.

Still, Frank Patrick insisted the rule should at least be given another try, and it would be in effect when the PCHA season opened on Friday, December 5, with New Westminster at Vancouver. In the *Vancouver World* on December 2, Barney Goss reported that brother Lester was at least willing to go that far. "Lester Patrick was reported yesterday as being absolutely opposed to the rule, but Lester denies the impeachment. He went so far as to say that he did not think it should be either approved or condemned on the one showing and is anxious that it should be further tried out before it is officially adopted or canned."

Si Griffis was still referring to the rule as "legalized loafing," but Goss was a fan:

There are few real objections to the rule, and it has many merits. It was devised to speed up the games for the benefit of the spectators and it has that effect. The test game was burdened by but thirty-two stoppages during its progress and the contest was over at least one-half hour earlier than the usual time when governing games.... There was action every minute the players were on the ice, and it is action and speed the spectators want. The rule is much more trying on the physique of the players, but they have compensation in the fact that they can get a rest any time they are seriously in need of it. It looks like a mighty good rule, and until it is demonstrated that its faults overshadow its merits it should prevail.

New Westminster beat Vancouver 7–5 on December 5, but despite the home team's loss, the local papers all reported on Saturday that the offside/forward pass rule was a big hit with fans. The *Vancouver Sun* said only that the "new offside rule makes a favorable impression and may be adopted." The *Province* and the *Daily News Advertiser* both had more.

"The new offside rule made a hit with the fans last night for it eliminated a lot of stoppages in the middle area," the *Province* reported. "The players showed a little hesitation at times in making the forward pass but frequently they got away with it for good gains. Toward the end the players tired under the terrific pace ... and resorted to considerable loafing offside. It had been agreed before the game that loafing would be permitted in the centre section but Referee [Skinner] Poulin had occasion to pull the players up a number of times near the finish for laying offside inside the lines."

With regard to loafing, the *Daily News Advertiser* thought: "If this habit can be checked the success of Frank Patrick's new rule is assured. Both teams played faster hockey as a result of the adoption of the new system and when they become more accustomed

to this style of play undoubtedly there will be more speed to the play."

The *Daily News Advertiser* added that the new rule "will be experimented with further before a decision is reached by the Coast League magnates," but as it turned out, PCHA executives held a special meeting that same Saturday night and approved the change by a unanimous vote. "We believe that the rule has worked satisfactorily and I am sure that the fans on the Coast appreciated the change," the *Daily News Advertiser* quoted Frank Patrick as saying in its Sunday edition on December 7, 1913. "We want to speed up the game and I believe that we will accomplish this purpose in adopting the new rules."

And after just one more game (a 6–2 victory for Victoria at home over New Westminster on December 9), the players themselves had come around. As the *Province* reported the following day:

> While most everybody else was satisfied with the workings of Frank Patrick's new offside rule in the first two games of the season, the players expressed themselves mostly as against the rule, but last night there was a marked change on the part of the puckchasers. After the game the Victoria players, one and all, came out with the declaration that the new rule was a distinct improvement to the game, while the Westminster players also fell into line. That is the best indication of the success of the rule. The players asserted that it made the game faster and freely admitted that the centre-ice play was improved by the freedom given in the way of passing the rubber.

Within a few days, newspapers in the east were reporting on a telegram Frank Patrick had sent to NHA president Emmett Quinn in Montreal on

Quote ... Unquote

"Taylor was the ultimate hockey player. There'll never be another like him. He was blessed with the complete skills, quite apart from the unique excitement he generated every time he stepped onto the ice. I watched him very closely, and some of our ideas, such as creating the two blue lines to open up the center-ice area for passing, were inspired by his marvellous style."

— **Frank Patrick** on Cyclone Taylor, quoted by Eric Whitehead in *The Patricks: Hockey's Royal Family*

December 11, 1913. Among other things, Patrick's message strongly recommended the adoption of the PCHA's new rule. The papers believed the NHA was now likely to make the change itself.

But it never did.

It would take until the second season of the NHL, in 1918–19, before blue lines were painted on the ice in eastern rinks and forward passing was allowed.

Setting Up the Scorers

On November 6, 1913, the *Daily Times* in Victoria ran a story about some of the rule changes coming to the PCHA for the 1913–14 season, announced that morning by Lester Patrick. Though nothing was written about the new offside/forward passing rule, the paper did note that an official scorer would be appointed in each of the league cities. "His duty will be to keep a record of the goals scored, by whom, the assists, and penalties of each league match played in that city."

Interestingly, while the NHA would refuse to adopt the center-ice zone for forward passing, they did vote at their league meeting on November 23, 1913, to have their official scorers keep track of assists as well as the players who score the goals. "This is done," reported the Montreal *Gazette* the next day, "with a view to encouraging more combination play in the matches."

Still, the official compilation of assists in hockey definitely seems like a Frank Patrick innovation. Especially in light of the fact that the PCHA had begun recording assists for the 1912–13 season, the year before the league allowed forward passing. Indeed, newspapers in Vancouver and Victoria were listing assists in their stories and summaries of PCHA games throughout that campaign. Barney Goss provided the background in his column in the *Vancouver World* from March 3, 1913:

> Just prior to the opening of the season I devised the system of scoring which has prevailed in The World this year, by giving assists to players from whom passes of the puck resulted directly in goals. It was done on the suggestion of Frank Patrick, who wanted to see if giving credit to the player making a pass equal to that given the player taking the pass and scoring the goal therefrom would not result in eliminating a tendency of "hoggishness" on the part of individualists who wanted their names well up in the scoring columns....
>
> When the system was inaugurated in The World there were a lot of hide-bound gentlemen, who, never seeing anything good off the beaten track, scoffed at the idea and predicted an early failure for it. It has been carried out consistently throughout the season and it has been an unqualified success. The plan has the complete endorsement of Frank and Lester

Patrick and of Jimmy Gardner, managers of the three teams in the association; they find their players ready to operate in combination when they know they are going to get credit this year in the official records of the association....

The work has been greatly lightened by the referees and judges of play, who have seen the merit it contains and when announcing to the occupants of the press box the name of the player scoring, have fallen into the habit of announcing the name of the player making the pass when the goal was the result of combination play.

While the PCHA tabulated — and trumpeted — assist totals for the rest of its existence, the NHA seems to have been inconsistent with the idea over the years, concerned that the publication of goal and assist totals made players too greedy for points. So much so that assists weren't tabulated as an official statistic when the NHL took over from the NHA until the new league's second season of 1918–19. Statistical researchers such as Ernie Fitzsimmons and Bob Duff have used newspapers of the era to calculate assist and point totals for most of the NHA era and for the first season of the NHL as well.

The Primary Assist

The 1912–13 PCHA season opened on December 10, 1912. (The NHA season wouldn't open until December 25.) The first game had New Westminster playing Vancouver. It was the first game Cyclone Taylor played in the PCHA. He would score a goal and set up another in Vancouver's 7–2 victory, and the general opinion in local newspapers was that he'd more than lived up to the advance notices from his five seasons

as a star in the east. But the first goal of the game was scored by another eastern newcomer, Jack McDonald, who was coming off a Stanley Cup win with the Quebec Bulldogs earlier in 1912. Setting up McDonald — and thereby earning the first assist in hockey history — was the man who'd come up with the idea: Frank Patrick.

In the *Vancouver World*, the historic listing appeared only in the official summary:

1—Van.   McDonald (from Patrick)...6:08

There was nothing about it in the *World*'s game story.

Other papers, perhaps, weren't aware of the history but noted the play nonetheless. "Jack McDonald got away with the first goal on a pass from Frank Patrick, who brought the puck down the ice," reported Vancouver's *Daily News Advertiser*.

There were further details in the *Province*:

Ran McDonald earned the first penalty for hooking Taylor when the Cyclone was making a thrilling dash and, while Ran was off his namesake [Jack McDonald] went down the ice with Frank Patrick, accepted the pass at the proper time and shoved the rubber past [Hugh] Lehman for the first goal.

1–2–3–4

When awarding assists, it seems the PCHA didn't give out more than one (and often none) on any goal. But the thought of awarding a second assist must have been making the rounds toward the end of the 1916–17 season. There seems no other explanation for this rant in a Hockey Gossip column in the *Vancouver Daily Province* on February 27, 1917:

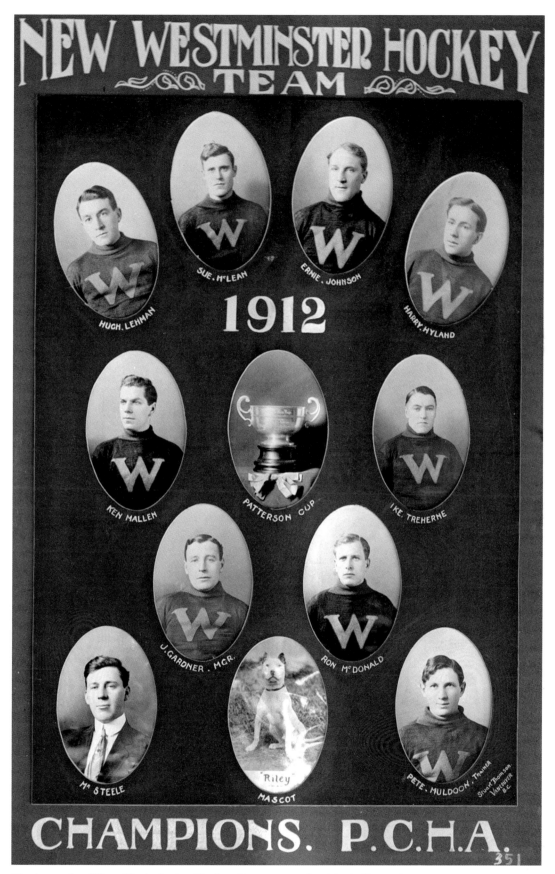

Photograph of New Westminster Hockey Team, 1912, the PCHA Champions.

The argument which some folks try to advance that double assists should be given in hockey will cause little excitement in hockey circles. The fans want the goals irrespective of how they are scored. It's not the team nor the player with the most assists that wins a title. The goals determine the issue.

Assuming that assists are due players who participate in a play that result[s] in a goal … if [Cyclone] Taylor passes to [Barney] Stanley who passes to [Gord] Roberts who passes to [Mickey] MacKay who passes to [Frank] Patrick who scores, why stop at double assists? They all had a hand in the play you must admit.

But why argue? … It is not necessary to credit assists to get a line on a player's ability.

The Coast League has been directly responsible for the introduction of some useful rules in the game … but this does not necessarily follow that all experiments must prove successful. There is little merit in single assists and none whatsoever in double assists so why worry?

When the NHL began to officially track assists in 1918–19, there was never more than one given on any goal for the next four seasons. But perhaps the rule was changed after that, because the first goal in NHL history to feature two assists was recorded on the second night of the 1922–23 season when the Toronto St. Pats visited the Ottawa Senators on December 20, 1922. With Ottawa leading 3–1 early in the second period (en route to a 7–2 victory), Punch Broadbent scored his second goal of the night and assists were awarded to Jack Darragh and George Boucher.

According to the game report the next day in the *Ottawa Journal*, "Darragh broke away and flipped the disc to Boucher who shot and Punch pounded on the rebound and scored [at] 3:55." In Montreal, the *Gazette* provides a little more detail: "Darragh and Boucher pulled off a nice piece of combination and Darragh shot. [Toronto goalie John Ross] Roach saved, but Broadbent, who had been trailing, tore in and flicked the rebound in for Ottawa's fourth goal."

Most accounts of the history of assists in the NHL will note that from 1930–31 through 1935–36, up to three assists could be awarded on a single goal. However, the first instance of a goal being credited with three assists actually occurred on March 13, 1928. This time, the Senators were visiting Toronto, who were the Maple Leafs by then. When Danny Cox scored for Toronto at 15:30 of the first period for the first goal in what would wind up a 1–1 tie, the NHL's original game sheets show assists were given to Eddie Rodden, Art Smith and Gerry Lowrey. No explanation appears to be given in any Toronto newspaper that can be checked online, the *Globe* and the *Daily Star* noting only Rodden's excellent work on the play and saying nothing about Smith or Lowrey. The news that a hard hit from King Clancy — probably a slash — broke Cox's leg during the second period may have overshadowed any description of his earlier goal.

But it is true the NHL moved to limit assists to no more than two on any goal prior to the 1936–37 season. As reported in newspapers the next day, this was among the items up for discussion at an NHL meeting in New York on October 19, 1936:

> Owing to criticism levelled at scorers in some quarters for their generosity in issuing assists, a rule was adopted limiting to two the assists on any goal scored. There were occasions last season in Gotham when four assists were given on a single marker.

At least one version of the Canadian Press story, appearing in the final edition of the *Windsor Daily Star* on October 20, claimed there had been five assists awarded on a single goal. There doesn't appear to be any record of that, nor of any games with four assists during the 1935–36 season. Still, there had been a game between the Maple Leafs and the New York Americans at Madison Square Garden on January 10, 1935, in which Busher Jackson, Baldy Cotton, Andy Blair and Charlie Conacher were all credited with assists on a Toronto goal by Joe Primeau. Three assists were credited on three of the Americans' goals in the 5–5 tie that night.

The assist rule was clarified once again at an NHL meeting on September 24, 1937, when it was noted, "Not more than two assists can be given on any one play," but also that "an assist may be credited to a player if a goal shall have been scored off a rebound from a goalkeeper."

Still, as late as 1945, there were discussions about limiting assists to just one per goal. Such a resolution was passed at a meeting between NHL and Canadian Amateur Hockey Association officials in Montreal on June 15, 1945, but at the next NHL meeting on September 7, 1945, agreements were reached standardizing the rules of hockey across all professional and amateur leagues, including that two assists would be allowed where such assists were earned.

Standing on His Head

It seems such a natural part of the game today — goalies on their knees, or sprawled on the ice, rolling or spinning, doing anything to make the save — that it's hard to believe someone had to invent it. But in the beginning, goalies were required to remain standing at all times to stop the puck. Clint Benedict's habit of falling to the ice in NHA and NHL games is often

credited for the change in this rule, but it was the Patrick brothers in the PCHA who spearheaded this change too.

Eric Whitehead credits Lester Patrick with this one. "It doesn't make sense," he portrays Lester as saying in *The Patricks: Hockey's Royal Family.* "A goalkeeper should be allowed to make any move he wants, just like the rest of us. He should be allowed to make the most of his physical abilities."

Lester may well have expressed these very sentiments, but Whitehead claims the change was made prior to the first PCHA season of 1911–12. It wasn't. The Patricks didn't change the rule until a league meeting in Vancouver on November 10, 1916. Reporting on it the next day, both the *Victoria Daily Times* and the *Vancouver Sun* said:

> Hereafter the goal-keeper will be able to stop the puck in any way he pleases and, according to the meeting, can even stand on his head if he wants to in saving the rubber.

The change wasn't quite as "anything goes" as that. As Whitehead relates, "The rule change allowed a goalie to stop the puck in any way he chooses, 'except by throwing his stick, but must not hold the puck or pass it forward with his hands.'" The *Ottawa Citizen* of November 13, 1916, reports the change "carried without opposition."

Like the forward pass, it seems the NHA was also considering the same new rule at the exact same time. The *Daily British Whig* in Kingston, Ontario, reported on November 3 that the "NHA proposes to allow goal-keepers to get down on their knees or adopt any other means in defending their goals." However, nothing about this was announced after the league meeting on November 11. (The biggest rule change to come out of the meeting was the awarding of a goal if any

Lester Patrick poses for a portrait as the emergency goaltender for the New York Rangers in 1928.

player threw his stick at the puck to prevent a goal from being scored.)

There was some mention later that the goalie rule might be discussed further at an NHA meeting in December, but joining the PCHA in changing the rule that penalized a goalie for dropping to his knees would have to wait until early in the first NHL season, on January 9, 1918. On that day, NHL president Frank Calder sent the following message to team managers and referees:

> Section 13 of the rules, and that portion of Section 9 dealing with the goal-keeper are hereby deleted, thus permitting the goal-keeper to adopt any attitude he pleases in stopping a shot. Please be governed accordingly.

The Center-Ice Red Line

When the NHL finally adopted blue lines to allow forward passing in the neutral zone, the lines were placed much closer to center ice than they had been in the PCHA. The NHL designated only a 40-foot passing area in the neutral zone rather than the 60-foot area in the coast league. The blue lines wouldn't be moved farther apart until the 1926–27 season.

Meanwhile, when the PCHA amalgamated with the Western Canada Hockey League for the 1924–25 season, among the first things league officials announced after their meeting on August 26, 1924, was that they were going to allow forward passing in all three zones. In the previous season, forward passing had been allowed in the neutral zone and the defensive zone.

Forward passing wouldn't be allowed in all three zones in the NHL until the 1929–30 campaign, after the record-low scores of 1928–29. Teams combined for just three goals per game that season, and there were 120 shutouts among the 220 games played, including 15 scoreless ties. George Hainsworth set records with 22 shutouts and a 0.92 goals-against average, while seven other goalies in the 10-team league reached double digits in shutouts. Among the 10 goalies who played at least 37 of their team's 44 games that year, none had an average above 1.85. Clearly something had to be done.

But previously in the WCHL, and now in the NHL, while the puck could be passed forward in any of the three zones, the rules prohibited players from passing the puck across the blue line. This meant the only effective way for a team to clear the puck out of its own zone was to either shoot it out and give up possession or try to skate it out. And to make things more difficult for a team to skate it out, coaches were soon instructing their defensemen — who had tended to lag behind the play to focus on defense — to move right up inside their opponent's blue line. Art Ross with the Boston Bruins seems to have been the first to employ this new strategy during the 1930–31 season. By the following year (long before the term was used to identify a team with a man advantage due to a penalty), people began referring to this hockey version of the full-court press as "the power-play." Later, they would also refer to it as "ganging" or "gang play."

The obvious solution might have been to allow teams to pass the puck across their own blue line and out of their defensive zone. But it seems the NHL was not yet ready for long passes all the way through the neutral zone. Even so, what modern commentators usually refer to as a "stretch pass" — which wasn't introduced to the NHL until the 2005–06 season — was actually discussed quite often during the 1930s. In fact, the minor-league Canadian-American Hockey League experimented with long passes all the way up to the opponent's blue line during the 1935–36 season. Other leagues during this time may have as well.

Art Ross, in addition to his role as general manager of the Boston Bruins in 1935–36, had also served as president of the Canadian-American Hockey League. A few years earlier, on March 22, 1932, his Bruins had experimented with another idea for freeing up the ice in a season-ending game against the New York Americans.

For that 1931–32 season, Ross had been trying to convince other NHL governors that it would speed up the game to split the ice into two zones instead of three. His plan was that, instead of two blue lines, a single red line at center made more sense. Offsides would only be called at center, and players would be free to attack their opponent's goal at will once the puck had crossed the red line. There were definitely fewer whistles — and a lot more goals — when the Bruins beat the Americans 8–6 in that March 22 experiment. Still, with two last-place teams merely playing out the string, no one was really sure how much effect the rule change had on what the *Boston Globe* called the poorest game of the season.

It wouldn't be until the 1943–44 season that the NHL officially added a red line at center ice. Frank Boucher, coach of the New York Rangers, was the man behind the plan. It didn't replace the blue lines, as Art Ross had envisioned, but it would allow players to pass the puck out of their own zone and into the neutral zone … provided that pass didn't cross the new center-ice red line.

At first, Boucher had come up with an idea very similar to what Ross had proposed. Like Ross, he wanted just one blue line at center ice. In a story in the *Windsor Star* on February 17, 1942, Boucher recalled trying out his plan a few years earlier in an Eastern Amateur Hockey League game between the New York Rovers (a Rangers farm club) and the Atlantic City Seagulls.

"It was an interesting game," said Boucher. "I think the final score was something like 7–3. The players said that they found it was easier to stick-handle out of one's own zone because the men were spread out so much. Today it is next to impossible to stick-handle out of your own end of the ice with five members of the opposition crowding you."

Boucher didn't see much point in going to a single blue line with World War II raging and the NHL losing so many players to military service. He thought moving to smaller rosters to combat the wartime shortages might be enough to open up the game. But a little more than a year later, he was proposing his new red line idea.

As Boucher explained in the Montreal *Gazette* on May 11, 1943:

> If a team backed up into its own end of the ice was allowed to pass out [as far as a center-ice red line], it would keep the other team from crowding up to the blue line. Most of the criticism is against having 11 men jammed into one-third of the playing area. With a line of this kind, they would have to stay back or run the risk of being caught flat-footed up the ice. I would leave the blue lines as they are. Once the puck is passed up to the new red line — just forget about the red line entirely. Go on playing exactly as before.

In his book, *When the Rangers Were Young*, which Boucher wrote with sports writer Trent Frayne and published in 1973, Boucher said he had discussed what to do with his peers, Art Ross and Hap Day. One idea they considered was to allow a forward pass as far as the opposite blue line, but this was still considered too radical. Boucher came up with the red line at center as a compromise. "If one blueline's too near and the other's too far, what about halfway

Art Ross circa 1964. His failing eyesight in later life would lead to the checkered red line.

Red Line Reactions

"Opinion was unanimous that the rule has restored balance to the game and improved it immeasurably. There was much less whistle blowing, fewer offsides and play ranged from one end of the ice to the other with amazing speed."
— Dink Carroll, Montreal *Gazette*, November 1, 1943, following the opening game of the 1943–44 season at the Montreal Forum between the Canadiens and the Boston Bruins on October 30 (Boston 2–Montreal 2)

"The new NHL ruling, allowing forward passes to the centre-ice red line found favor with the fans, possibly because Canadiens made much more use of it than the Bruins. Several times they caught the Bruins off-balance with fast-breaking plays, starting from quick pass outs from close to the net to centre ice."
— Canadian Press, November 1, 1943

"The new red line across centre ice seems to be so much fooferaw, or ice and 'dasher' dressing. Pretty, and all that, but otherwise ignored by all, including linesmen and the referee. The game is just as it has been since the continuous gang play became of paramount interest to coaches."
— Andy Lytle, *Toronto Daily Star*, November 1, 1943, following the opening game at Maple Leaf Gardens between the Maple Leafs and New York Rangers on October 30 (Toronto 5–New York 2)

"The new rules permitting passing to center ice and preventing jamming up on the face-offs didn't hurt the Wings, [and] speeded the game at least 30 percent."
— Lewis H. Walter, *Detroit Evening Times*, November 1, 1943, following the opening game at the Detroit Olympia between the New York Rangers and defending Stanley Cup–champion Detroit Red Wings on October 31 (Detroit 8–New York 3)

"The new rule seems an improvement on the old rule and yet not so much of an improvement as we had expected. Before the game Coach Dick Irvin of Canadiens had warned us, saying, 'There's not such a great difference. We're still being hemmed in by other teams and we're hemming them in.'"
— Harold Kaese, *Boston Globe*, November 17, 1943, following the first game of the season at the Boston Garden between the Montreal Canadiens and Boston Bruins on November 16 (Montreal 2–Boston 2)

"Hockey men declare that if Howie Morenz was playing today under the new red line rule he would shoot 60 goals a season. The old Flying Frenchman could take a pass at center ice and have only half the rink to skate.
— *Brooklyn Daily Eagle*, November 20, 1943

"Institution of the centre-ice red line is beginning to look like one of the hockey rules that's here to stay. There is praise for the red line on every side. Coaches and players agree it opens up great new possibilities for attack. The customers admit it makes a faster game in all respects. The red line puts a premium on skating ability, and if we're not mistaken that's what the game is all about. The red line was brought in this season to break up the power play, which was achieving unwelcome domination of hockey strategy. . . . From the evidence provided so far in the Winnipeg Services league, for one competitive group, the red line has achieved its purpose."
— Herb Manning, *Winnipeg Tribune*, December 14, 1943

Howie Morenz.

in between? We can put a line at centre ice and we'll paint it red to avoid confusion."

Boucher's new plan was first suggested at a meeting of the Canadian Amateur Hockey Association (CAHA) and was accepted at a joint meeting of the NHL and CAHA rules committee on August 14, 1943. A month later, at the end of the three-day semiannual meeting in Toronto on September 12, 1943, the NHL governors approved the change. (They also approved a change to the faceoff format so that players would face their opponent's end of the ice rather than the side of the rink.)

Reaction to the new rule came in mid-October when teams got to training camp. Art Ross and his player-coach, Dit Clapper, were holding the Bruins' training camp in Quebec City, and both men expressed their approval during workouts. The red line made its official debut on Sunday, October 17, 1943, when the Bruins faced the Quebec Aces in an exhibition game. After a 3–3 tie, Ross was quoted in the *Boston Globe* on October 19: "There is no question that this change will make for even faster hockey. It will prevent gang plays. It will eliminate many whistles. It will put a premium on hockey smartness, both on the part of forwards and defensemen."

King Clancy, who refereed the game, was equally enthusiastic. "I'd say it was the biggest change hockey ever made, and perhaps the best," he told sports editor Bill Westwick of the *Ottawa Journal* for its October 21 issue. "That red line in centre ice and the added freedom in passing up to it from either end is bound to make the game better."

Among the few critics of the red line was Clancy's former Toronto teammate Hap Day, then the coach of the Maple Leafs. Holding training camp for his team in St. Catharines, Ontario, Day didn't think the rule would make much difference:

> After all, it wasn't hard for a team to hold six men inside their own blue line under the old ganging play. The defending team frequently wasn't unable to shoot the pucks up the ice for minutes on end particularly when they were a man short due to a penalty. What chance would they have if they posted still another man out at centre ice for a possible pass? Even if a defending team does manage to get a pass out to centre the pass receiver has to get the puck on his stick and get under way. His check will usually catch him before he can get along.

Other than Day's complaint, the only real criticism of the center-ice red line was that it was too small. The new line was only two inches wide, while the blue lines were 12 inches. The NHL took care of that problem on October 27 when it announced the league would widen the red line to 12 inches as well. But the Toronto camp was still grumbling. Writing about the Maple Leafs' 2–2 tie with the St. Catharines Saints that night for the next day's *Globe and Mail*, Vern DeGeer snarked: "The new 12-inch centre ice pass zone line was displayed for the first time. By the end of the second period we were satisfied that the NHL rulemakers have definitely added to the confusion of the customers by even dreaming up this rule in the first place."

At first, the new center red line led to a lot more breakaways and more goals being scored. Boucher would write, "This was a development that intrigued the fans but horrified a lot of traditionalists who claimed the red line was making a mockery of defence, if not destroying the whole structure of the game."

Soon enough, defenses adjusted but the game continued to have more back-and-forth flow, which was what the rule intended. The NHL has long considered the 1943–44 season to be the birth of its modern era. The suffocating defensive game of the 1930s and early 1940s wouldn't really return until the advent of the left-wing lock and other stifling defensive styles of the late 1990s and early 2000s … which would lead to allowing the long stretch passes the center red line had originally been created to avoid.

Check, Please …

For 10 Saturdays, starting on January 5, 1957, CBS Television in the United States began a four-year run of national hockey broadcasts. After 30 years with the Bruins, Art Ross had retired in 1954. His deteriorating eyesight meant he could no longer attend games, but he liked to listen on the radio, and he was pleased he would be able to watch the CBS broadcasts from his living room in the Wadsworth suite, his apartment in the annex building behind Boston's Hotel Kenmore.

It may have been during that very first CBS broadcast. Perhaps it was later. The date was never recorded for posterity. But while watching on his small black-and-white television set, Ross noticed that — especially when the cameras showed a player in a close-up shot — it was impossible to tell if the lines on the ice were red or blue. So Ross phoned NHL president Clarence Campbell and suggested the center red line be dashed, or checkered. Within a few years, the checkered red line was a standard feature in hockey rinks all around the world.

As a player, Art Ross had always fought for the highest salary he could get and supported his fellow players who did the same. As a coach and general manager, he fought just as hard to keep salaries down and was always conscious of the bottom line. When his son, John, would re-tell the story of the checkered red line, he'd say Ross realized what he should have done.

"I should have called him up and said, 'Hey, Clarence, I've got a great idea. It'll cost you $500 to use it!'"

A view of the red-and-white center line during the opening face off of the final NHL game played at Maple Leaf Gardens, in Toronto Saturday, February 13, 1999.

CHAPTER 4

International Incidents

Few hockey fans in Canada paid much attention to the international game before the so-called Summit Series of 1972. Still, the forerunner of the International Ice Hockey Federation was formed in 1908 and Canadian teams began talking about hockey trips to Europe as long ago as 1912.

▼

World Cup of Hockey ... in 1912?

Until the country's NHL stars met the national team of the Soviet Union in September of 1972, Canadians hadn't shown a lot of interest in international hockey. From the first Olympic hockey tournament, held in Antwerp, Belgium, in April 1920 — prior to the Games there that summer and four years before the first Winter Olympics — until the early 1960s, Canadians mostly expected any amateur team sent to compete against the Europeans to dominate them.

Things changed a little after the Soviets entered the scene in 1954, winning the World Championship that year and an Olympic gold in 1956. Canadian amateurs were still more than able to hold their own for a while, but starting in 1963, the Soviet Union won nine major championships in a row. The newly created Canadian National Team — made up mainly of university players willing to put off their entry into pro hockey — was competitive but couldn't keep up with the Soviets. It was then that Canadians began

demanding for a matchup between the best NHL pros and the top Soviet players, who were amateur only in that they didn't get paid.

Canadian fans were stunned by how well the Soviets played against the NHL stars in September 1972 and began clamoring for more international hockey. Soon there was Super Series '76, with Soviet club teams facing NHL teams during the 1975–76 season (this was followed by eight similar series through the 1990–91 season). And there was the Canada Cup in the fall of 1976, which was followed by tournaments in 1981, 1984, 1987 and 1991 before it became the World Cup of Hockey in 1996.

But it all could have started 60 years before the so-called Summit Series of 1972, when there was talk of a new international trophy that would, according to a headline in the *Montreal Daily Star* on February 26, 1912, "Put the Stanley Cup in the Shade."

The article that followed described the proposed trophy:

Peter Mahovlich scores on Vladislav Tretiak during the third period of Game 2 of the Summit Series on September 4, 1972 at Maple Leaf Gardens in Toronto, Ontario.

Mr. T. Emmett Quinn, President of the National Hockey Association of Canada, has received an offer for a World's Championship Hockey Trophy, from a private gentleman, whose name will not be divulged till a decision is reached by the Association as to whether they will accept the trophy or not.

The trophy will be intrinsically worth Five Hundred Dollars, and one of the most gorgeous that has ever been seen in Canada.

It is a trophy that will be open for competition to teams from Canada, the United States and Europe, and is expected to put the Stanley Cup entirely in the shade as a trophy of importance.

The proposal for the donation of the trophy will have to be submitted to a meeting of the Association, which will probably be called shortly, and there is little doubt but that body will appreciate the offer.

Ice hockey executive Thomas Emmett Quinn, President of the National Hockey Association.

On March 1, 1912, the Montreal *Gazette* reported there would be a special meeting of the NHA in the Windsor Hotel that evening. Among other items on the agenda, league officials would "deal with the offer of an anonymous donor to give a new trophy for open competition."

As it turned out, arrangements for a postseason exhibition series in New York and Boston and the need to make up a protested game between the Montreal Wanderers and Ottawa Senators from earlier in the season dominated the discussion that night. As the *Gazette* reported the following day, "The new trophy which is said to have been offered for competition instead of the Stanley Cup was not discussed at all."

Early IIHF

The International Ice Hockey Federation (IIHF) was founded on May 15, 1908, in Paris, France. It was known at the time as the Ligue International de Hockey sur Glace (LIHG). Representatives from Belgium, France, Great Britain and Switzerland signed the founding document. Later that year, Bohemia (which became Czechoslovakia after World War I) joined as the fifth member.

The first international tournament organized by the LIHG took place in Chamonix, France, in 1909. The first official European Championship was held in Switzerland in January of 1910. Four teams took part, playing a single round robin. Great Britain finished first with a record of 2-0-1, followed by Germany (2-1-0),

Bohemia Ice Hockey Team, Champions of Europe 1911.

Belgium (1-1-1) and Switzerland (0-3-0). France, which had won the tournament in 1909, did not attend. The Oxford Canadians, a team founded in 1905 by Rhodes scholars from Canada studying at the prestigious British university, played exhibition games at the 1910 tournament and defeated Switzerland 8–1, Germany 4–0 and Belgium 6–0.

The LIHG became the IIHF on March 14, 1911, and officially adopted the Canadian rules for amateur play.

International Interest

The proposed new world championship trophy never seems to have been discussed again after the NHA meeting on March 1, 1912. When the *Ottawa Evening Journal* reported the story days earlier on February 26, it had described the trophy as international, but only for competition between Canadian and American teams. The *Journal* reported that the Montreal donor "refused to give his name," but the paper speculated it was likely Sam Lichtenhein, owner of the Montreal Wanderers.

Whether or not this mystery trophy was ever intended for European competition, hockey in Europe definitely seems to have been on the minds of Canadians in 1912 and 1913. Perhaps it had to do with the success of the Oxford Canadians, who were winning English titles and competing successfully against European national and club teams at the time. Or maybe it was the fact that the LIHG/IIHF had adopted the Canadian rules. Whatever the reason, in October of 1912, several newspapers across Canada reported on the junior team in Orillia, Ontario, making plans for a trip to Europe in the spring of 1913. The *Toronto Daily Star* told the story best on October 24, 1912:

Orillia, Oct. 24.—Arrangements for the proposed trip of the Orillia junior hockey team to Europe next March are progressing favourably, and have now reached a stage that the trip is practically assured, providing the team has a successful season during the coming winter.

Mr. John C. Miller, who so successfully organized and conducted the tour of the Canadian lacrosse team to Australia in 1907, is carrying on the negotiations for the trip. He has heard from clubs in London, Manchester, and Edinburgh in England and Scotland asking for games. Last week he received a letter from Mr. Van Buren of Brussels, Belgium, secretary of the International Hockey Association of Europe, in which the Orillia team is officially invited to attend and participate in the series of games which are played annually to decide the championship of Europe.

The other clubs that take part in the series are the champions of England, France, Belgium, Switzerland, Germany, Bohemia, and Austria.

Mr. Miller fully expects the final arrangements to be completed before the end of the year. The games in Europe will take place in March, the team leaving here immediately after the close of the [Ontario Hockey Association] season.

This trip will be a splendid outing for the members of the team, and will be worth many times the cost to each of the lucky players, as well as being a splendid advertisement for Orillia.

Few people in the know were worried about Orillia having a successful season in the OHA. After all, the Younkers, as the team was called, were coming off two consecutive appearances in the provincial junior

The Orillia Younkers of 1912–13. Back row: Ken McNab, Chief James, Dick Reid, George Moore, Pete Thornton. Front Row: Love Jupp, Quinn Butterfield, Norm Cooke, Andy Tudhope.

finals, although they had lost them both. In 1911 Orillia was defeated by the Kingston Frontenacs, who were led by future Hockey Hall of Famer Scotty Davidson. They lost to the Toronto Canoe Club at the end of February 1912. Still, the *Winnipeg Tribune* on October 31, 1912, hoped Orillia's European hosts wouldn't suddenly expect the Younkers' appearance to confer world championship status upon their annual European Championship.

"It is to be hoped," the *Tribune* said, "that writers across the sea will not emulate the American sports critics and style the game in which the Canadians play 'world championship contests.'" The writer complained that American sportsmen were always trying to hype the visit of any Canadian hockey team, no matter how weak it was, into a best-on-best battle, and warned that because Orillia was only a junior team, "the players cannot be expected to show Europeans first class Canadian Hockey." Still, "Junior hockey in Canada … should just about compare with the best in

Europe so that Orillia would be legitimate contenders for the European championship."

Interestingly, although probably due to the fact that both of its local newspapers were weeklies, the first word of the proposed European trip in an Orillia newspaper appears to have run in the *Orillia Times* of October 31, 1912. In a front-page story about the meeting scheduled for that evening to organize the Younkers for the upcoming season, the story mentioned John C. Miller and said the Younkers "would probably make a tour of Europe," with games in England and Scotland "as well as on the continent," at the close of the season in March. Nothing about the trip was reported when the *Times* ran its story about the meeting two weeks later, on November 14, but that day's *Orillia Packet* said, "After completing the OHA series, they will visit England and Europe."

Orillia would play in Group 11 during the 1912–13 OHA junior season. (The OHA had 11 junior groups that year.) Originally the group contained Barrie,

Midland and Newmarket, along with Orillia, but Barrie and Midland both eventually dropped out, leaving only the other two. Orillia opened the new season with an exhibition game at home against Barrie on December 26, 1912. The game was played on soft, slow ice, but Orillia jumped out to a 6–0 lead and went on to a 9–6 victory.

On New Year's Day in 1913, the Younkers avenged their loss to the Toronto Canoe Club in the 1912 final with a 9–3 victory at home. Then in OHA group play, Orillia opened its two-game regular season with Newmarket by scoring a 7–3 win on the road on January 14. The Younkers closed it with a 12–0 romp at home on January 21.

Next up would be the first round of the provincial playoffs, with games against St. Andrew's College of Aurora, Ontario, in Orillia on February 7 and in Toronto on the 11th. The day before the series started,

The 1913–14 Younkers inside Orillia's Palace Skating Rink. After losing in the OHA Junior Finals in 1911 and 1912, the Younkers won back-to-back championships in 1913 and 1914.

the *Brantford Expositor* of Brantford, Ontario, touted the Younkers "as coming OHA champions" and alerted its readers to their "additional incentive [in] the fact that Mr. George Moore, a merchant of Orillia [and the team's manager] has promised to take the boys on a trip to Europe if they win the championship for their home town." And after they scored 14–2 and 7–5 victories in the two-game, total-goals series, the *Expositor* reported, "The Orillia juniors are still continuing their march towards the junior OHA championship, and their trip to Europe."

Next for Orillia were romps of 9–3 and 16–4 over Collingwood on February 13 and 18 to set up a semifinal series with Oshawa on February 26 and 28. On the day of the first game, the *Daily British Whig* in Kingston, Ontario, had this in its Sport Review column:

> If St. Michael's hockey club win the senior OHA championship, it will, in all probability, take a trip to Europe, playing in England, France, Switzerland and Germany. Negotiations have been in progress for some time with the European hockey authorities and latest advices are that the trip is feasible. The Orillia team have also been promised a trip to the Old Country in case it wins the junior championship of the OHA.

But this appears to be the last mention of any European visit.

St. Michael's would go on to lose the senior championship to Toronto R&AA (Rugby and Athletic Association) in early March, but Orillia kept on winning. The team scored 8–0 and 7–4 wins in the Oshawa series, and then took the junior championship with a 7–4 win over Woodstock in a game at Stratford on March 4 and another 7–4 win over Woodstock at home in Orillia two nights later.

Younkers?

According to Orillia historian David Town, author of the book *The Incredible Younkers*, *Younker* was a popular slang word circa 1910. It was originally Dutch for "young man." The *Canadian Oxford Dictionary* defines *younker* as "n[oun]. archaic = YOUNGSTER. [Middle Dutch *jonckher* from *jonc* YOUNG + *hēre* lord]." Similarly, various online dictionaries define the word as "a youngster (dated)," and "obsolete. a young noble or gentleman." As to why Orillia took the name, Town thinks it was probably "just a cooler name than Colts," the nickname of the hockey team in Barrie, which was Orillia's biggest local rival.

As for the 1912–13 Younkers, the team had Norman Caswell (Norm) Cooke and Norman Johnston in goal. The defense was Gordon Perryman and Richard (Dick) Reid at point and team captain Kenneth Leroy (Ken) MacNab at cover point. Quinn Butterfield played center and rover, with Robert Lovering (Love) Jupp, Peter Francis (Pete) Thornton and Andrew Haron (Andy) Tudhope as other forwards. Dick Reid was only 17 during the 1912–13 season, while the rest were young men of 18 and 19.

There is no talk of a trip to Europe in any newspaper stories about Orillia's championship, and after the Younkers split a series against the OHA All-Stars (winning 9–0 in Toronto on March 12, but suffering their only loss of the season 4–3 at home two nights later), the *Sault Daily Star* of Sault Ste. Marie, Ontario, had this to say about the team's postseason plans:

Manager George Moore of Orillia Junior champions is undecided between a trip to North Bay, the Soo, Cobalt, and Haileybury, or to Guelph, Hamilton and Cleveland to wind up the season for his champions.

The team did play a final game, defeating Hamilton 8–3 on March 20.

But Hamilton, Ontario, was a long way from Europe.

A lengthy story about a town banquet for the team that appeared in the *Orillia Times* on April 24, 1913 — two days after the event took place — made no mention at all about why the team never went overseas.

Other European (Mis)adventures

There was talk again of the team from Toronto's St. Michael's College making a trip to Europe before the 1913–14 season. It may not have been serious, but the *Ottawa Citizen* reported the following on October 30, 1913:

> None of St. Michael's crack team will turn professional according to Manager Frank Dissette. They will again figure in the Ontario Hockey Association.
>
> Who wouldn't be a member of St. Michael's team? They have $9,000 in the bank and do not know what to do with it. It is proposed to send the team to Europe to blow the money.

But a report about the Montreal Wanderers in the Montreal *Gazette* from November 14, 1913, seems much more legitimate. Under the headline "European Trip Promised," the article stated that Sam Lichtenhein, owner of the Wanderers, had arranged to send a

Lester Patrick.

business agent to Berlin, Munich and Hamburg to set up a hockey tour of those cities in early March after the 1913–14 season was over.

"All the club's players will make the trip," the article said, "as well as an All-Star team to play a series of games." There would be eight matches in all, and the teams would be away for eight weeks, "two of which will be devoted to vacation." There were said to be good artificial ice rinks in all three cities mentioned, and the terms for finances would be "expenses and a percentage of the gate receipts."

Newspaper stories from earlier in 1913 indicate that Lichtenhein had been proposing an even more elaborate European trip for the Wanderers. In mentioning (and dismissing) the possibility in the *Victoria Daily Times* on January 11, 1913, the writer of the story noted: "Three years ago the Ottawa Hockey Club took up such a trip, and even went so far as to have its representative investigate conditions across the pond.

His report was that while the scheme was practicable, insofar as ice was concerned, there was absolutely no hope of securing the return of the money invested."

Sam Lichtenhein's European tour was also discussed in the *Winnipeg Tribune* on January 25, 1913. That story said, "Word has been received from New York that England, France, Germany, Austria and Holland will formally request a hockey promoter from Canada to take teams abroad to play exhibition games in the countries named." Lichtenhein was said to be interested.

"These countries," the article continued, "for the last few seasons have been manifesting more and more interest in the sport and are anxious to see Canadian professional [teams], the most proficient exponents of the game in action. They have witnessed amateur hockey, but have heard so much about the speed and expertness of the 'pros' that they demand a sample of it."

In both the Victoria and Winnipeg articles, Lester Patrick expressed the opinion that, while he was "tickled" to learn that hockey was becoming so widespread, he didn't think such a tour was feasible. In order to visit all the European countries named, he felt it would be almost necessary for the players on any two teams involved to pass up the entire season in Canada. "How many hockey players," the *Victoria Daily Times* had Patrick wondering, "will Lichtenhein get who are willing to sacrifice their salaries for a whole season in the Canadian leagues to tour Europe for their expenses only?" The *Winnipeg Tribune* said Patrick believed the European idea wasn't as feasible as something he and Frank were considering: taking a couple of teams to Australia, where the winter season occurred during what were the summer months in Canada.

The first indoor skating rink in Australia opened in the city of Adelaide on September 4, 1904, and the first true hockey game in the country was played in Melbourne on June 9, 1906. There was even an annual national tournament in Australia by 1909. At the time of the Patricks' proposal, Australian-born Tommy Dunderdale (a future Hockey Hall of Famer) was starring with Lester Patrick's Victoria team … but none of the PCHA clubs ever made a trip Down Under.

Orillia and Australia

Orillia native John C. Miller organized the Canadian lacrosse trip to Australia in 1907 and was said to have been organizing the Orillia Younkers' European adventure in 1912–13. He'd been the president of the Canadian Lacrosse Association in 1907 and manager of Orillia's senior lacrosse team. The 15-man team he put together for the Australian trip was not a true Canadian team (as some newspapers were only too happy to point out), but was composed of eight current or former Orillia players and seven others from across Ontario.

The team left Orillia on June 4, 1907, and played nine games (reportedly with a 7-2 record) while traveling across Canada. They set sail for Australia from Vancouver and Victoria on June 21, on the SS *Aorangi*, and arrived in Honolulu, Hawaii, on June 28 before sailing on to Fiji and then Australia. They arrived in Brisbane on July 14 prior to their first game on July 20. They played 16 games in either eight or nine cities across Australia through August 28, with a record of either 16-0 or 15-1. They then returned via Colombo, Ceylon (now Sri Lanka), through the Red Sea and the Suez Canal, and then by train through Europe before sailing home from Liverpool. They arrived back in Canada at Quebec City aboard the *Empress of Ireland* on October 24.

In the *Bradford Times* in 2017, Luanne Campbell Edwards wrote about the Australian tour. Her great uncle, Dr. Lewis H. Campbell, had been 41 years old at the time, but he was one of the players on the trip, which included a hockey game played against a local team at the artificial ice rink in Melbourne. "It was a funny game as they have little or no rules, no offside," wrote Dr. Campbell in his diary. "We won by 12–1."

Bound for Belgium

A Canadian hockey team finally visited Europe in the spring of 1920, when the Winnipeg Falcons represented the country at the first Olympic hockey tournament. Antwerp had bid to host the 1920 Olympics in 1912, but no decision was reached before the outbreak of World War I. Shortly after the Armistice, on November 11, 1918, the International Olympic

Committee offered Antwerp first choice to hold the Games in 1920 if the Belgians still wished to do so. The move was seen as a way to honor the suffering of the Belgian people during the war.

The Belgian Athletic Federation met on March 15, 1919, to discuss hosting the Olympics. It was decided to go ahead … provided the Games could be postponed until 1921. Stockholm (which had hosted in 1912) and Havana were said to be interested in hosting in 1920, and a few days later, newspaper reports indicate that Rome and perhaps Geneva were also in contention. (Online sources say Amsterdam, Lyon, Atlanta, Budapest, Cleveland and Philadelphia were in the running too.) But by April 3, 1919 — as newspapers would report the following day — Antwerp was

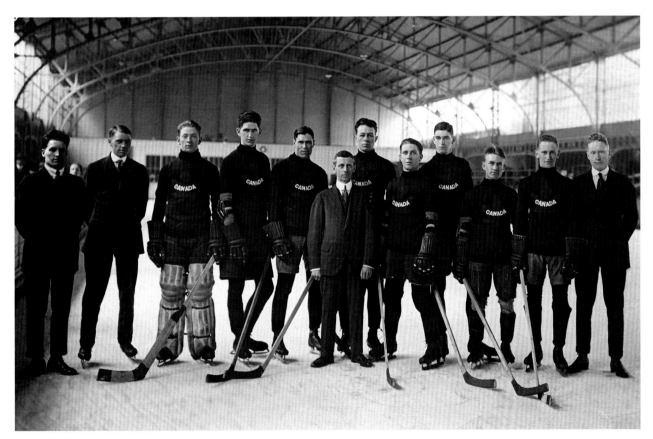

Winnipeg Falcons team photo at the 1920 Summer Olympics.

good to go for 1920, and the city was confirmed as the Olympic host.

On December 16, 1919, the official program and schedule for the Antwerp Olympics were announced. The bulk of the competition was slated for mid-July to late September, but events would kick off in April with a hockey tournament. Figure skating, which had previously appeared as part of the 1908 London Olympics, would later be added to the spring schedule as well.

By February 4, 1920, several newspapers were reporting that the Ontario Hockey Association was taking the lead in impressing upon the Canadian Olympic Committee the urgent necessity of deciding on Canada's representative in hockey at the Belgian Olympiad. Three days later, there were reports that James G.B. Merrick, chairman of the Canadian Olympic Committee, was in favor of sending the Allan Cup champions.

The Allan Cup, Canada's amateur hockey championship, would be decided on March 29, 1920, and by March 20, three of the four teams left in the competition — the Winnipeg Falcons, Sudbury Wolves and Toronto Granites — had all indicated they would be willing to make the trip to represent Canada should they win the championship. Only the University of Toronto team had yet to state their intentions. The U of T knocked off both the Granites and the Wolves en route to the eastern berth, but an 8–3 Falcons win on March 27 followed by a 3–2 win two nights later gave the Winnipeg team the Allan Cup by an 11–5 margin in the total-goals series.

The Allan Cup champions (whoever they might be) had been booked to sail for Liverpool from Saint John, New Brunswick, aboard the SS *Melita* on April 3, so when the Falcons won, the team had no time to return to Winnipeg. Fortunately, hockey fans in Toronto helped raise money so the players could buy some of the things they needed. Toronto mayor Tommy

Church wrote a letter asking local businesses for their help, and the city of Winnipeg raised $500, which was sent to the team. The government of Manitoba added $2,000. Proceeds from the Allan Cup tournament were also used to help finance the Falcons' trip.

The United States was sending an all-star team to Antwerp made up of players from Minnesota, Pittsburgh and Boston. A few of the Americans were born and raised in Canada, but they'd played in the States for several years and were said to have become American citizens after serving in the U.S. Army during World War I. National teams representing Belgium, France, Sweden, Switzerland and Czechoslovakia were also at the first Olympic hockey tournament.

The Falcons roster was mainly players of Icelandic descent. They had faced a lot of prejudice while growing up in Winnipeg, and perhaps for that reason, they decided to take it easy on their European opponents. *Toronto Star* sports editor William A. Hewitt (father of Foster Hewitt), who had accompanied the Falcons as a representative of the Canadian Olympic Committee, said: "One of the customs our boys instituted was to coach and assist all our opponents. We virtually trained the Swedes, Czecho-Slovaks, Belgians and French teams." Team captain Frank Fredrickson would later say: "We tried to limit ourselves to 14 or 15 goals against the European teams. Believe me, it was difficult!"

The Falcons beat Czechoslovakia 15–0 in their first Olympic encounter on April 24, 1920, while the United States ran up a 29–0 win over Switzerland. Because of the luck of the draw and an unusual tournament format, when the Falcons met the Americans in their second game the next day, it was essentially a semifinal match, with the winner all but assured of a gold medal when they faced their next European opponent.

Canada versus the United States was going to be the greatest hockey game ever played in Europe, and it was a tough ticket at an Antwerp arena that held just 1,600 people. Hewitt sent special reports on the games to the *Winnipeg Free Press* and wrote that this game "proved such an attraction that the Palais de Glace tonight was unable to accommodate one-tenth the number of people who sought admission."

In describing the scene, Hewitt wrote:

> The streets in the neighborhood of the rink were crowded from 6 o'clock, although the game was not advertised to start until 9 o'clock. The doors were finally closed about an hour before the match.... Special squads of soldiers were employed to get the players into the rink…[and] gentlemen in evening clothes on the outside implored the players to allow them to carry their skates and sticks so that they could obtain admission. It would have been a great joke to his Winnipeg friends to have witnessed the entry of Monsieur Mike Goodman, escorted by a detachment of soldiers and three men in full evening dress and top hats, carrying his skates, stick and grip — and they all got away with it, too, as valets to 'Monsieur le Canadienne.'

For those who got inside, the night was definitely memorable. "No one will forget easily the Sunday evening at the Ice Palace where [Canada] battled against the United States," read a translation of a Belgian recap of the tournament. "A full house, agitated [and] feverish, so much the public was sensitive to the spectacle and the intelligence inspired by this show of force."

"I have never seen anything like this sports competition," wrote a reporter for a Swedish newspaper. "Every single player on the rink is a perfect acrobat on skates. They jump over sticks and players with ease and grace. They turn sharply with perfect ease and without losing speed. They skate backwards just as easily as forwards. The small puck was moved at an extraordinary speed around the rink. The players fought for it like seagulls that flutter after bread crusts from a boat. The players attacked each other with a roughness that would have knocked you into the next week."

The Americans were a strong team individually, but they weren't a true team like the Falcons and that proved to be the difference in a 2–0 Canadian victory. "Their play was constantly more disciplined," read the Belgian recap. "Never a single player looking for individual glory, these men, in their united action, playing their assigned and required places, never to the detriment of the overall play, a team success exceeding individual achievement…. These qualities ensured a brilliant triumph of Canada."

The next night, Canada defeated Sweden to win the gold medal. The final score was 12–1. The only surprise was that the Swedes scored a goal. "They were without a doubt the best of the European teams," Frank Fredrickson would say. "They were very friendly fellows and we liked them a lot." In reference to the Swedish goal, he added: "I guess it's safe to say we gave it to them."

Hockey at the First Winter Olympics

The NHL showed little interest in the Winter Olympics in 2018 and 2022. Things weren't a whole lot different before the first Olympic Winter Games were held in Chamonix, France, in 1924. Back then — for a little while, at least — it was the Canadian Amateur Hockey Association that was less than thrilled about interrupting its season for international competition.

News of the 1924 Winter Games first appeared late in 1922. "The French Olympic Committee," reported the *Globe* newspaper in Toronto on November 10, 1922, "announces that the seventh renewal of the

The Toronto Granites, representing Canada, won the gold medal at the 1924 Olympics.

Olympic games will open … on January 20, 1924, with the program of winter sports."

The uncredited *Globe* writer, in his Scanning the Sports Field column, reminded readers that "Canada, will not, of course, have declared a champion hockey team until perhaps two months later. [So] the hockey competition will probably be deferred until April, as at the Olympiad of 1920 when the Falcons of Winnipeg won the Allan Cup and represented Canada, winning the world's championship."

But there would be no deferment.

On January 11, 1923, the *Toronto Star* reported: "It is not expected that Canada will be represented in the Olympic hockey tournament … next January to defend the honors won by the Falcons of Winnipeg, according to Secretary Fred Marples of the Canadian Amateur Hockey Association. Mr. Marples states that he has received word that the Olympic committee has refused to change the date of the tournament to later in the year, when Canada would have a representative team

to send, and under the circumstances, does not expect the Canadian hockey body will send representatives."

The subject would be revisited during the Allan Cup final in Winnipeg that spring, and obviously, opinions changed. On March 21, 1923, the CAHA decided unanimously at its annual meeting to recommend to the Canadian Olympic Committee that the winners of the Allan Cup for this season should represent the country at the Olympic Games the next winter.

The Toronto Granites won their second straight Allan Cup the following day, and by March 24, it seemed certain they would represent Canada. Their participation was virtually assured at a banquet held at the Granite Club on the night of March 27, 1923, after the team's return to Toronto, when city officials and the government of Ontario promised to help fund the trip. The chairman of the Canadian Olympic Committee added that the federal government had been asked to up its contribution of $15,000 from previous Olympic years to $30,000 in 1924.

Scenes from the 1924 Winter Olympics ice hockey final match, between Canada (in white) and the United States.

Rumors in April that France might not get the 1924 Games after all, or that winter sports might be excluded if they did, soon proved false, and on May 27, 1923, the Granites formally withdrew from the senior section of the Ontario Hockey Association for the winter of 1923–24. This cleared the way for them to represent the country in France as the Canadian Olympic hockey team in January and February of 1924.

Unlike when the NHL has participated, there was now no schedule to interrupt when the Granites went to the Olympics...although there was some concern about losing the OHA's best team (and therefore its biggest draw) for the entire season. Still, there wasn't really any other way to accommodate a trip that would see the Olympic hockey team set sail for Europe on January 11, 1924, and not arrive back in Toronto until March 4.

Thirteen players had suited up for the Granites during the 1922–23 season, but not all would be able to take the nearly two months off work that was required for the Olympic trip. That was fine, since only nine players would be taken to France anyway. The Granites' biggest star, Harry Watson, would go. So would fellow future Hockey Hall of Famer Hooley Smith, as well as another future NHL star, team captain Dunc Munro. Team veterans Bert McCaffrey and Beattie Ramsay, as well as Jack Cameron and Ernie Collett (both goalies), would also make the trip. Harold McMunn of the Winnipeg Falcons (though not from the 1920 Olympic team) and Cyril Slater of the Montreal Victorias were added to the roster as well.

Various members of the Olympic team (as well as some Granites from the previous season) saw action in a series of exhibition games on this side of the ocean to get into shape between December 1, 1923, and January 10, 1924. Sources often show the the Granites playing 14 games, though it seems they actually played 15. They won all but two, and in both cases (defeats at the hands of the Hamilton Tigers and Sault Ste. Marie Greyhounds, who had been the Granites' toughest opponents en route to the 1923 Allan Cup), the losses were offset by victories in either previous or subsequent games against their two top rivals. In truth, Canada could have sent the Tigers or the Greyhounds — and probably any number of other senior teams — to the Olympics and still won the gold as easily as the Granites did.

Once they got overseas, Canada's 1924 Olympic hockey team didn't display quite the same charitable outlook as the Winnipeg Falcons in 1920. Even playing under unfamiliar conditions on a huge, open-air ice surface with tiny boards to cordon off a playable rink, Canada crushed the European teams they faced in the first round at Chamonix. They opened the tournament with a 30–0 win over Czechoslovakia on January 28, 1924, then defeated Sweden 22–0 the next day and followed up with a 33–0 rout of Switzerland the day after that.

A semifinal game against Great Britain on February 1 provided Canada with slightly more competition but still resulted in a 19–2 victory. Even the United States didn't put up much opposition in the gold-medal game on February 3, 1924, as Canada won 6–1.

Victory for the Victorias

When the Winnipeg Falcons went to Belgium in 1920, they played just three Olympic games. In France in 1924, the Toronto Granites played five Olympic games in Chamonix and one post-tournament 5-on-5 exhibition — beating Great Britain 17–1 — on an undersized rink in Paris.

During that time frame, no real Canadian team ever toured Europe along the lines of the discussions from the 1910s. There were the Oxford Canadians, who had disbanded with the outbreak of World War I in 1914 but reformed in 1920. From 1921 to 1923 the team included future Canadian prime minister Lester B. Pearson and future Governor General Roland Michener, but the Oxford Canadians were based in England. The first truly Canadian team to tour Europe would be the Montreal Victorias, who played 14 games in six different countries in February and March of 1927.

According to a story in the *Montreal Star* on September 17, 1926, there had been some concern that the Victorias, "one of the oldest organizations of the winter sport still in existence in Canada," would not even ice a team for the 1926–27 season. However, "any

JOE LAMB

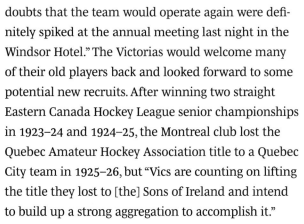

doubts that the team would operate again were definitely spiked at the annual meeting last night in the Windsor Hotel." The Victorias would welcome many of their old players back and looked forward to some potential new recruits. After winning two straight Eastern Canada Hockey League senior championships in 1923–24 and 1924–25, the Montreal club lost the Quebec Amateur Hockey Association title to a Quebec City team in 1925–26, but "Vics are counting on lifting the title they lost to [the] Sons of Ireland and intend to build up a strong aggregation to accomplish it."

Talk of a trip to Europe didn't begin until the week of November 8, 1926. An offer had been made by a representative of the government of Sweden, and on November 15, the *Montreal Star* reported, "S.C. [Sadie] Holland, president of the Vics, received a cable direct from Sweden concerning the trip saying that a definite guarantee of all expenses would be covered by the Swedish Government … if the Vics decide to make the trip."

At that point, the plans included only five games in Sweden, two in Berlin and one in Vienna. The *Star* said the team would meet to decide the matter following their practice that evening at the Montreal Forum. "Naturally the players are all anxious for the journey, but the loss of time from their business is one drawback, while their obligations to the Quebec Senior Group will also have to be carried out."

Four days later, the Montreal *Gazette* noted that 14 Victorias players were willing to make the trip and could make the necessary arrangements for the time away from work. It was further reported that only eight players would be taken (nine ended up going), "which leaves a delicate task for the selection committee should the trip materialize." That same November 19, the *Star* ran a story saying that many "old and prominent members of the Victoria Hockey Club" had been consulted and were in favor of going. "You're only young once," one of them was reported as saying.

EARL ROBINSON

M

On November 24, 1926, the *Star* said the tour was a "practical certainty" following a meeting of the club executive the previous night. The Victorias would leave from New York on January 22 and play their first game in Sweden on February 6. (It was later reported they'd arrive in Gothenburg on January 31, although they appear to have docked on February 1 and not disembarked until the following morning.) "The journey will not mean that their scheduled games in the Quebec Senior League will be forfeited," the story added. The team would begin the season with the players who would be making the trip, "and a strong sextette will be left here to carry on" after the traveling team departed.

The Victorias arrived in New York on January 19, 1927, and played a game against the Canadian Club of New York at Madison Square Garden that night.

They scored an easy 7–0 victory against the team that would host them for the next few days before the Canadians boarded the Swedish American liner *Stockholm* for their overseas journey. According to a story that appeared in the *Montreal Star* on February 16, the passage was a rough one and "a few of the boys were fairly wobbly."

In a later *Star* story on February 22, a letter from Sadie Holland explained that after leaving the ship in Gothenburg at 9 a.m. on February 2, "and after being photographed for the movies," the team was given a tour of the city aboard a sightseeing bus and entertained at a luncheon before boarding a train for Stockholm at 12:30 p.m. They arrived at 9:15 that night. The *Montreal Star* of February 3 reported that large crowds turned out at every station along the route to cheer the Canadians, who were given "a tremendous welcome" when they reached the capital city. An official welcoming banquet was held at seven o'clock on February 3.

The next morning, there was a bus tour of Stockholm, followed by a practice "at the Stadium, which is quite a fine ground enclosed in a beautiful brick building of Swedish design." The winter weather was unseasonably warm, and the ice "was quite soft and partially covered with water." Raoul Le Mat, the American who had introduced hockey to Sweden circa 1919 and who worked for Metro-Goldwyn-Mayer studios in Stockholm, was at the practice. He was "awfully decent to us all," wrote Holland, and "took slow motion pictures of the boys in action."

The Victorias were well treated during their stay in Sweden, being invited to tea by the King on February 10 and playing before the Crown Prince, to whom they were all presented after their game on February 12. This was apparently not the team's only brush with royalty while in Europe. According to a look back at the tour in the Montreal *Gazette* on February 23, 1935, a German princess was so intrigued by the Victorias while they were in Davos, Switzerland, that she attended all their practices.

When the tour wrapped up in London on March 9, 1927, the Victorias had won all 14 games in Europe, outscoring their opponents 155–10. As reported in the *Gazette* story in 1935 (which said the team played 17 games and outscored its opponents 157–11), "The opposition's counters were frequently merely a friendly gesture on the part of the Canadians." For example, while playing in Milan, "the Vics were told that a round of champagne awaited them at the banquet for every goal scored against them. The Vics, being an abstemious lot, permitted the Italians to score once." In fact, the actual score of their game versus HC Milano on February 27 was 15–2, so perhaps there were two rounds of champagne that evening.

The Victorias returned to Canada on board the *Montclare*, arriving at Saint John, New Brunswick, on March 21. They reached Windsor Station in Montreal by train about 6:30 in the morning the next day. Recaps of the tour in Montreal papers later in March of 1927 show the team's record as 15–0 with 162 goals scored, but that includes the 7–0 win in New York before going overseas.

"We all thoroughly enjoyed ourselves," said Sadie Holland in a story in the *Montreal Star* on March 23, "and the treatment we received was simply marvellous." The experience, he thought, was one that could not be bought with money. As to the hockey, he believed the Europeans were still a long way behind Canada.

"It seems ridiculous and a waste of money for Canada to send its Allan Cup winners to compete for the Olympic hockey championship," said Holland. "We did not experience much difficulty in defeating the Vienna sextette, champions of Europe, winning 8–0 and 7–0, and when it is taken into consideration that we did not use heavy defensive methods, not being called upon to do so, one can imagine the difference between a Canadian championship team and the ones we played."

The Victorian Era?

McGill students, led by James Creighton, had been instrumental in what is considered the first organized hockey game, played at the Victoria Skating Rink in Montreal on March 3, 1875. Even so, McGill University didn't officially form its own team, and play its first game, until January 31, 1877. This is said to make McGill the first organization to found a hockey team.

Unless it wasn't.

At least a few articles about the Montreal Victorias in Montreal newspapers over the years give an age

The Vic-tory Tour

The Montreal Victorias' European tour of 1927, game by game:

Date	Opponent	City	Score
Jan 19*	Canadian Club	New York	7–0
Feb 6	All-Sweden	Stockholm	17–1
Feb 9	IK Göta	Stockholm	5–0
Feb 11	Djurgårdens IF	Stockholm	6–2
Feb 12	Södertälje	Stockholm	6–0
Feb 14	IK Göta	Stockholm	19–3
Feb 15	Södertälje	Stockholm	10–1
Feb 18	Prague	Berlin	8–0
Feb 19	Berliner SC	Berlin	13–0
Feb 22	Wiener EV	Vienna	8–0
Feb 23	Wiener EV	Vienna	7–0
Feb 26	HC Davos/EHC St. Moritz	Milan	18–0
Feb 27	HC Milano	Milan	15–2
Mar 1	HC Davos/EHC St. Moritz	Switzerland	9–0
Mar 9	All-England	London	14–1

* Pretour game

for that organization that would date it back to 1874. And indeed, there is a story from the Montreal *Gazette* on Monday, February 7, 1876, that refers to a game of hockey being played the previous Saturday at the Victoria Skating Rink "between nine men belonging to the Montreal Foot Ball Club … and nine members of the Victoria Skating Club."

Admittedly, this Victoria Skating Club team may not yet have been officially considered a hockey team, though there are certainly advertisements in the

Montreal Star hyping a game on February 12, 1880, between the Quebec Hockey Club and the Victoria Skating Club. Still, the first specific mention of the Victoria Hockey Club doesn't seem to appear in the Montreal *Gazette* until January 11, 1882. The story that day reports on the first annual meeting of the team, which would indicate it was formed in 1881.

Further complicating matters is the fact that in *Hockey: Canada's Royal Winter Game* (1899), Arthur Farrell writes that the formation of both the Victorias

The Vic-tory Tour continued

Vics' European statistics courtesy of the Society for International Hockey Research. (Note that the game-by-game scores from Europe add up to 155 goals, but the scoring statistics add up to 156.)

Player	GP	G	A	Pts	PIM
Earle Robinson	13	46	7	53	4
Wes King	11	27	9	36	2
Joe Lamb	14	28	4	32	7
Dave Campbell	13	24	2	26	—
Frank Carlin	13	13	2	15	2
Bob Bell	12	8	5	13	—
Torry Shibley	12	4	6	10	2
Teddy Bowles	12	6	2	8	1

Goalie	GP	W-L-T	MIN	GA	SO	GAA
Rollie Beaudry	14	14-0-0	840	10	8	0.71

and McGill, "the first regularly organized hockey clubs in the world," occurred "about 1881," but in *How to Play Hockey*, which he wrote for the Spalding sporting goods company in 1907, he states the Victorias were formed in 1880. So either 1880 or 1881 seems a likely date for the birth of the Victorias as a distinct hockey team, which would be three or four years after the formation of the McGill hockey team. Still, it's possible the Victoria Hockey Club considered its birth to date back to the earlier Victoria Skating Club hockey team circa 1874, which would make it the oldest.

Early NHL Attempts

On February 9, 1935, the Montreal *Gazette* reported that, the day before, Léo Dandurand said the Canadiens were "virtually certain" to go to Europe after the current NHL season and Stanley Cup playoffs were over. Dandurand had been approached by a promoter with the offer to make a hockey tour of England and the continent with another NHL team. The Canadiens' owner/coach/general manager had submitted the conditions under which the team would agree to go and said that if they were met, the trip was "on" as far as the Canadiens were concerned. The schedule called for eight games, with two each in London, Paris, Berlin and Milan. The Canadiens asked for a stipulated guarantee and an option on a percentage of receipts.

It was reported that 10 players, one manager and one trainer would be carried on the trip by each of the two teams. A referee would also be taken, with one of the managers to fill in as a second game official when needed. Players would be given an allowance for hotel and meal expenses. It was said that either the Boston Bruins or New York Rangers might accompany the Canadiens. Both of those teams were coached by one of the Patrick brothers — Lester in New York and Frank in Boston — and the *Gazette* article noted:

> In previously proposed European invasions by professional teams the Patricks were moving spirits in the negotiations and in both instances sought Canadiens as one of the two clubs to go overseas. Back in 1924, Frank Patrick wanted Canadiens to join him in a professional hockey venture in London in connection with the Empire Exhibition at Wembley. Three years ago, Lester Patrick and his Rangers had a bid to visit England and the Continent and immediately asked Canadiens to go along. On both former occasions, lack of a suitable rink in London was the main objection against such tours.

It's difficult to confirm plans for a trip in sources from 1924. As to the 1935 tour, a story from New York dated March 5 appeared in the *Gazette* the next day, with Lester Patrick admitting only that the Rangers were considering making the trip with the Canadiens. "Much depends on how far we go in the playoffs," said Patrick. "Then too the players will be travelling more or less on their own, and I want to make sure they will suffer no monetary loss." A Canadian Press story on March 6 said games might also be played in Vienna and Budapest.

The trip was the brainchild of Armand Vincent, a Montreal promoter who had been in Europe working on his plan for several weeks. The news even reached the *Miami Herald* that same March 6, in a syndicated column by John J. Romano, who wrote in great detail about Vincent (who was in Paris at the time) and his grand plan to use minor-league hockey players from North America to stock a new pro league in Europe. But by March 25, 1935, Vincent was in London, where

Leo Dandurand.

he announced he'd been unable to arrange for a tour by the Canadiens and Rangers.

Vincent still hoped to put something together for the following season, and two days later, plans were announced for the Canadiens and another team to make a 15-game European tour in 1936. It was said there would be three games in London and two each in Berlin, Munich, Garmisch-Partenkirchen, Prague and Vienna, plus one game in Budapest and another in Zurich. But this tour never happened either.

Canadiens vs. Red Wings: 1938

After two straight Stanley Cup championships, the Detroit Red Wings failed to make the NHL playoffs in the spring of 1938. On March 26, 1938, the Chicago Black Hawks beat the Canadiens 3–2 in overtime to eliminate Montreal in their opening-round series. That same Saturday night, Canadiens coach Cecil Hart announced tentative plans for a visit to London and Paris by his team and the Red Wings.

"The plans have not been completed as yet," reported the Montreal *Gazette* on March 28, "but some agreement is expected to be reached within one or two days." Visits by Canadian and American amateur teams "have been a regular thing for several years now," the story noted, "but the British Rinks Association, which will sponsor the trip, believe that hockey-conscious France and England will throng to witness the famous Canadiens and the almost as famed Detroit team."

On March 29, 1938, Armand Vincent announced from London that arrangements had been completed for the Canadiens and Red Wings to make the journey. But in reporting the news on March 30, the *Gazette* said that when Cecil Hart was informed, his comment was, "That's funny. They announce over there that the trip is all set, and we don't know anything about it over here." There would be a few more glitches over the next few days, but this trip would happen. The teams played an exhibition game in Sydney, Nova Scotia, on April 7, and two in Halifax on April 8 and 9, and then set sail aboard the *Ausonia* after the third game.

The two teams arrived in London on Tuesday morning, April 19. In reporting on their arrival the next day, the *Gazette* said the Wings and Canadiens got on the ice for practice and that "managers Cecil Hart and Jack Adams were satisfied with their players' condition after the Atlantic Crossing." The *Gazette* also noted that the London papers were discussing the high salaries of the hockey players "as compared to the meagre pay English soccer players receive." Indeed, the Star Lights column in the *Daily Mirror* reported in its April 20 edition: "George Mantha, Babe Siebert and Big Toe Blake, members of Montreal Canadiens Ice Hockey Club, who with Detroit Red Wings, arrived in London yesterday, earn £1,500 a season apiece. The party of twenty-three players are valued at £110,000."

Jack Adams as general manager and coach of the Detroit Red Wings during the 1938–39 NHL season.

(Those numbers might be a little high, as the exchange rate of US$4.89 for the British pound in 1938 would work out to $7,335 at a time when NHL salaries were capped at $7,000.) However, the *Sunday Pictorial* noted on April 24 that, unlike British footballers, "ice pros … don't get any percentage of transfer fees."

News of the first game on April 21 attracted less attention in that day's London *Daily Telegraph* than did the arrival of the Australian cricket team, who would play test matches that summer, but still: "The first professional ice hockey match to be seen in England takes place at Earl's Court tonight, when the Montreal Canadiens and Detroit Red Wings meet in the first of a series of six matches. These fixtures are creating great interest in view of the possibility of the game over here becoming professionalised, and with the rules similar to our own, the game should be easy to follow."

A comic featured in the Brooklyn Citizen *on March 6, 1935.*

A crowd of 8,000 fans filled the arena, and "London vociferously hailed its first demonstration of professional hockey, complete with power plays and with overtime thrown in for good measure," read the Canadian Press report of the game. The Canadiens won 5–4, and just in case the rules weren't similar enough, "the game was interspersed with explanations to the crowd by Jack Adams." It was said the fans cheered both teams loudly but seemed to favor the Canadiens. Before the game, Montreal goalie Wilf Cude, who was born in Wales but raised in Winnipeg, "was wreathed with a horseshoe of leeks [the leek is the national emblem of Wales] by a London beauty queen and given an ovation."

The second game, in Brighton two nights later, was also said to have packed a big crowd, although an exact attendance figure isn't given. In referring back to the first game, a London paper called *The People*, under the headline "Pro. Ice Hockey Is Best," noted on April 24: "The Earl's Court authorities must be complimented for taking the risk of bringing the two teams over here. That they were justified is proved by the fact that for the first time ever the Stadium was crowded for an ice event."

The Canadiens and Red Wings moved on to Paris for three games and then returned to England to play four more before the tour wrapped up on May 14. Immediately after the final game, the teams left for Southampton, where they boarded the RMS *Aurania* to return to Montreal. "We've had a successful and enjoyable trip," said Cecil Hart to the Canadian Press for a story on May 16. "The boys played wonderful hockey and I'm sure they've sold the professional game in a big way to British and French fans."

One dissenting view came from former Montreal *Gazette* sports editor Dunc MacDonald, who was then in England as the assistant director for Harringay Arena and White City Stadium. His opinions were shared by *Gazette* columnist Marc T. McNeil on May 18, 1938:

They had a sellout crowd at Earl's Court, but the rink only holds 7,500. The press was lukewarm in its reception of the pro game. Canadiens and Detroit staged a fake fight which did not go over so big with the crowd, but their passing plays did get fine notices. Neither Canadiens nor Detroit tried too hard and that reflected on their showing as a whole. The English are pretty hard to fool; even about things they know little of. I think the biggest disappointment for the press and public alike was the lack of body-checking.

Naturally, Hart and Adams were not going to take any chances on injury. But over here the press has made everyone believe NHL hockey is murderously rough, and there was nothing in the Earl's Court show to support that idea.

After arriving home in Montreal on the night of May 23, Cecil Hart was a little more philosophical. While maintaining that it was a wonderful trip (the next day's Montreal *Gazette* said, "The players themselves were unanimous in declaring it was the greatest experience of their lives"), Hart thought, "Europe is not ready for pro hockey," adding it would be at least five or 10 years before the pro game would catch on in England. Still, he was amazed at the size of the crowds, which he knew could have been much larger. "We turned thousands away," he said. "I never saw anything like it. If they ever get any big rinks over there the game is a cinch to go."

Crowd Controlled

Cecil Hart wasn't just playing up the size of the crowds for the Montreal audience once he got home.

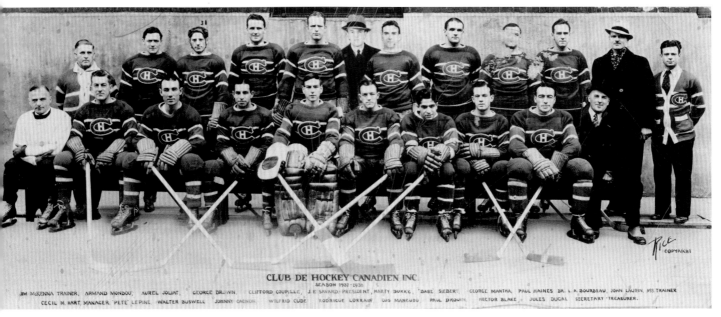

CLUB DE HOCKEY CANADIEN INC.
SEASON 1937-1938

JIM McKENNA TRAINER, ARMAND MONDOU, AUREL JOLIAT, GEORGE BROWN, CLIFFORD COUPILLE, J.E. SAVARD PRESIDENT, MARTY BURKE, BABE SIEBERT, GEORGE MANTHA, PAUL HAINES DR. L.A. BOURBEAU, JOHN LAURIN, ASS. TRAINER.
CECIL M. HART MANAGER 'PETE' LEPINE, WALTER BUSWELL, JOHNNY CACHON, WILFRID CUDE, RODRIGUE LORRAIN, GUS MANCUSO, PAUL DROUIN, HECTOR BLAKE, JULES DUGAL SECRETARY-TREASURER.

Team photo of the Montreal Canadiens during the 1937–38 season.

Back in London, they'd been saying the same thing. Under a headline on May 20, 1938, reading, "Insufficient Seating for Huge Record Crowd," a writer bylined only as "Lowlyn," in a newspaper called the *Kensington News and West London Times*, said:

> It is impossible to describe the scenes witnessed outside Empress Hall last Saturday evening on the event of the last Ice-Hockey match of the season.
>
> Arriving rather early, I was amazed to see crowds turning away into Lillie road, almost as if the match might have been postponed. However, there were the thousands of unfortunate ones who had left it too late in not booking a seat. You may remember I gave a warning last week about this being the last chance — and it is no mere exaggeration to say that on this occasion it was not hundreds that were turned away, but positively thousands.

As Cecil Hart explained in the Montreal *Gazette* on May 24, 1938:

> We were idle from Tuesday of one week until Saturday and I wanted to play Thursday night. "We'll pack 'em in," I said. But no, they were afraid of hurting the Saturday gate. So when we turned 4,000 away Saturday night, the rink promoter came to me and said, "Hart," he said, "I wish I'd taken your advice."
>
> "Mr. Langdon," I said, "with your money and my brains you'd be a success." "What's that?" he shouted — then he ordered two quarts of champagne.

Quote ... Unquote

"Professional ice hockey, introduced to England at Empress Hall, London, last night, had a packed house gasping at its speed, dexterity and toughness. . . . The puck was carried from one end to the other so fast that amateur defences in this country would have been left standing. . . . Mr. Hart, Canadiens trainer and manager, told me that the boys were a bit stiff after their nine days at sea. But if they were stiff, playing at that speed, most of us must be permanently rigid."

— **Denis O'Sullivan**, the *Daily Mirror*, London, England, April 22, 1938

Canadiens vs. Red Wings: Rosters

The players on each team earned $250 in addition to a free trip to Europe.

	Montreal	Detroit
G	Wilf Cude	Normie Smith
D	Walter Buswell	Doug Young
	Babe Siebert*	Ebbie Goodfellow*
	Red Goupille	Pete Bessone
F	Paul Haynes	Larry Aurie*
	Johnny Gagnon	Marty Barry*
	Toe Blake*	Mud Bruneteau
	Pit Lépine	Carl Liscombe
	George Mantha	Eddie Wares
	Rod Lorrain	Alex Motter
	Paul Drouin	Syd Howe*
	Hec Kilrea	

* Hockey Hall of Fame

Cardigan worn by General Manager and Head Coach Cecil Hart of the Montreal Canadiens during the 1937–38 NHL season.

Canadiens vs. Red Wings: Results

Canadiens and Red Wings European tour of 1938, game by game (final: 5-3-1 Canadiens):

Date	City	Arena	Score
April 7*	Sydney	Sydney Forum	Montreal 3 Detroit 2
April 8*	Halifax	Halifax Forum	Montreal 6 Detroit 5 (OT)
April 9*	Halifax	Halifax Forum	Detroit 7 Montreal 2
April 21	London	Empress Hall	Montreal 5 Detroit 4 (OT)
April 23	Brighton	Sports Stadium	Montreal 5 Detroit 5
April 25	Paris	Palais des Sports	Montreal 10 Detroit 8
April 27	Paris	Palais des Sports	Detroit 4 Montreal 3
April 29	Paris	Palais des Sports	Montreal 7 Detroit 5
May 5	London	Empress Hall	Montreal 6 Detroit 3
May 8	Brighton	Sports Stadium	Detroit 10 Montreal 5
May 10	London	Empress Hall	Montreal 5 Detroit 4
May 14	Brighton	Sports Stadium	Detroit 5 Montreal 2

* Pretour games

What the Puck: Part One

From the *Sunday Pictorial*, London, England (May 1, 1938):

> Montreal Canadiens and Detroit Red Wings play third of [professional] ice hockey matches at Earl's Court next Thursday ... if they have enough pucks left ... explanation is that pros use different kind of puck, and souvenir hunters have been busy.
>
> Six were pinched in first London game ... nine at Brighton — including one referee dropped on way to dressing-room which small boy took — and five more in Paris ... Manager Cecil Hart has cabled for fifty more to New York ... and begs puck-snatchers to lay off until end of tour.

Bruins vs. Rangers: 1959

United Press International broke the story on November 30, 1958, that the New York Rangers and Boston Bruins would play in 11 European cities from April 29 to May 27, 1959. (In actual fact, the tour would visit only 10 cities and wrap up on May 24.) The news was announced by IIHF president John "Bunny" Ahearne, but the tour had been organized by Othmar Delnon, a Swiss promotor and former Swiss hockey player.

The Bruins left Logan Airport in Boston aboard a BOAC flight for London scheduled to depart at 9:25 on the night of April 27, 1959. Back in January, the NHL had barred the teams from traveling on the same plane, so the Rangers left separately on an earlier flight that same evening. Both teams arrived in London on the morning of April 28 and played their first game the next night. Upon arrival, Rangers general manager Muzz Patrick was asked if the teams would play any British-league opponents while in London. "There would be no point to it," he said. "It would not be fair. All our boys are big league and the best in the world."

The first game was played at Wembley Arena, then known as Empire Pool. The Bruins beat the Rangers 7–5, but New York's *Daily News* reported only 1,500 fans attended, while "another 8,500 boycotted the session because admission prices were doubled."

High prices and low attendance would plague the entire tour, with large crowds turning out in only a few cities. In the *Montreal Star* on May 11, 1959, Red Fisher wrote of 19,000 fans watching two games in Geneva but only 700 at one of the games in Paris, just 1,300 for two games in Antwerp and only 1,000 people who "raised echoes in a 12,000-seat arena" in Brussels. "Some of the blame," Fisher reasoned, "must be traced to the hockey promoters … [who] hoisted the prices 100 percent." But he also thought it was a mistake not to play any of the local teams. "The Bruins and Rangers are strangers to Europeans, and with nobody to root for, apathy sets in."

After playing 23 games in just 26 nights, the teams flew home from Switzerland and arrived back in the United States on May 28. Herb Ralby in the *Boston Globe* that day noted: "The tour drew big crowds in Switzerland and Vienna and fairly well in Germany. But poorly elsewhere." (Other reports say the tour

Gump Worsley of the New York Rangers makes the save with Toronto's George Armstrong and the Rangers' Camille Henry close by.

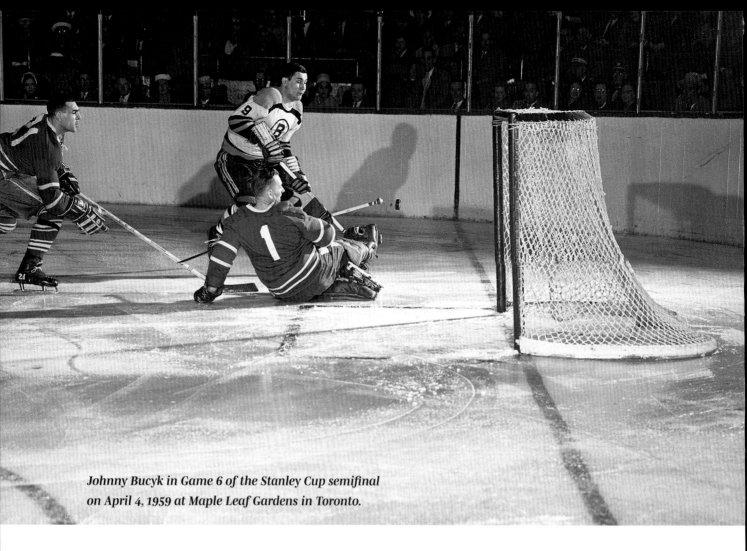

Johnny Bucyk in Game 6 of the Stanley Cup semifinal on April 4, 1959 at Maple Leaf Gardens in Toronto.

finale in Vienna drew only about 1,000 people.) Still, Bruins general manager Lynn Patrick, Muzz's brother, told Ralby, "Considering the lack of advertising, we did pretty well."

After returning home to North Bay, Ontario, Leo Labine of the Bruins told *Daily Nugget* sports editor Rolly Ethier for a story on June 2: "The tour was alright. We enjoyed ourselves and saw most of the sights but I wouldn't trade it for living in Canada." Labine, who thought he scored about 20 goals in 23 games, blamed the poor attendance on "the lateness of the season, high ticket prices ($9 a seat in most places), poor bookings and the lack of sufficient advanced publicity."

Even so, in Jack Kinsella's column in the *Ottawa Citizen* on June 12, 1959, Muzz Patrick said: "I never enjoyed a trip more in my life. I'm telling you right now, if we go again next year, I'll be first guy in line."

Show Me the Money!

According to Muzz Patrick, he and his brother Lynn had been guaranteed US$70,000 for the trip. "We agreed before hand," Muzz said in Jack Kinsella's June 12 *Ottawa Citizen* story, "I was to be real tough and Lynn was to be the nice guy." And so, after the poor attendance at the early games in London, Muzz demanded the $70,000 payout immediately. "No pay, no play," said Muzz, "and he turned over the guarantee to me." The younger Patrick brother put the pile of mostly $50 and $100 bills into a briefcase. "I watched that briefcase," Muzz laughed, "and Lynn watched me."

When the two teams got to Paris, the money was split up, with each player receiving $1,000 above all their expenses. "The players spent their money on side trips and really seeing the continent," said Muzz. "I was really surprised, and especially with some of the players. I never thought they'd be that interested."

Lynn Patrick.

European Vacations

Before returning from Europe, Boston's Jerry Toppazz-ini and the Rangers' Lou Fontinato visited the Italian homes of their grandparents, whom they'd never seen before. "They got a real kick out of it," Muzz Patrick said, "and so did their grandparents." Patrick said that Bronco Horvath and Johnny Bucyk tried to do the same thing, "but they weren't allowed to enter Yugo-slavia and were turned back." Given their Ukrainian and Hungarian heritage, perhaps Patrick had the country wrong?

Herb Ralby in the *Boston Globe* reported that Horvath and Bucyk visited Venice. In 2010, Bucyk told Kevin Paul Dupont of the *Globe* that he and Horvath skipped the end-of-tour dinner in Vienna to visit Italy. "Didn't cost us any extra, because the airline let us

rewrite the tickets and we got home the same time as the rest of the boys. I think we went to two cities."

Missing from the Bruins' party when they got home to Boston were Fern Flaman and Jim Morrison. Flaman was joined overseas by his wife, and the two took their own vacation. Morrison chose to take a boat home instead of flying.

Hull and Bathgate

On April 7, 1959, the *Boston Globe* reported: "Chicago Blackhawks' officials said Ed Litzenberger and Bobby Hull could join the Bruins and Rangers on a forthcom-ing European tour — but weren't sure they had been asked." Hull, Litzenberger, Eric Nesterenko and Pierre Pilote of the Black Hawks would all join the Rangers for the trip.

Bobby Hull was 20 years old. He'd already played two seasons in the NHL, but scored only 13 and 18 goals those years. Still, he would fill in as the Rangers' big scorer in place of another future Hall of Famer, Andy Bathgate, who had established career highs in 1958–59 with 40 goals and 88 points. "I'd had a good year and I was pooped out," Bathgate recalled about his decision not to go overseas in a 2009 story about the 1959 tour on *NHL.com*. "My wife had just had a baby and I needed to be with her in Vancouver. I didn't want to be traveling by myself at that time."

Hull certainly made the most of his opportunity. "Eddie Litzenberger joined me from the Blackhawks and I played on a line with him and Eddie Shack," said Hull. "Shack was all over the ice, like a can of worms. Every shift, I would tell him to stay wide on his wing, get around the defenseman, and before he went behind the net, look in the slot and I'll be there. I had to tell him that every shift ... but sure enough, he did it and I scored 50 goals in 22 games. I came home from Europe and told my father I was going to lead the

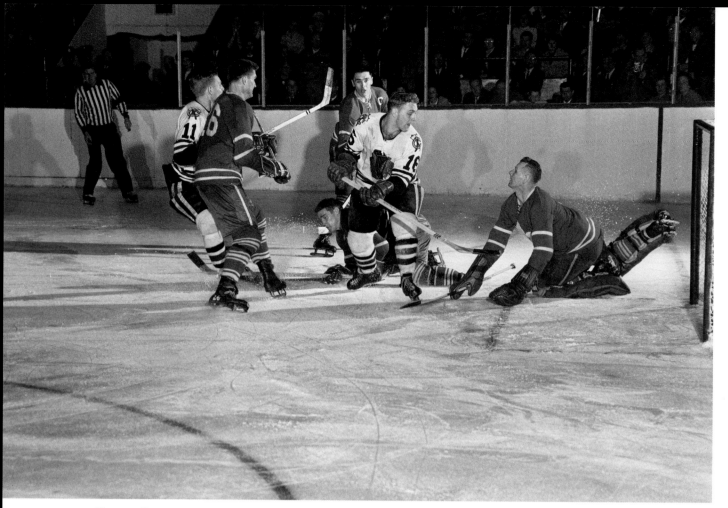

*Bill Hay, Allan Stanley, Tim Horton, George Armstrong, Bobby Hull and Johnny Bower
in game action from December 12, 1959 at Maple Leaf Gardens.*

NHL in scoring and he said, 'Yeah, you and how many other guys?'"

But Hull did indeed have a breakout season in 1959–60. He led the league in goals (39) for the first of seven times in his career and topped everyone in points (81) for the first of three times. "That's where I learned how to play," said Hull of the European trip. "I wanted to see all of Europe that I could and I suppose I played smart hockey.... When I came back, I was a more complete player and it went on from there.

"Had I not made that trip to Europe and played as well as I did, gaining all that confidence, who knows where my career would have gone?"

Gordie Howe

Gordie Howe was also invited to tour Europe with the Rangers and Bruins, though it's unclear whom he would have suited up with. As reported in the *Detroit Free Press* and other newspapers on Tuesday, April 7, 1959, "The veteran star was asked to accompany the two teams but said Monday he had decided against it.

"I talked with my doctors about my injured ribs," said Howe, "and we feel I should rest them as much as possible. Too, we have a new baby girl and I'd rather spend the time at home."

What the Puck: Part Two

A Canadian Press story out of New York on April 28, 1959, reported that the New York Rangers and Boston Bruins would be "doing a little experimental research" during their 23-game European tour. The teams would be taking along "two gross of a new type of puck designed by Clair F. Kinney of Toronto." Kinney was a Toronto scientist and hockey fan whose new puck design featured one bright orange side, which he hoped would make them easier for goalies and fans to see. "After using the disks," the story said, "the teams will report to league president Clarence Campbell … whether they consider them an improvement over the pucks now in regular play."

Kinney had also invented a yellow hockey tape, and on May 18, 1959, UPI reported that the Amateur Hockey Association of the United States, in a joint convention with the Canadian Amateur Hockey Association, was proposing the use of yellow tape and orange pucks. However, according to the *Detroit Free Press* on June 9, Muzz Patrick gave a scathing review of the 288 orange pucks the Bruins and Rangers had taken to Europe at an NHL meeting in Montreal the day before.

"We paid all that excess weight charges on those dizzy things and they were a pure flop," said Patrick. "The players said they couldn't see the puck and wouldn't use them after the first try. They would be good only on black ice. European teams are going to use them, however, because we gave them away free."

As the story concluded, "Pucks still will be black next season, the NHL officials formally voted."

Before the Zamboni

In writing about the Bruins-Rangers tour in the Montreal *Gazette* on February 26, 1959, Vern DeGeer noted that a New York story "inferred that this tour would give Europeans their first look at major professional hockey." DeGeer further reported, "It reminded coach Toe Blake of the Habs that the big fellas of the ice lanes made a brief swing of England and France 21 years ago."

DeGeer then dedicated the first half of his Good Morning column to memories of the 1938 tour and concluded by saying: "It was [at Jeff Dickson's Palais des Sports in Paris] that the tourists saw barrel carts

Bruins vs. Rangers: Rosters

	Bruins	Rangers
G	Harry Lumley*	Gump Worsley*
	Don Simmons	
D	Bob Armstrong	Jack Bownass
	Leo Boivin*	Lou Fontinato
	Fern Flaman*	John Hanna
	Larry Hillman	Adam Keller†
	Jim Morrison	Gus Mortson†
		Pierre Pilote*†
F	Dunc Brodie†	Jimmy Bartlett
	John Bucyk*	Hank Ciesla
	Jean-Guy Gendron	Les Colwill
	Bronco Horvath	Gord Labossiere†
	Leo Labine	Dean Prentice
	Larry Leach	Bobby Hull*†
	Fleming Mackell	Ed Litzenberger†
	Don McKenney	Eric Nesterenko†
	Dick Meissner†	Eddie Shack
	Doug Mohns	Red Sullivan
	Gord Redahl	Bill Sweeney†
	Dutch Reibel	
	Vic Stasiuk	
	Jerry Toppazzini	

Red Storey,* who had resigned as an NHL referee after being criticized by league president Clarence Campbell during the playoffs that year, made the trip to Europe to serve as referee.

* Hockey Hall of Fame   † On loan from Chicago

† Prospect/Minor Leaguer

Bruins vs. Rangers: Results

Bruins and Rangers European tour of 1959, game by game (final: 11–9–3 Rangers):

Date	City	Score
April 29	London, England	Bruins 7 Rangers 5
April 30	London, England	Rangers 4 Bruins 3
May 2	Geneva, Switzerland	Rangers 4 Bruins 3
May 3	Geneva, Switzerland	Bruins 12 Rangers 4
May 4	Paris, France	Rangers 6 Bruins 2
May 5	Paris, France	Bruins 6 Rangers 4
May 6	Antwerp, Belgium	Bruins 6 Rangers 3
May 7	Antwerp, Belgium	Rangers 6 Bruins 3
May 8	Antwerp, Belgium	Rangers 8 Bruins 4
May 9	Zurich, Switzerland	Rangers 7 Bruins 6
May 10	Zurich, Switzerland	Bruins 4 Rangers 2
May 12	Dortmund, West Germany	Rangers 4 Bruins 2
May 13	Dortmund, West Germany	Bruins 6 Rangers 4
May 14	Essen, West Germany	Bruins 6 Rangers 4
May 15	Essen, West Germany	Rangers 4 Bruins 3
May 16	Krefeld, West Germany	Rangers 8 Bruins 0
May 17	Krefeld, West Germany	Rangers 7 Bruins 2
May 19	West Berlin, West Germany	Bruins 6 Rangers 6
May 20	West Berlin, West Germany	Rangers 3 Bruins 2
May 21	West Berlin, West Germany	Bruins 8 Rangers 2
May 22	Vienna, Austria	Bruins 2 Rangers 2
May 23	Vienna, Austria	Bruins 5 Rangers 3
May 24	Vienna, Austria	Bruins 4 Rangers 4

An early ice flooding machine at Maple Leaf Gardens. The hot water barrel was later replaced by the more famous Zamboni or Olympia Ice resurfacing machines.

flooding the ice surface between periods. Toronto first tried this wrinkle a couple of years later, leading up to the general flooding practice at all NHL arenas and many minor pro rinks in the United States and Canada today."

DeGeer wrote for the *Globe and Mail* in Toronto from 1938 until 1949, so he may well have recalled the early ice-flooding barrels used at Maple Leaf Gardens between periods of games from that time. Still, it's unclear whether Toronto began using them before Montreal did.

At an NHL governors meeting in New York on September 12, 1940, the league introduced a rule change that "the ice surface be sprayed between periods, instead of scraped or brushed, except when two teams have a mutual understanding that spraying

is not necessary." Two months later, in reporting on the Canadiens' season-opening 1–1 tie with Boston the previous night in the Montreal *Gazette* on November 4, 1940, Harold McNamara wrote about Tommy Gorman's "new ice-making machines" being on view between periods. "They're sort of hot-water wagons dragging sacks behind," wrote McNamara, "and they do a great job on the ice."

That same year, Frank Zamboni had partnered in a family ice rink in southern California. He invented a workable ice-resurfacing machine in 1949 and received a patent for it in 1953. Figure skating legend Sonja Henie had been using a Zamboni in her ice shows since 1950, and the Boston Bruins became the first NHL team to use one in the fall of 1954.

CHAPTER 5

Media Moments

Uniform numbers helped new fans identify players by
the 1911–12 season, and radio began to take the game to
larger audiences in 1923. Before Hockey Night in Canada
had fans glued to their televisions on Saturday night, fans
were tuning on TVs in England and the United States.

Get Yer Programs

The addition of numbers to hockey uniforms is often credited to Frank Patrick and the PCHA in its inaugural season of 1911–12. It would seem that PCHA players did wear numbers somewhere on their sweaters that season. But so did the players in the NHA.

In his 1980 biography, *The Patricks: Hockey's Royal Family*, Eric Whitehead refers to the numbering of players as the PCHA's first rules innovation. "That was done in the 1911–12 season," writes Whitehead, "in the opening game in Victoria between the Aristocrats and New Westminster Royals. It was perhaps poetic justice that the Patrick who sparked this idea was [father] Joe, whose generosity and consummate faith in his boys [he had agreed to use the proceeds from the sale of the family lumber company to finance the new artificial ice arenas needed in Vancouver and Victoria] had made everything possible."

Whitehead describes Joe Patrick as having produced a picture in *London Illustrated* of runners in a cross-country race. Noting the numbers pinned to the backs of their shirts he suggested that hockey fans new to the sport might find this a useful way of identifying the players. "And on the following Saturday at the PCHA inaugural [the first PCHA game was actually played on Tuesday, January 2, 1912], the hockey players were similarly marked."

It's hard to confirm from the early game reports if and when PCHA players started wearing numbers, though the Society for International Hockey Research has numbers recorded for everyone on all three PCHA rosters for the 1911–12 season. Still, even if most of what Whitehead writes is true, the NHA would also unveil numbers on its sweaters that season, so it's difficult to say who came up with the idea first. If PCHA players were wearing numbers on that inaugural night, it would seem they beat the NHA to the punch ... but only by a single day.

The 1911–12 NHA season started slightly before the PCHA's, with its first game on December 29, 1911. (Not December 30, as usually recorded.) On December 27, a few days prior to the NHA opener between the Montreal Wanderers and Quebec Bulldogs, NHA president Emmett Quinn visited Quebec City and reportedly made public for the first time the amended rules for the coming NHA season.

Among the new rules for that season were that teams would have nine players in uniform for every game, each team was to be composed of six players (no more rover), and each player was to bear a number on the left arm of their sweater. Interestingly, the rule changes reported that day had already appeared in newspapers as early as October 12, 1911, the day after an NHA meeting in Montreal, and the stories that day said the players would wear large numbers on the back and front of their sweaters.

However, in its report of the Wanderers' 9–5 season-opening win in Quebec, the Montreal *Gazette* on December 30 noted, "The numbers of the players were not on hand, so this innovation will receive its initial trial next week." It's unclear if numbers were worn in Ottawa when the Bulldogs visited the Senators on January 3, 1912, but that same night in Montreal numbers were definitely worn when the Wanderers blanked the Canadiens 5–0.

But the change didn't have the desired effect.

According to the next day's *Gazette*, "The players were all numbered but there was no board with the names corresponding to the numbers to enlighten the uninitiated, so the public was little the wiser for the innovation." The *Montreal Star* felt the biggest problem with the numbers on the sleeves was that they were too small.

On the day of the next Montreal home game (Ottawa versus the Wanderers on Saturday, January 6), the *Star* was pleased to report that Emmett Quinn had agreed about the small numbers. "He immediately decided to have them made larger, and make the players wear them on their jerseys, not only on the back, but on their chests." The *Star* reporter believed this would result in spectators being able to distinguish the players much more easily that night, "providing as always that the numbers are delivered in time."

February 22, 1913, game between Quebec Bulldogs and Montreal Canadiens.

Apparently, they were.

Even though the only player shown with a number in a series of cartoons depicting the action in Monday's *Star* was Wanderers goalie George Broughton, who was drawn wearing the number 1 on an armband, the game story said: "The big numbers on the back and front of the players were a great improvement." The writer further noted, "Those spectators who had bought a six o'clock edition of Saturday's *Star* [where the uniform numbers had been reported] were able to tell the men at a glance even if they did not know them."

In a last reference to the numbers, the *Star* writer added, "A huge bulletin board giving the men and their respective numbers or small cards giving them and distributed amongst the spectators as they enter the rink might be a further improvement." And on Saturday, January 13, before that night's game between the Senators and Canadiens, a headline in the *Star* read, "Player Numbers to Be Shown on Blackboard at Arena." A small story added, "It is announced that the Arena management will provide a blackboard this evening which will contain the names of the various players and the numbers which they will carry so that the spectators will be able to follow the play without trouble."

Even these blackboards and bulletin boards would prove insufficient, and soon enough, team or rink owners began providing cards and programs with the names and numbers of the players. But the owners would realize they were giving away something for free they might otherwise be able to profit from and would later capitalize on the uniform numbers by selling their programs.

Hello Out There ...

Since at least 1896, when the Winnipeg Victorias traveled east to face and defeat the Montreal Victorias in a one-game challenge for the Stanley Cup, hockey fans have been coming up with ways to follow the game when they couldn't be there in person. Telegraph lines first made this possible. Special wires were often set up in hotels, where people could gather in comfort to hear scores and details, or outside of train stations and newspaper offices, where people had to stand in the cold.

"Hundreds would gather to get the latest bulletins," superstar Cyclone Taylor would recall from his childhood for biographer Eric Whitehead. "The mobs would hang around at night in sub-zero temperatures just waiting for the operator to leave his key and come dashing out with an announcement.... He'd chalk the score up on a blackboard and then go back to his office, and we'd just stand there and talk hockey and wait for the next bulletin."

Soon fans wouldn't have to wait in the cold if they didn't want to ... as long as they had a telephone. Newspaper offices in the early 1900s often put extra operators on duty to give out score updates to those who called in. But beginning in 1922, newspapers had a more efficient way of getting scores out to anyone living within a thousand miles of their office. They could do it through the magic of radio. Even before there were any live broadcasts of hockey games.

In March of 1922, three Vancouver newspapers — the *Province*, the *Sun* and the *World* — were all racing to get their own radio stations on the air. The *Province* was first, on March 13, followed by the *Sun* two days later, and then the *World* on March 23. Content included such things as news reports, stock prices and musical programs. From March 17 to March 28, 1922, the nightly program also included almost up-to-the-minute reports on the Stanley Cup Final between the Vancouver Millionaires and the Toronto St. Pats as it took place in Toronto.

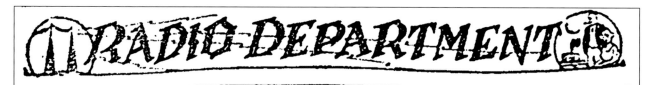

HOCKEY OVER RADIO NEW STAR FEATURE

Latest "Wrinkle" in Broadcasting Now Installed at Station CFCA.

In the Air To-Night

All times stated in Toronto time

7.00 p.m.
WWJ- DETROIT
Orchestra. Town crier.
Between 7.00 and 8.30, Rodolph Valentino will speak on "What's Wrong With the Movies?"
WDAP- CHICAGO
Closing markets.

7.30 p.m.
WEAF—NEW YORK

From the Toronto Star *radio page, February 9, 1923.*

From the newspaper accounts, it's unclear exactly how much information was being provided. After Game 1, for example, the *Province* said only that "great interest was shown in the world series hockey results," and that "after the bulletins were broadcast, numerous telephone calls were received, stating they were very clearly heard." Were just the scores provided? Or was some effort being made to recreate (or at least read) the play-by-play accounts that telegraphed reports had long been able to transmit? And were they providing more by Game 2?

It's hard to imagine anyone reporting that "it was as good as being at the game," as they had in the *Sun*, if all listeners were getting were score updates from the second game. But the *Sun* was reporting that again after Game 3. When the *World* reported on its triumphant first broadcast, which was made the day of Game 3 on March 23, it bragged of "Hockey Results Told as Fast as Plays Were Made" but provided no further details of what that actually meant.

After a 6–0 win for Toronto in the fourth game on March 25, the St. Pats and Millionaires were even at two games apiece in the best-of-five series.

Interestingly, the *Sun* noted on March 27 that it would be "giving a complete and comprehensive story of the final world series hockey game," but by the time the game was played on March 28, it appears the *Sun* station had given up on daily broadcasts, and the *World* reported only the final result, which was a 5–1 Stanley Cup–winning victory for Toronto. The *Province* continued to provide a fairly full service, but it's still a little unclear what the listeners heard. The broadcast began at 5:45 p.m. Vancouver time (8:45 in Toronto), and the March 29 radio column once again seems most interested in the fact that "hockey fans who listened in on The Province radio bulletins got results very clearly." Apparently, the first word over the wire was that Babe Dye had scored for Toronto (which he did just three minutes into the game). "A running account," the *Province* reported, "was sent out just as it came in, and in the pauses between periods musical selections were sent out."

Whatever it was that fans in Vancouver were tuning in to more than 100 years ago, it was far from the multiplatform experience we've become used to today. But everything has to start somewhere!

... We're on the Air

Foster Hewitt seemed able to recall the story of his first hockey broadcast in great detail. How he, on short notice, rushed out to Toronto's Mutual Street Arena to broadcast the play-by-play of an Ontario Hockey Association senior playoff game between a team from Kitchener and Toronto's Parkdale Canoe Club hockey team.

Hewitt's early interest in radio had led him to a job with the *Toronto Star* (where his father, W.A. Hewitt, was sports editor) in 1922. Soon he was working as a reporter at the *Star*'s radio station, CFCA, which went on the air that June. As Hewitt recalls:

> On the afternoon of March 22, 1923, I had left my desk, which was shared by fellow reporter Gordon Sinclair, when I heard the voice of Basil Lake, the radio editor. "Foster, will you come in here for a minute. I have a job for you tonight." As I recall the conversation 44 years later, it went something like this:
>
> "I hope you're not suggesting anything strenuous, Basil. I'm beat. I've had a hard day. I'm all in."
>
> "This isn't too hard, Foster. In fact it may pep you up. Anyway I can't avoid it. All plans are made. The notice is in the paper."
>
> "What is it? Not another orchestral program?"
>
> "No, no. There won't be any music in it, Foster. Instead, I'd like you to go to Mutual Street Arena."

Hewitt tells this story in his 1967 autobiography, *Foster Hewitt: His Own Story*. Though he never says so directly, Hewitt certainly implies that this was the date not only of his first hockey broadcast but of the first broadcast in hockey history. He goes on to describe the stuffy conditions inside the tiny glass booth set up at rinkside. He recalls being cooped up there "with knees almost touching my chin" through a 60-minute game that then required three 10-minute overtime periods before there was a winner. The story of this game has been a part of both hockey and Canadian history for decades.

There's just one problem with it.

It isn't true!

Or at the very least, it isn't accurate.

In truth, the CFCA broadcast on March 22, 1923 — likely by Foster Hewitt — was made from telegraphed reports sent to the station by W.A. Hewitt from Winnipeg, where the Toronto Granites would defeat the University of Saskatchewan to win the Allan Cup for the second straight season. It was actually the last in a series of hockey broadcasts of NHL and OHA games that had begun on CFCA on February 8, 1923. And the man who made the first broadcast was Norman Albert, a *Toronto Star* employee working that night for the newspaper's radio station. Albert would soon disappear from the historical record and remain lost to a rather tangled history for nearly 50 years. And, really, for almost another 50 years after that.

The game on February 8, 1923, was an Ontario Hockey Association intermediate-division playoff game between North Toronto and Midland. Fewer than 3,000 fans were at the 8,000-seat Mutual Street Arena that night. Defenseman Lionel Conacher, who was already nationally famous as a multisport star and would be named Canada's athlete of the half century in 1950, scored six goals in North Toronto's 16–4 victory.

"The announcer who described the play," reported the *Star*'s radio column the following day, "was right by the side of the rink and as he spoke, his voice was shot into space." (It was, in fact, sent out by phone over the Bell Telephone wires from the arena near Queen

Foster Hewitt at a Toronto Maple Leafs/Chicago Black Hawks game on WCFL Radio in Chicago.

and Jarvis to the CFCA studio in the Star building at 18 King St. West, then amplified and transmitted over thousands of miles.)

"The vivid description of Norman Albert," reported the *Star*, "gave listeners the chance to mentally see the fast action."

Albert had worked for the *Star* since 1917. He was the secretary to managing editor John R. Bowen. "They settled on me [for the broadcast]," Albert told sports writer Dick Beddoes for a story in the *Globe and Mail* on February 16, 1973, "because in addition to my secretarial duties, I also did some sports reporting at night." In fact, Albert wrote the story of the North Toronto–Midland game that appeared in the next day's *Star*.

Not surprisingly, the hockey broadcast proved tremendously popular, and so six days later, on February 14, Albert was back at the Arena, this time for an NHL game involving the Toronto St. Pats and the Ottawa Senators. Albert was on the air at 9:45 p.m. with a recap of the first and second periods (future Hall of Famers Jack Adams, Reg Noble and Babe Dye had Toronto in front 5–1) followed by live play-by-play of the third. Listeners heard the St. Pats hold on for a 6–4 victory.

CFCA was on the air for at least 12 more live third-period broadcasts (including three other NHL games) over the next five weeks, but Albert was on the air only one more time in 1923. Foster Hewitt would take his place.

NEWS RADIO PROGRAMS

HOCKEY AND WOODWIND PROGRAMS OVER CFCA

Tip Top Tailors and Canada Dry — England Clear Again

Once again conditions for radio reception were at their best last evening, making a fine record for the last three days. Pacific coast stations were in evidence around midnight, KJR of Seattle being very strong.

CKOC (311), Hamilton, 4.20 p.m., stock reports; 4.45, shoppers' hour; 7, feature.
CKPR (267), Midland (80 miles), 12.25 noon, stock quotations, news, weather; 6.55 p.m., stock quotations, news, weather; 6.50, unnamed club; 7, studio; 7.30, CKPR old time fiddlers; 8, studio, Midland municipal band; 8.15, hour of music.
CFCT (476), Victoria (2,150 miles), 1.30 a.m., Reliable Order of Nightbirds.
CNRC (434.8), Calgary (1,700 miles), 11.30 p.m., studio program by Cyril Hampshire, pianist, with assisting artists.
CNRV (291), Vancouver (2,125 miles), 1 a.m., Les Crane and his Canadians.
CNRM (411), Montreal (325 miles); CNRO (434.5), Ottawa (235 miles); CNRQ (340.7), Quebec (435 miles), 7.15 p.m., Aunt Bessie; markets; 8, Chateau Laurier orchestra; 8.30, pianist; trio; CNRO symphony; male quartet; tenor; 11, Chateau Laurier dance orchestra.

EASTERN STATIONS

WADC (238), Akron (210 miles), 8 p.m., the Northern Lights &...

For nearly six years CFCA has been broadcasting hockey games. Last night it gave a vivid word picture of the third period of the great struggle between Marlboros and Newmarket for the Junior O. H. A. hockey title. Every detail of Newmarket's valiant efforts to cut down the Dukes one-goal lead in the last period was presented to radio fans in an interesting way by Norman Albert, who is doing CFCA's hockey announcing, during Foster Hewitt's absence. Mr. Albert from his perch on the rafters, saw and described everything. It was a splendid game to broadcast. The North Yorkers went into the third period behind on the round and their gallant fight to even the score will be long remembered by both the fans present at the game and the fans who were kept so well informed by CFCA's play-by-play description of the struggle.

From the Toronto Star *on March 8, 1928, telling how Albert was filling in on the air for Foster Hewitt.*

"It was a natural for Foster to go into broadcasting," Albert told Beddoes. "He was the sports editor's son and he didn't do any harm."

However, Hewitt's name doesn't appear in print in the *Toronto Star* in connection with the hockey broadcasts until April 10, 1923, when an article that first ran in the *Dunnville Chronicle* on April 6 was reprinted. Still, when checking the games that CFCA broadcast, it becomes clear that Hewitt had called his first game on February 16, 1923. The details of the game that night between the Toronto Argonauts and the Kitchener Greenshirts match well with Hewitt's recollections. Tied 3–3 after the third, the game required four full-time (not sudden death) five-minute overtime periods before the Argonauts emerged with a 5–3 victory over the Greenshirts.

The broadcast of the game was described as "an epic" in the *Star* when the same (unnamed) announcer returned to the air the following week.

A legend was already in the making.

But what of Norman Albert?

He remained with the *Star* until 1927 when the rival *Toronto Telegram* hired him as their financial editor. He occasionally served as a referee for OHA

games, and he returned to the CFCA airwaves briefly in 1928 when Foster Hewitt was in Europe with his father and mother and the Toronto Varsity Grads hockey team at the time of the 1928 Winter Olympics. Albert left the newspaper business in 1950 to join an investment firm on Bay Street and was fairly well off when declining health forced him into retirement in 1966. Sadly, Parkinson's disease would leave the man who called hockey's first live play-by-play broadcast barely able to speak when he passed away on Christmas Day at the age of 77 in 1974.

It's Hockey Night Tonight

The first national hockey broadcasts in Canada have long been attributed to the nationwide hookup for the opening game from Maple Leaf Gardens on November 12, 1931. Some sources point to the General Motors Saturday night broadcasts that began in January 1933 and were later taken over by Imperial Oil. These were the roots of *Hockey Night in Canada*.

It turns out, however, that the first national broadcast (much like the earliest broadcasts in 1923) was made from Mutual Street Arena. Fittingly, it was a game

Foster Hewitt.

between the Toronto Maple Leafs and the Montreal Canadiens. The date was January 17, 1929 — almost three years before the opening of Maple Leaf Gardens.

Although radio station CFCA was owned by the *Toronto Star*, it was sports writer Bert Perry in Toronto's *Globe* newspaper on January 8, 1929, who noted at the end of his column:

> When the Montreal Canadiens make their second visit of the season here on Jan. 17 the game will be broadcast over the Canadian National Broadcasting Company's chain of stations from Halifax to Vancouver. It will be the first time that a Dominion-wide hook-up on a hockey game has been tried in Canada. Some fifteen Canadian stations will relay the play-by-play account to every corner of the country. The fans in Halifax, Edmonton and Vancouver will get the details right from the Arena Gardens as clearly as Toronto listeners-in.

When W.A. Hewitt — father of Foster — mentioned the story a week later in the *Toronto Star*, he had more (and slightly different) details:

> A joint broadcast of unusual interest to Canadian hockey fans will be held on Thursday night of this week when the Maple Leafs–Canadiens NHL game will be sent out on the air from Arena Gardens, Toronto. The broadcast is to be given under the joint auspices of the Toronto Daily Star and the Canadian National Railways over Stations CFCA of the Toronto Daily Star at Toronto and the Canadian National Railway's chain of stations at Quebec, Montreal, Ottawa, Toronto and Winnipeg with CJGX, the Winnipeg Grain Exchange station at Yorkton, Saskatchewan. Foster Hewitt will be at the microphone. This will be the first time that a hockey broadcast of such magnitude has been attempted and the hook-up will interest hockey and radio fans in all parts of Canada.

Foster Hewitt began his nationwide broadcast at nine o'clock in Toronto around the start of the second period. The Leafs and Canadiens ended up tied after three periods, and when 10 minutes of overtime settled nothing, they skated off with a 1–1 tie. In one story on the sports pages of the *Star*, the game was described as "dull for the most part, with both goals coming in the first four minutes of the second period." (Danny Cox, assisted by Hap Day, scored for Toronto; Sylvio Mantha for Montreal. Howie Morenz was out with an injury.) A story just after the Radio page noted that Hewitt "described the game in a graphic way."

By the end of the 1930–31 hockey season (still seven months prior to the opening of Maple Leaf Gardens), Foster Hewitt was calling all the most important games on the radio from coast to coast. He called the Memorial Cup final between the Winnipeg-based Elmwood Millionaires and the Ottawa Primroses on March 23, 25 and 27; the Allan Cup games between the Winnipeg Hockey Club and the Hamilton Tigers on March 31 and April 2; and the last three games of the Stanley Cup Final on April 9, 11 and 14 as the Canadiens beat the Black Hawks in five games.

Writing in the *Toronto Star* on April 15, 1931, W.A. Hewitt had this to say:

> The hockey season which ended last night with a coast-to-coast network broadcast of the Stanley Cup final was another triumph for CFCA (Toronto Star). Over 50 hockey games were broadcast during the season by Foster Hewitt and these included all the Maple Leaf Hockey Club scheduled games, the finals for the OHA championships in all series, the Allan Cup finals at Winnipeg, the Memorial Cup finals at Toronto and Ottawa and the Stanley Cup finals at Montreal. Foster Hewitt's voice is now as familiar in Vancouver and Halifax as it is in Toronto and throughout the province of Ontario.

And if you don't trust Foster's father to be giving you the straight goods, consider the following from A.R. Dingman in the *Vancouver Province* that same day:

> Radio has again been the means of bringing to the people of Canada a close-up of a national athletic contest of major importance. Last night over the lines of the CPR,

station CKWX brought to Vancouver the fifth and deciding game of the world's championship Stanley Cup hockey series in which Canadiens of Montreal mastered the dashing young team of the Chicago Black Hawks.

> Foster Hewitt of Toronto was on the "mike" in the Montreal Forum.... Foster gave a most realistic description of the play. Many homes in Vancouver had their dining tables transferred to proximity to the radio, where for nearly two hours the performance of these two great teams was told via the air route.

Hockey night in Canada, indeed!

Looking Back at Listening In

Foster Hewitt must have known that Norman Albert preceded his first hockey broadcast in 1923, but over the years he did very little to dissuade people from believing he had been the first. And his confusion over the dates of his first broadcast would lead to another misconception about early broadcasts. This would eventually bring Albert's name back into the picture.

On March 14, 1923, radio station CKCK, owned by the *Regina Leader* newspaper, aired a playoff game between the Regina Capitals and Edmonton Eskimos of the Western Canada Hockey League. The man who called the game that night was Lionel Dyke "Pete" Parker. Many people in Western Canada recalled Parker's game, and as the date of March 22, 1923, for Hewitt's initial broadcast became established, there were those who believed Parker's performance must have been first.

Among those most strongly in Parker's corner was Tom Melville, whose family had moved from Scotland to Weyburn, Saskatchewan, in 1910, when Melville was only two years old. He may well have heard Parker's first broadcast. He'd certainly heard of it. Melville would work for Regina newspapers from 1933 until 1998, and he made Parker's case to hockey authorities in the late 1960s.

In the *Regina Sun* on December 5, 1993, Melville recalled: "In the late 1960s an eastern company used television to promote a series of phonograph records dealing with Canadiana. Frank Selke Jr. did the TV commercial. Among his statements was one that said people could listen to an excerpt from a hockey game played in Maple Leaf Gardens as broadcast by Foster Hewitt 'the first-ever hockey broadcaster.'"

Melville "had been fighting for a long time to get recognition for Parker, who was living in retirement in Kelowna." Melville wrote to Selke and told him he was wrong. Selke told Melville he was surprised to learn that Hewitt was not number one and promised to look into it. Selke — probably by looking through old issues of the *Toronto Star* — discovered the February 8, 1923, broadcast by Norman Albert.

Though he doesn't say so, Melville was likely surprised to learn of Albert, and he relayed the information to Parker in Kelowna. "Getting information from the telephone office in Toronto, [Parker] came up with a number for Norman Albert and called him."

Albert told Parker he had indeed broadcast the third period of a game that night as an experiment for the radio station owned by the *Toronto Star*, the paper for which he worked. Perhaps this all happened a little bit later than Melville recalled. Or maybe it just took a while for the story to emerge, since it's not until 1972 that Albert appears to have finally gotten his due. Bruce Levett, sports editor for the Canadian Press, spoke to both Albert and Hewitt for a story that appeared in many newspapers across Canada in late June of that year.

"Who broadcast the first radio account of a hockey game?" wrote Levett. "Tradition says it was Foster Hewitt on March 23, 1923 [note that the dates of March 22 and 23 would often get confused]: files seem to indicate it was Norm Albert on Feb. 8, 1923. But neither of the pioneer broadcasters knows for certain."

"People are always telling me I was the first, but I've never claimed that, Hewitt says. But then, I never argued the point."

Hewitt may not have come clean, but the rest of Levett's story makes it pretty clear that Albert knew the truth! "If that game (Feb. 8) was the first," he told Levett, "then I guess I was the first."

In Albert's recollection, CFCA manager William Main Johnson had actually asked Hewitt's father to make the first broadcast. "Bill couldn't do it," Albert remembered, "and looked around for son Foster, who was out on another assignment. He offered the job to the late Lou Marsh, who turned it down. There was nobody else available, so Main Johnson asked me. I had been doing a lot of sports reporting and had a loud, clear voice."

As Albert remembered it, he broadcast the game from "a little hut about the size of a coffee table" beside the penalty timekeeper's bench. "I sat bent over and we broke in halfway through the game, somewhere in the second period. [The broadcast definitely began with the third period.] I think we followed the Hambourg Trio, I seem to recall a bass drum and a violin." The *Star*'s radio listings from February 8, 1923, do show a concert program from 8 to 9 p.m. that night, but no act called the Hambourg Trio.

Levett reported that Albert was philosophical about his lack of recognition. "If I had stayed with the *Star*, I might have laid claim to being first — but what's the point now? [Still] if anyone doesn't believe you when you write this, send them to me. I'll straighten them out."

And so Norman Albert briefly returned to the limelight, only to pretty much disappear again after he died on Christmas Day in 1974. But the story of hockey on the radio was still being told wrong. This was because no one had yet discovered that Foster Hewitt's first broadcast was actually on February 16, 1923, nor Albert's pioneering NHL broadcast of February 14, nor the other early broadcasts in Toronto. Bill Fitsell may have been the first to report on these, in the *Kingston Whig-Standard* on November 23, 1985, when he took Scott Young to task for his lazy research in Young's Hewitt bio, *Hello Canada!* Yet for nearly another 20 years, anyone telling the story still seemed to believe that Albert was hockey's first broadcaster, Pete Parker the second and Hewitt the third … even though Hewitt had been on the air nearly a month before Parker.

In Parker's first broadcast on March 14, 1923, he was on the air for the full 60 minutes, so regardless of whether he'd been first, second or third, his supporters now claimed he was the first man to broadcast an entire hockey game. But that's not true either. On February 22, 1923, radio station CJCG in Winnipeg, owned and operated by the *Manitoba Free Press*, aired the complete game as the Winnipeg Falcons defeated the Port Arthur Hockey Club 4–1. It seems that none of the stations in Toronto, Winnipeg or Regina had been aware of what the others were doing, and the name of the Winnipeg broadcaster was never reported.

Foster Hewitt, of course, would go on to call thousands of games, on radio and television, before ending his play-by-play career with the 1972 Canada-Russia series. Norman Albert had his two other games in 1923 and his handful of broadcasts in 1928. As for Pete Parker, his was the first complete broadcast of a professional hockey game, and he would be on the air the next winter calling more during the 1923–24 season. Six more, according to a *Leader-Post* story from March 31, 1991, but apparently none beyond that. Parker seems to have been out of radio entirely by the 1930s,

and when he passed away in Kelowna on February 11, 1991, Parker's obituary in the *Leader-Post* said nothing at all about his radio career.

Later, on September 13, 1997 — the 75th anniversary of CKCK — the *Regina Leader-Post* ran a transcription of an interview taped in 1962 with the station's first (and longtime) employee, Bert Cooper. In his interview, Cooper spoke of Parker and their first hockey broadcast. He said a nurse in a sanitorium in Fort Qu'Appelle suggested hockey on the radio as something her patients would enjoy. Cooper got permission from the owner of the Regina Capitals, who said he would go along with it … as long as they didn't announce it ahead of time. He didn't want to cut into potential ticket sales.

> I [Cooper] told Pete Parker, assistant to the manager of the *Leader-Post*. He was quite a sports fan, and he was a baritone singer. He had a deep low voice, an excellent voice, and he loved hockey, and he knew hockey. We built a booth at the south end of the rink…. That night I announced, "We're now switching you to Studio No. 2, where you'll hear the voice of Pete Parker, our new announcer." I gave Pete the cue, and he went ahead, and you could hear the hockey sticks, and the crowd, as plain as can be.
>
> Pete Parker was a minister's son. One of the Edmonton Eskimos came down the ice with the puck, and time and time again, he couldn't get it in the net. And he swore. Pete Parker had the window open, and he shouted down to the player, 'Cut it out, we're broadcasting!'

Quote ... Unquote

"Harold Noble, in hymns, proved to be a noteworthy factor in [radio station] WLWL's well-selected program, with a voice of lyric quality. While he was singing, just a few notches away on the radio dials, we were hearing about the uppercuts that were enlivening the fistic proceedings out Jersey way, which WOR made known. Simultaneously, WMSG was telling us all about the hockey game — which may be exciting (over the air) to some folks, but which sounds dull to others. It is much easier to visualize a punch on the nose than a slam on the shins — over radio. But when we get television, hockey will become more popular with the listening brigade who like to see heads cracked in the name of athletics."

— **Eric H. Palmer** in his column Outside Listening In, the *Brooklyn Daily Times*, December 21, 1926

Hockey Night in History

It's unclear who coined the phrase "hockey night in Canada," or when it was first applied to the national broadcast of games on the radio. (The name was well established by the time national broadcasts moved to television in 1952.) Maple Leaf Gardens called Saturday night "Ontario's hockey night" and "Canada's hockey night" in newspaper ads during the 1930s, and it's likely the name came from that.

After the success of Foster Hewitt's national broadcasts in 1930–31, General Motors sponsored the national broadcasts of Maple Leafs home games, which began with the opening of Maple Leaf Gardens on November 12, 1931. These officially became known by the 1932–33 season as the *General Motors Hockey Broadcast*. GM continued as the main sponsor through the 1935–36 season, with Imperial Oil taking over in 1936–37. Ralph Mellanby, in his book *Walking with Legends* (2007), claims the program acquired the name *Hockey Night in Canada* around that time, and that it was Foster Hewitt who came up with it.

Hewitt had already been introducing his broadcasts with the familiar phrase "Hello Canada, and hockey fans in the United States" (Newfoundland was added to the intro by 1937 or earlier), and at least two western newspapers (the *Calgary Herald* and the *Saskatoon Star-Phoenix*) referred to Hewitt making Saturday nights famous as "hockey night in Canada" in November of 1936. Still, the radio program was officially known as the *Imperial Oil Hockey Broadcast* until at least the 1939–40 season. Even so, references to "hockey night in Canada" had become more common by 1937. Stories in 1940 about the broadcast being introduced with "It's hockey night in Canada!" make it sound as if that was already a familiar refrain by then, and the name seems to have become official by the 1941–42 season.

Three Stars Get Started

The story has long been told that the tradition of naming three stars in a hockey game dates back to the 1936–37 season, when Imperial Oil became the sponsor of Canada's national hockey broadcasts. Imperial Oil did take over the broadcasting rights from General Motors that year, and although the three-star selections must have gotten a big boost, it all started a few

Ace Bailey poses as a Maple Leaf.

Red Beattie as a member of the Boston Bruins in December 1930.

years before then. In fact, the three stars began with the start of the 1932–33 season, which was the first year that hockey coverage was known as the *General Motors Hockey Broadcast*.

Imperial Oil introduced 3-Star Gasoline in September of 1931. "Following many months of planning and preparation," reported the Montreal *Gazette* on September 3, "three of Canada's largest manufacturing plants, the Imperial Oil Refineries at Dartmouth [Nova Scotia], Montreal East, and Sarnia [Ontario], changed over production to Imperial 3-Star Gasoline during the past few days. This change-over is said to be one of the biggest undertakings in industrial history.

"Twenty large tankships, thousands of railway tank cars, and hundreds of motor tank trucks were employed during the past week or ten days to distribute the new Imperial 3-Star Gasoline throughout Eastern Canada, thus paving the way for its introduction today."

By May 1932, the company was promoting its new gasoline in Canadian newspapers with a series of sporty ads using images of divers, boxers, tennis players and baseball players. When the next NHL season began in the fall of 1932, Imperial Oil hired Toronto sports personality Charles Querrie to select the three stars of games at Maple Leaf Gardens for a new series of promotions. Following the opening game of the season, a 1–1 tie between Toronto and the Boston Bruins, on November 10, 1932, Querrie's first three-star selections appeared in large print ads in Toronto newspapers. His selections continued throughout the 1932–33 season, and the next year, similar 3-Star ads appeared in newspapers in Toronto and Montreal. Imperial Oil also sponsored 3-Star ads for football games in the fall of 1933.

The First Three

The game between the Maple Leafs and Bruins on November 10, 1932, was a penalty-filled affair — as games between these two rivals often were in those days. There were 23 minor penalties plus a game misconduct, handed out to Toronto's Charlie Conacher late in the third period. King Clancy, with assists to Baldy Cotton and Ace Bailey, scored a power-play goal for Toronto at 8:40 of the first period (although none of the times given for the penalties match up correctly to account for Boston being shorthanded). Red Beattie, from Eddie Shore and Harry Oliver, scored for the Bruins at 9:25 of the second. Clancy, Beattie and Bailey were Charles Querrie's choices as the three stars. Here's what he wrote for the ad copy:

> When the Maple Leafs and Boston Bruins struggled through to a tie score under

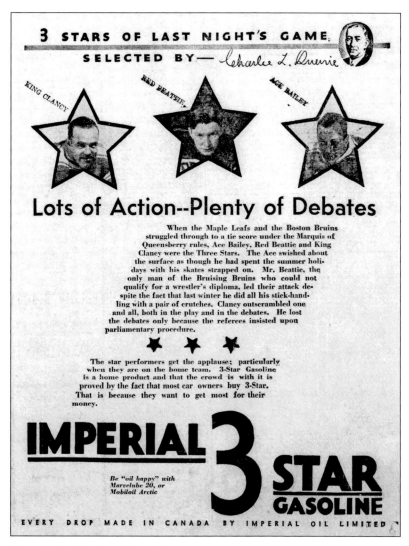

Toronto Daily Star, *November 11, 1932.*

Marquis of Queensbury rules, Ace Bailey, Red Beattie, and King Clancy were the Three Stars. The Ace swished about the surface as though he had spent the summer holidays with skates strapped on. Mr. Beattie, the only man of the Bruising Bruins who could not qualify for a wrestler's diploma, led their attack despite the fact that last winter he did all his stick-handling with a pair of crutches. Clancy out scrambled one and all, both in the play and in the debates. He lost the debates only because the referees insisted upon parliamentary procedure.

Hockey Night on Television

The history of television is much older than most people realize, with roots going back to the 19th century. The first public display of a commercially developed type of television occurred on March 25, 1925, by John Logie Baird at Selfridges department store in London, England. The first display of an electric television system (which would, essentially, lead to the development of modern television) was made by Philo Farnsworth in San Francisco on September 7, 1927.

The history of hockey on television in Canada usually says that experimental broadcasts were made in Toronto in the fall of 1951, or at the Memorial Cup in the spring of 1952. Both may have occurred, but the first experimental broadcast was actually made during a game between the Maple Leafs and the Montreal Canadiens in Toronto on March 21, 1951.

"Wednesday night," reported the *Globe and Mail* on Friday, March 23, "the Canadian Broadcasting Corporation, which hopes to begin TV operations in Toronto later this year, set up an experimental operation at the Gardens — the first time a hockey game had been televised in Canada."

Ace

It's an eerie coincidence that Bert Perry of the *Globe* newspaper in Toronto was writing about the nicknames of pro hockey players on December 14, 1933. It was the second in an eight-part series of Nicknames in Sports the *Globe* was running at the time, and it's eerie because just one page before, the *Globe* had stories about the reaction to Ace Bailey being injured. Born Irvine Wallace Bailey in Bracebridge, Ontario, on July 3, 1903, the right winger was fighting for his life in a Boston hospital. Two nights earlier, in a game between the Bruins and Maple Leafs, he had hit his head on the ice following a dirty hit from behind by Eddie Shore.

The story behind Bailey's nickname is cheerfully provided among dozens of other hockey monikers without reference to his current ordeal. Perry writes this on the origins of the famous nickname:

> Ace Bailey of the Leafs owes that name to the fact that two coaches were arguing as to the respective merits of a couple of their players, and one of them declared that his man was the king of them all. "He may be the king," said the other, "but in Irvin [sic] Bailey I have an ace that will take your king any old time," and so it has been Ace Bailey ever since.

Irvin "Ace" Bailey cartoon as drawn by Lou Skuce likely for the 1929–30 NHL season.

Quote ... Unquote

"She told me the Prince spends hours attending hockey games in London, but that she never had seen one, except on television."

— **Conn Smythe** after sitting with the future Queen Elizabeth II during an exhibition hockey game at Maple Leaf Gardens on October 13, 1951 (as told to Al Nickleson, the *Globe and Mail*, October 15, 1951)

Two cameras were positioned in Foster Hewitt's gondola while representatives of the CBC, Imperial Oil and McLaren Advertising watched from the radio control room. Hewitt provided an exclusive TV play-by-play description for the first period before moving on to his radio story of the game. "The results were excellent," says the *Globe* story. "Images were sharp and clear, and the ability of the cameramen to follow the play belied the fact that this was the first time they had worked a hockey game." Fergus Mutrie of the CBC said that from a technical standpoint, they could begin broadcasting games from Maple Leaf Gardens as soon as TV operations were set up in Toronto. "We're ready any time we get the green light."

Hugh Horler from McLaren, which was the ad agency for Imperial Oil, added that his client was very anxious to sponsor televised hockey if it proved practical. "Televised hockey is one of the first sports events people will be interested in," said Horler. "From the Imperial Oil angle, this experiment has shown just what could be done."

Although only about 10 percent of Canadians owned television sets, the CBC broadcast its first TV game from Montreal on October 11, 1952. Joining the action already in progress, René Lecavalier described

the play-by-play in French as the Canadiens beat the Red Wings 2–1. The first *Hockey Night in Canada* TV broadcast from Toronto was made three weeks later, on November 1, with Foster Hewitt at the microphone when the Maple Leafs beat the Bruins 3–2.

The First Game on Television

Hockey on television got its start in London, England. On January 26, 1937, the *Daily Telegraph* had a headline on page 8 reading, "Televising Ice Hockey Players." Goalie Art Child and center Jimmy Chappell, 1936 gold-medal Olympians for Great Britain and current members of the Earls Court Rangers, were to be on the air at 3:20 and 9:10 p.m. that day. "It is hoped to introduce a 10ft square of ice into the studio for demonstration purposes," the paper reported. There was no follow-up the next day.

More than a year and a half later, what is believed to be the first television broadcast of a hockey game took place on October 29, 1938. "With television cameras trained on them and an unseen audience watching their efforts, Harringay Racers play Streatham in a National Tournament match at Harringay Arena to-night," reported the *Evening Standard*. An ad in the paper indicated the game would begin at 8 p.m. The London Television listings in the *Daily Herald* show the game at both 8:30 and 9:35, while a story in the *Daily Telegraph* reported that "the second and third periods are to be televised." Harringay won 7–3, although those watching on television missed the best part of the action, which occurred late in the first period.

"It is unusual for a goal-minder to be sent to the penalty box," reported the *Sunday Dispatch* on October 30, "but Streatham suffered twice to-night in less than 60 seconds. After 17 minutes of play with no score [Louis] St. Denis was penalised for 1min., and the substitute let through two rapid goals for the Harringay

The Harringay Racers, the 1937–38 English National League Champions.

men, and then he, too, was sent off. The puck went into the visitors' net twice more, and this episode, which lasted less than three minutes, resulted in a four goal deficit for the Streatham side, which they failed to make up."

The NHL's TV Debut

Television broadcasting in New York began with the opening of the 1939 World's Fair at Flushing Meadows in Queens on April 30 of that year. According to a newspaper story from the *Altoona Tribune* in Altoona, Pennsylvania, on February 24, 1940, when James R. Luntzel of the National Broadcasting Corporation was in town, programs included "wrestling matches, style shows, [and] dramas, with leading stars of the stage and screen." Luntzel also boasted that television was bringing "thrilling hockey games right into the homes of listeners and lookers."

Indeed, the very next day — Sunday, February 25, 1940 — station W2XBS (now the NBC flagship station WNBC) broadcast the New York Rangers game against the Montreal Canadiens from Madison Square Garden. With the TV listing showing the coverage running from 8:45 to 10:45, and given that the NHL game sheet from that night shows an 8:45 start and a 10:39 finish, it appears the game was broadcast in its entirety. There were only 7,500 fans in attendance, and most online sources say about 300 people watched on television. (NBC estimated there were about 3,000 TV sets in the New York area in a *New York Times* story on May 21, 1940.) The Rangers — en route to the Stanley Cup that season — won the game 6–2. Bryan Hextall led the way with a pair of goals to open the scoring in the first period.

The television listings in some papers confirm that Bill Allen provided the play-by-play, but there is little in the newspapers from February 26 to provide much

The Rangers and the Canadiens in game action from February 4, 1940 at Madison Square Garden.

insight into the broadcast. Doug Watt, in his Listening In column in that day's *New York Daily News*, noted: "If a puck were as large as a football, television's first hockey match would have been swell. But although the capers of the skaters were visible, the televised game between the Rangers and Canadiens, from Madison Square Garden, was hard to follow."

Alas, while there would be further broadcasts of hockey games in New York over the next two seasons, and more from New York and other U.S. cities prior to the first Canadian broadcasts, the FoxTrax glowing puck was still 56 years in the future.

Injuries
and Oddities

Hockey has always been a rough game,
but not all injuries happen on the ice. Horses
and dogs; cars and canoes; sidewalks and
snowblowers have all played a part. And
sometimes, you just have to be silly.

Man vs. Horse

Having turned 36 on June 2, 1987, Larry Robinson indicated he would rather take the summer to rest when it was learned on June 23 that he would be named to the Team Canada roster for the upcoming Canada Cup. Robinson wouldn't change his mind, but with two years left on his contract with the Montreal Canadiens, he confirmed in July he would be back with the team when training camp opened in September.

But Robinson wasn't on the ice when the Canadiens began practicing on September 12. He wouldn't hit the ice until late October, and wouldn't play his first game for Montreal that season until November 18. That was because, on August 9, 1987 — when he might otherwise have been at training camp with Team Canada — Robinson fractured his right tibia (shinbone) while playing polo.

A six-time Stanley Cup champion, two-time winner of the Norris Trophy and one of the greatest defensemen of his era, Robinson grew up on a dairy farm in Marvelville, Ontario, in the Ottawa Valley. In an interview with *Weekend Magazine* in the *Globe and Mail* on October 13, 1979, Robinson said that, as a boy: "my original ambition was to be a veterinarian, growing up around animals the way I did. Not a big city vet, more a country doctor."

In the early 1980s, after living on the West Island of Montreal, Robinson decided to find a less urban setting for his family and moved to Saint-Lazare. As he explains in his book *The Great Defender* (2014) with author Kevin Shea: "I looked around and I didn't like some of the things I was seeing. I saw kids getting into things that made me uncomfortable. There were gangs of kids hanging out at the arcades, getting up to no good. I grew up on a farm and I wanted my kids to have the same values I was raised with."

Canadiens teammate Steve Shutt had recently bought a farm west of Montreal and then bought a horse. Robinson decided to do the same. Soon he and Shutt were introduced to families that had started the Montreal Polo Club. They tried it out, and both fell in love with the sport. Robinson took lessons for three years, and by 1985, he and Shutt were wearing the

Larry Robinson skates with the puck during game action on December 8, 1987.

"Quote ... Unquote

"Polo casualty Larry Robinson take heart: As a young cavalryman in India, Sir Winston Churchill had his shoulder crushed during a polo match. Though he walked with a slight stoop for the rest of his life, it didn't prevent him from becoming one of the great warriors and leaders in history."

— **Tim Burke**, the *Gazette*, Montreal,
  August 14, 1987

colors of the Montreal Polo Club at tournaments in Hudson, Quebec. Years later, Robinson told writer Joe Lapointe for a *New York Times* story on April 11, 2001, that he enjoyed polo because its patterns resemble those of hockey. Polo, said Robinson, "became almost a passion. It's a fascinating, frustrating game. You know what you want to do, but you can't always get the horse to get there."

It was while competing at Hudson in 1987 that Robinson was injured. "[He] saw the check coming in time to prepare for impact," writes Ian MacDonald in the Montreal *Gazette* on September 4, 1987. "But even a glancing shoulder block from a 1,200-pound foe can be devastating."

Robinson would tell the story differently in *The Great Defender*, but when talking to MacDonald, he explained: "I slid off the horse, as much from the pain

Big Bird

Larry Robinson tells the story behind his nickname in *The Great Defender*. It began during the 1976 Stanley Cup Final between Montreal and Philadelphia:

> It was during that Flyers series that I got tagged with the nickname Big Bird. The Flyers had a guy on their team named Don Saleski, and he had been called Big Bird because he somewhat resembled the Sesame Street character. In an interview, Serge [Savard] said, "We've got our Big Bird too. It's Larry Robinson." Back then, I had my hair permed. You have to remember the era, but after the game there were guys who would stand there blow-drying their hair and then use hairspray. I just wanted something that I could towel-dry and then go, so the perm worked for me — well, at least for a while. So in Serge's mind, being tall and thin with permed hair made me resemble Big Bird. And from there it stuck. It's not something I'm enamoured of, but I can live with it or without it. I still get people who want me to sign pictures with my name and Big Bird.

as the impact. I kinda rolled around on the ground, holding my knee. I figured I had done some damage but I had no idea my leg was broken."

Canadiens orthopedic specialist Dr. Eric Lenczner performed surgery on August 10. The operation required a six-inch surgical incision, a pin or screws, and a bone graft. Fortunately, there was no ligament damage, but it was predicted (fairly accurately, as it turned out) that Robinson would be sidelined for three months.

According to MacDonald's story, Robinson spent 10 days in hospital and 10 days at home before starting two-a-day therapeutic sessions with Canadiens trainer Gaétan Lefebvre. Robinson was working out on a stationary bike when he spoke to MacDonald. "Every time I see a Canada Cup game (televised), I wonder," said Robinson. "I get the itch.... If I had decided to take part in the series, the polo accident would never have happened. I would have been practising with the team that day."

Robinson recovered to play two more seasons with the Canadiens and then three with the Los Angeles Kings before retiring as a player in 1992. As a coach, assistant coach and consultant with New Jersey, Los Angeles, San Jose and St. Louis after his playing career, Robinson upped his Stanley Cup tally to 10. He now lives full time in Florida and still owns horses on a small farm at the Sarasota Polo Club.

Man vs. Dog

A little more than a week after the start of the first NHL season on December 19, 1917, the PCHA began its seventh season on December 28, with the Vancouver Millionaires visiting the Portland Rosebuds. The Rosebuds had won the PCHA title in 1916, but after losing the Stanley Cup to the Montreal Canadiens, they'd suffered through a difficult campaign and were

Tommy Dunderdale.

looking to rebound in 1917–18.

Tommy Dunderdale played most of his Hall of Fame career at center, but when Dick Irvin (another future Hall of Famer) left the Winnipeg Monarchs to go pro in Portland in 1916–17, he took over at center. Dunderdale spent the season rotating between all the forward positions. His scoring numbers were down that year and his penalty minutes way up. Now, with Irvin conscripted into the Canadian military, Dunderdale was back at center and a bounce back was expected. But on Christmas Day — three days before the start of the season — "Tommy was fooling with his bulldog," reported the *Oregon Daily Journal* on December 27, 1917, "and the latter playfully sank his teeth into the fleshy part of Dunderdale's right thumb."

Papers in Vancouver and Victoria on the day of the first game reported that Dunderdale had been playing with a child, and that it was believed the dog was seized with a fit of jealousy. While the Portland paper said only that Dunderdale's thumb was a little stiff, the British Columbia reports said he hadn't been able to practice because he was unable to close his hand sufficiently to grip his stick. He might not be available to play the season opener.

In the end, Dunderdale not only played but also scored the first goal just 19 seconds after the opening faceoff. (He also took the game's first penalty.) Portland beat Vancouver 4–2 in a game played with a thick fog over the Ice Palace rink due to an unseasonably warm night.

Going to the Dogs

Uwe Krupp wasn't the first German player in the NHL, but he was the first to make an impact. The 6-foot-6, 235-pound defenseman was selected 214th in the 1983 NHL Draft by the Buffalo Sabres after being spotted by Scotty Bowman while playing for his hometown Kölner HC. Krupp played 15 seasons in the NHL from 1986–87 through 2002–03 with Sabres, New York Islanders, Quebec Nordiques, Colorado Avalanche, Detroit Red Wings and Atlanta Thrashers, although his final seasons were marred by injuries.

Krupp's signature moment came when he blasted a slap shot past John Vanbiesbrouck at the 4:31 mark of the third overtime period in Game 4 of the 1996 Stanley Cup Final to give the Avalanche a sweep of the Florida Panthers. It capped a rather remarkable comeback from a serious injury.

On October 6, 1995, in the first game of the 1995–96 season, Krupp tore the anterior cruciate ligament in his left knee. It was expected he would be sidelined for 10 to 12 months, but he began skating again in early March and returned to action on April 6, 1996, after missing 76 games. Krupp got into the final

Uwe Krupp with the puck during an NHL game.

five games of the season and was good to go when the playoffs started. His rehabilitation had mostly involved walking and working out with the sled-dog team he owned.

In an alumni story on the New York Islanders website dated October 31, 2020, Krupp explained he had always had dogs in his life, but he stumbled onto dogsledding during his three years on Long Island from 1991 to 1994. He had six Siberian huskies and found a small community that trained them. Eventually, he entered them in races. (A 2001 *Sports Illustrated* story says Krupp bought his first Siberian husky when he was playing in his native Cologne, Germany, in the 1980s and started racing there.) When he moved teams, the dogs moved with him, going from Long Island to Quebec, Colorado and Detroit.

"We entered some competitions," said Krupp. "Mostly [my wife], but I used to go on training runs, or run three dogs around the course. It was a total departure from our normal life as a hockey player. It was refreshing I have to say."

But Krupp and the dogs ran into trouble after he signed a four-year, $16.4 million contract with the Red Wings in 1998. Krupp, who had undergone surgery for a herniated disc in 1997, began experiencing back pain early in December of 1998. He missed the rest of the season after playing just 22 games, but he was seen racing with his sled dogs. The Red Wings, who had not insured his contract, suspended him six months later, contending that dogsledding had compromised his rehab.

Krupp missed the next two seasons, and when he finally returned to action in 2001, he played just two games that October before injuring his rotator cuff. This time, he returned to play six games late in the season but played only the first two games of Detroit's 23-game playoff run to the Stanley Cup. Another back injury limited him to just four games played in his final season with the Atlanta Thrashers in 2002–03.

Krupp and the Red Wings waged a long court battle over the $8.2 million he felt he was owed for the two seasons he was suspended while rehabilitating his back injury. The case was finally resolved in January of 2003. Financial details were not disclosed.

Joe vs. Snow

Already sidelined since November 28, 2008, because of a herniated disc that was expected to keep him out until January, Colorado Avalanche captain Joe Sakic underwent surgery on December 9 to repair three broken fingers and a damaged tendon in his left hand after an accident with his snowblower earlier that day. It was expected Sakic would miss another three months, but he would never play again. Two

Joe Sakic lets a shot go against the Vancouver Canucks.

days after his 40th birthday on July 7, 2009, Sakic announced his retirement.

Man vs. Sidewalk: Part One

The 1992–93 season was one of turmoil and disappointment for the New York Rangers. It wasn't supposed to be that way. The arrival of Mark Messier from Edmonton in October 1991 was supposed to herald the end of what was then hockey's longest Stanley Cup drought, dating back to 1940.

It soon would.

But not yet.

The Rangers finished the 1991–92 season with the NHL's best record at 50-25-5, but the Presidents' Trophy wasn't the Stanley Cup. New York was bounced by the New Jersey Devils in the first round of the playoffs, and the disappointment carried over. The Rangers were 19-17-4 on January 4, 1993, when they fired coach Roger Neilson. It was said that Neilson's

philosophy displeased Messier, but things got worse under Ron Smith, his replacement. The Rangers failed to even qualify for the postseason when they finished with a record of 34-39-11.

Goalie Mike Richter had struggled. Back and rib injuries kept Messier out of a few games and limited his effectiveness in the ones he played. Worst of all, Brian Leetch, who was coming off a 102-point season and his first of two career Norris Trophy wins, had missed 34 games with nerve damage in his neck and shoulder. An injury that was supposed to sideline him for six weeks kept him out for nearly three months from mid-December until early March. He returned for only five games before another injury put him out for the rest of the season.

On the night of March 19, 1993, Leetch was returning to his Manhattan apartment from a restaurant following the Rangers' 8–1 win over San Jose. He'd been out with teammates Mark Messier and Tony Amonte, and while admitting he'd had a few beers,

Brian Leetch skates with the puck during a 1993–94 game.

Leetch maintained that alcohol didn't contribute to the fact he slipped on a patch of ice while getting out of a taxi. Not thinking the injury was serious, Leetch didn't do anything until he arrived at practice the next day. When he told the trainers what happened, they sent him for x-rays, and doctors discovered he'd fractured his ankle.

Man vs. Sidewalk: Part Two

Three years before he slipped on the sidewalk, Brian Leetch had suffered a more serious fracture of his left ankle near the end of the 1989–90 season. No one ever doubted his ability to return from either injury, but when Sprague Cleghorn broke an ankle for the second time and missed the entire 1917–18 season, hockey experts of that era figured his career was over.

Like Leetch, Cleghorn's second ankle injury was the result of slipping on an icy city sidewalk. The date was November 25, 1917. The *Montreal Star* ran a short story about the injury in a caption under a picture of Cleghorn in its paper the next day. Surprisingly — but perhaps because the NHL was officially formed that same November 26, 1917 — local papers seem to have reported very little about the injury to the longtime Montreal Wanderers star. But papers in other cities across the country were soon reporting that Cleghorn planned to sue the city of Montreal for $10,000 (it's unclear if he ever did or not) because the injury to his left ankle had likely ended his career.

Reporters seemed to consider it nothing short of amazing that Cleghorn had already managed to come back from breaking his left ankle in a game against the Toronto Blueshirts on January 20, 1916, when he got tangled up with Ken Randall and crashed into the boards. They thought it highly unlikely he could come back again after breaking his right ankle.

"There were plenty of people besides myself who figured that Sprague Cleghorn was through," said Cleghorn in the third of a four-part story of his life in *Maclean's* magazine on December 15, 1934. "Even after the second break had knitted and I was getting the idea into my head that maybe I could stage a comeback, the wise men of the game went around shaking their heads when such a suggestion was put into words."

The Wanderers had dropped out of the NHL after fire destroyed the Montreal Arena in January of 1918, but Cleghorn hoped to sign with the Canadiens and continue playing in his hometown. When Canadiens owner George Kennedy refused to offer him a decent contract, Cleghorn signed with Ottawa instead.

"Perhaps it was because I was keen to show Kennedy he was wrong. Perhaps it was just that I still had a lot of hockey in me and it had to come out. I don't know, but I was with Ottawa for three seasons and in two of those seasons Ottawa won the world's championship. I had to break both legs to get on a championship team for the first time in my career."

Sprague Cleghorn On and Off the Ice

Henry William Sprague Cleghorn was born in Montreal on March 11, 1890. His brother, James Albert Ogilvie Cleghorn, arrived 18 months later on September 19, 1891. They were the only sons in a family of five children who grew up in the affluent Westmount district.

There is little in the upbringing of Sprague and Odie Cleghorn to explain the hockey violence for which they would become known, though it may have had something to do with their father. William John

Cleghorn had been a championship lacrosse player in his youth and was still a well-known curler. "He always encouraged Odie and myself to play competitive games and to play them hard," wrote Sprague in the first part of the *Maclean's* magazine feature on November 15, 1934. "My mother did not like the idea so much. She never went to hockey games."

The Cleghorns played, mostly together, on teams in Westmount. Their reputation for mayhem was first established when they joined the New York Wanderers of the American Amateur Hockey League for the winter of 1909–10. A year later, the two brothers returned to Canada when they signed with the

Sprague Cleghorn.

Renfrew Millionaires of the NHA. A year after that, they joined the Montreal Wanderers. In the NHL, Odie starred with the Canadiens from 1918 to 1925 and finished out his playing career with three seasons as a player-coach with the Pittsburgh Pirates. Sprague played with Ottawa, the Toronto St. Pats, the Canadiens and the Boston Bruins through to 1927–28.

It was while the brothers played in New York that Sprague met Miss Evelyn Irene Mabie of Brooklyn (by way of Schenectady). The two were married on May 4, 1911, at the Little Church Around the Corner — officially known as the Church of the Transfiguration, an Episcopal parish church located at 1 East 29th Street, between Madison and Fifth Avenues in the NoMad (Madison Square North) neighborhood of Manhattan. The marriage may well have been as stormy as Sprague Cleghorn's hockey career. It ended in divorce on July 28, 1921, but seems to have been in trouble for at least a few years before that.

On Saturday, January 5, 1918, the following headline appeared on page 23 of the *Montreal Daily Star*: "Sprague Cleghorn Arrested This A.M. on Assault Charge."

According to the story, Cleghorn was arrested at his home at 145 Belgrave Avenue, in Notre-Dame-de-Grâce, by a Constable Trudel, on a warrant sworn out by his wife. "Cleghorn, who some time ago broke his leg, has been going around with a crutch according to the statement made at police headquarters by his wife…. There has been trouble between them for many months and things came to a head on the last day of the old year, and Cleghorn is alleged to have beaten his wife up with his wooden crutch. She accordingly took out a warrant charging him with assault and yesterday three policemen went to his house to execute it." The door was bolted, and Cleghorn refused to open it, so "police broke in the door and Cleghorn offered no further resistance

to the representatives of the law and was taken to police headquarters."

On January 14, 1918, under the headline "The Day in Court," the *Montreal Star* noted that in the case of Dame C.I. Mabie — the C must be a typo for E — v. H.W.S. Cleghorn, "Plaintiff's petition to sue in separation as to bed and board; granted, costs to follow suit." Cleghorn would be acquitted on January 21 when the charge of assault against him was dismissed after the evidence failed to show sufficient grounds to warrant conviction, but it would seem the couple would no longer be living together as husband and wife. Some of the circumstances of their estrangement would come out in the papers on July 29, 1921, the day after Evelyn Cleghorn was granted a divorce in New York:

> A chance visit of Mrs. Evelyn Cleghorn to Ottawa, Ont., last fall not only revealed to her the news of her missing husband, Henry William Sprague Cleghorn, one of the best known hockey players in the country [Cleghorn had been playing for Ottawa since 1918, and the *Ottawa Citizen* of November 13, 1920, had stated that Mrs. Cleghorn was in Ottawa, where she intended to spend the winter], but disclosed information that he was living there with another woman he introduced as his wife.

Upon hearing this testimony, and receiving depositions from witnesses in Ottawa that Mrs. Vivian Dalbec, named in the complaint as a co-respondent, had been introduced to them as Mrs. Cleghorn, New York State Supreme Court Justice Daniel Florence Cohalan granted the divorce decree. The *New York Times* reported that the judge directed Cleghorn to pay $1,000 per month in alimony, although every other account says $100, which seems much more in keeping with the fact that Evelyn Cleghorn had stated her husband's income from the sporting goods company he worked at in Ottawa was $5,000 per year. Sprague Cleghorn did not dispute the ruling, although he was no longer selling sporting goods for Hurd & Company, and his former employer referred to the $5,000 salary as ridiculous. There is no mention of his hockey income, but his salary wouldn't have been more than about $3,000 at that time.

When Sprague Cleghorn died on July 12, 1956, succumbing to injuries after having been hit by a car in Montreal on June 29, his obituary stated he was married three times, with two marriages ending in divorce and one wife predeceasing him on December 8, 1943. Odie Cleghorn was found dead in his bed on the morning of July 14, 1956, just a few hours before Sprague's funeral.

The Life and Death of Bruce Ridpath

The Toronto Hockey Club was one of two teams from the city that was supposed to enter the NHA for the 1911–12 season. The Torontos — usually called the Blueshirts or Blue Shirts — were officially admitted at a league meeting on October 11, 1911, although as early as July 19, 1911, the *Manitoba Free Press* had reported the new Toronto team was already beginning to do business.

John Purcell "Percy" Quinn was the owner of the Toronto Hockey Club. Quinn was born in Montreal on January 9, 1876, and grew up to become a lacrosse star with the Montreal Shamrocks. He was also involved in hockey as a coach and referee. An insurance executive by trade, and the older brother of NHA president Thomas Emmett Quinn, Percy Quinn was the president of the Dominion Lacrosse Association when he bought the dormant NHA franchise that would become the Blueshirts.

Percy Quinn owned the Toronto Hockey Club, but the man tasked with building the team for the 1911–12 season was Bruce Ridpath. Ridpath had little experience as a hockey executive, but he was a star player who worked off-ice as a bookkeeper and had managed his own successful career as a canoe champion.

David Bruce Ridpath was born in Lakefield, Ontario (just north of Peterborough), on January 2, 1884. He was the fifth of six sons, and ninth of 11 children, born to Samuel Ridpath, a tailor from England, and his wife, the former Jane Isbister of Scotland. Ridpath was still living in Lakefield at the time of the 1901 Canadian census with his by then widowed mother (Samuel died of a kidney ailment in 1895), two brothers, two sisters and one of those sister's husbands. By 1903, Ridpath had moved to Toronto, where he lived downtown with his brother John, a woodworker two years his senior, at 58 Gerrard Street West, near Bay Street.

Ridpath must have played hockey in Lakefield, but he first began to make a name for himself during the winter of 1903–04 with Toronto's Western Athletic Club in the junior division (Group 4) of the Ontario Hockey Association. A year later, the 21-year-old Ridpath moved up to senior hockey with the Marlboros — the top team in Toronto. The Marlboros had lost future Hall of Famer Tommy Phillips from their championship roster of the previous winter when he moved back to his hometown of Rat Portage (now Kenora), Ontario. Ridpath helped the Marlboros make up for the loss of Phillips and win their second straight OHA senior championship in 1905.

Turning down several pro offers, Riddy, as he was so often called, spent a second season with the Marlboros in 1905–06, but one year later the siren call of the professional clubs sounded again. "Bruce Ridpath of last year's Marlboros will play professional

The Toronto Hockey Club during the 1907–08 Ontario Professional Hockey League season. Bruce Ridpath is in the back row on the right.

hockey this year," reported Toronto's *Globe* newspaper on November 23, 1906, "but not for the teams abroad that want him. A few days ago he refused an invitation to go to Pittsburgh, and last night he said no to a telegram from … the Canadian Soo team who was inquiring for Ridpath's terms." Riddy would remain in Toronto for the 1906–07 season, but this time as a paid member of the city's first professional hockey team.

Only a few weeks earlier, on October 27, 1906, the *Toronto Star* had scoffed at the possibility of a professional hockey league being formed in Western Ontario. The paper stated specifically that "Toronto can be counted out." However, on November 23, 1906, the *Star* noted there had been a meeting of

professional hockey players the previous night at the Mutual Street Rink and that a club had been formed.

"Hugh Lambe, the old St. George cover point, was appointed secretary-treasurer," the *Star* reported, "and an Executive Committee elected consisting of [former Marlboros players] Rowley Young, Pete Charlton, and Bruce Ridpath." The team would not play in a league but would arrange its own schedule of games, "with International League teams on their way to and from Pittsburgh, and also with the teams of the Eastern League in Montreal and Ottawa."

The *Pittsburgh Press* reported that day that the Toronto pro team would be organized "on the joint stock principle, the profits to be split up among the players, who will manage the team themselves." If true, this would have been Bruce Ridpath's introduction to hockey management.

Although the Toronto Pros, as they've come to be known, had only modest success on the ice during the winter of 1906–07, they must have drawn big enough crowds (despite the small capacity of the Mutual Street Rink) that the pro players in the city took a leading role the following year in organizing the Ontario Professional Hockey League along with teams in Guelph, Brantford and Berlin (later Kitchener). Toronto won the OPHL title that season and gave the Montreal Wanderers a surprisingly tough battle in a one-game challenge for the Stanley Cup before the defending champions pulled out a 6–4 victory. Ridpath, who scored one goal for Toronto, was described as the fastest man on the ice and was said to have played "a sterling game." The next season, he scored seven goals for Toronto in a game against Brantford on January 30, 1909.

Ridpath spent two seasons with Toronto in the OPHL, but near the end of the 1908–09 campaign he was one of several so-called ringers who were signed by the Cobalt Silver Kings of the Temiskaming Hockey League to help them win the league title over their archrivals in Haileybury — who brought in a few ringers of their own. This perceived desire to follow the money above all, with little or no loyalty to their local teams, was what bothered the defenders of amateurism most about professional athletes and was difficult for even the supporters of the pro game to defend.

Ridpath was paid "the princely sum of $500" to play the final two games for Cobalt in the eight-game Temiskaming league season. He also played two playoff games as the Silver Kings defeated Haileybury for the championship. In all likelihood, Ridpath would have returned to Toronto for the 1909–10 season, but when it became apparent there would be no pro hockey in the city that winter, he signed instead with the 1909 Stanley Cup–champion Ottawa Senators. As he had done when he joined the Marlboros, Riddy helped his new team overcome the loss of another future Hall of Famer. This time it was Cyclone Taylor, who had signed to play in Renfrew.

Ridpath helped the Senators defend their title in two challenge series contested early in the 1909–10 campaign, and after losing the Cup to the Montreal Wanderers at the conclusion of the inaugural season of the National Hockey Association, he helped Ottawa win it back in 1910–11. Riddy scored a career-high 22 goals during a 16-game season that winter to rank fourth in the NHA.

Perhaps because of the administrative ability he had displayed in organizing his canoeing career, combined with his skill as a hockey player and his off-ice job as a bookkeeper, Ridpath was brought back to Toronto to both star on and build the Toronto Hockey Club, which was slated to enter the NHA in 1911–12. Spoken of informally at least as the prospective manager of the Toronto team as early as the middle of July 1911, Ridpath was said to be hot on the heels of talent for the December opening of the NHA season in late August when he appeared at a regatta in Winnipeg. But whatever work he was doing to build the Torontos came, literally, to a crashing halt on November 2, 1911.

Ridpath stepped off a northbound Toronto streetcar at the intersection of Alexander and Yonge, just steps from his home at 548 Yonge Street (only a few blocks from the future site of Maple Leaf Gardens) and was attempting to cross the street from east to west behind the streetcar when he was knocked down by a southbound motorist and pinned beneath the car. After being freed, Ridpath was carried to a nearby drugstore, where two doctors were summoned. They called for his removal to St. Michael's Hospital.

Ridpath had sustained a major injury at the base of his skull, although not a fracture. He also had a concussion and bruises on his arms and face. During the night, he suffered an internal hemorrhage. "His condition is bad," said a doctor quoted by the *Toronto Star* the following morning. "In fact his recovery is doubtful, although not hopeless."

Ridpath remained no better than semiconscious for days and was not thought to be out of danger for several weeks. Finally on December 4, 1911, Dr. Walter McKeown announced: "Bruce Ridpath will be out of the hospital in a week. It has been a splendid case and his strong constitution pulled him through a shock that would have killed most men." When asked when he might play hockey again, the doctor admitted he couldn't say, "but he certainly won't play this winter."

Ridpath, who required another month or so of recovery at home, would talk about a comeback for the next two years, but his days as a competitive athlete were over. It's highly unlikely he would even have been in condition to carry on as team manager (what we would refer to today as general manager) during the 1911–12 season, but a lengthy delay in the construction of the new 8,000-seat artificial-ice Arena Gardens being built on the site of the old, cramped natural-ice rink on Mutual Street resulted in the NHA's voting to exclude both the Torontos and the Toronto Tecumsehs for the upcoming season. The two teams would wait another year to enter the league, and by the time the work of building the Blueshirts got under way again during the summer of 1912, Riddy was back on the job.

Ridpath was once again in the Canadian west in August of 1912. While visiting his brother Thomas in Lethbridge, Alberta, he told a local reporter that his team would be "made up of young stars picked up from the OHA." Not every new Blueshirt came from the OHA, though future Hall of Famers Frank Foyston, Hap Holmes and Scotty Davidson had played there, while other future Hall of Famers Jack Walker,

Harry Cameron and Frank Nighbor, who signed with Toronto, already had limited professional experience. Ridpath had certainly built his team well. Though he would give up his job as coach to Jack Marshall early in the 1912–13 season, and relinquish the manager's job early the next year, the team Ridpath put together would be Stanley Cup champions by its second season of 1913–14.

Bruce Ridpath was never fully healthy again after being hit by that car in 1911, and he was just 41 years old when he died in Toronto on June 3, 1925. He had suffered a stroke at the home of a friend on May 18 and was taken once again to St. Michael's Hospital. Ridpath never regained consciousness. It was thought that his old accident may well have contributed to his death.

Extreme Canoeist

By more modern standards, Bruce Ridpath was certainly no Wayne Gretzky or Guy Lafleur. He was never named to the Hockey Hall of Fame, but Ridpath was surely a star on the level of Gretzky's Edmonton teammate Glenn Anderson or Steve Shutt in Montreal. Yet hockey was only his second-best sport.

It was in a canoe where Ridpath truly excelled.

"Riddy first sprang into fame as a racing and stunt paddler down at the old Toronto Canoe Club at the foot of York Street," *Toronto Star* sportswriter Lou Marsh would recall in an obituary on June 4, 1925. "He was a champion at straight racing work but when it came to stunts he was a marvel.... He was the first man, in this part of Canada at least, who could jump on the gunwale of a canoe, make it turn a flip clear of the water and then bounce back into it without shipping more than enough water to give a gold fish a bath."

Ridpath was also said to be able to walk on water at a clip of five miles per hour by using a pair of

An Imperial Tobacco card of Bruce Ridpath.

A *Toronto Star* story from November 15, 1907, referred to Ridpath being "engaged at a high salary to appear in his canoeing specialties at the Berlin Hippodrome" and "recently appearing before the royal family." Another *Star* story from December 4 quoted from one of his reviews in Berlin:

> A water-acrobat is the newest drawing-card at the Circus Busch. Mr Ridpath, an American, bustles around in his pitchim canoe in the water of the manege [an enclosed area in which horses and riders are usually trained] of 4 m depth in such a clever way that one could desire him to teach all water-sportsmen, etc, this art. All accidents on the water would then be considerably decreased.

Another article in the *Star* from December 11, 1907, reported that Ridpath never missed a performance, playing once per day. As to his being an American, "He was billed as 'D. Bruce Ridpath of Chicago, the aquatic wonder.' The Germans thought Chicago was better known than Toronto, and billed the young Canadian as coming from that place."

Physician, Heal Thy ... Opponent

Gord Roberts broke into the pro ranks at the age of 18 with his hometown Ottawa Senators of the Canadian Hockey Association (CHA). He scored his first goal 30 seconds into his first game and finished the night with three as the Senators crushed All-Montreal 15–5 on January 13, 1910. Two nights later, Roberts scored again in a 15–3 win over the Montreal Shamrocks, which would count as the first game for each team in the NHA after the two clubs abandoned the CHA. In a two-game Stanley Cup series against the Edmonton Eskimos later that week, Roberts scored four goals

"water shoes" he built and designed himself. (They resembled miniature kayaks he would wear on each foot.) Ridpath was so good at his various stunts that he was often in demand to give exhibitions of his tricks at canoe club regattas all across Canada and the United States. He even toured Germany from September 18 to November 23, 1907, performing in Berlin and Hamburg.

A hockey card representing Gordon Roberts on the Montreal Wanderers.

Roberts, who was said to be able to curve his shot, had scored six goals in a game twice in his six years with the Wanderers and was second in the NHA with 31 goals (behind Tommy Smith's 39) in a 20-game season in 1913–14. In his first season in the PCHA in 1916–17, Roberts led the league with a career-high 43 goals (in 23 games), which would hold up as the most in league history.

On Saturday, January 20, 1917, in a 6–3 win over Spokane in Vancouver, Roberts scored a goal in the second period, but he made more news with a unique assist in the first after Spokane's Dubbie Kerr was hit in the face with the puck and suffered a nasty cut above one eye. "Play was stopped," reported Vancouver's *World* newspaper on January 22, "and Roberts was called on to get out his bag and patch Kerr up." Said the *Vancouver Daily Sun*, "Doc Roberts of the Vancouver team patched it up and like any practicing physician will probably send Dubbie a bill at the end of the month."

Father Leveque

In the fall of 1935, the Boston Bruins played the Montreal Canadiens in an eight-game exhibition tour prior to the 1935–36 NHL season. Between October 28 and November 10, the teams played games in Saint John and Moncton, New Brunswick; Halifax, Nova Scotia; Charlottetown, Prince Edward Island; and Quebec City. A year later, the Bruins faced the Montreal Maroons in a six-game series in Saint John, Moncton and Halifax between October 26 and November 4.

After an informal gathering of NHL governors at Montreal's Windsor Hotel on Saturday, May 8, 1943, Boston's Art Ross was asked to tell "the Father Leveque story" from the 1936 Bruins tour with the Maroons. Dink Carroll reported on it in the *Gazette* on May 11, 1943:

in the first game in an 8–4 Ottawa victory and three goals in a 13–7 win in the second.

After finishing the season with the Senators, Roberts entered McGill University that fall. He signed with the Montreal Wanderers to finance his way through medical school. Roberts played six seasons, and upon graduation from McGill, he established himself in a medical practice in New Westminster, British Columbia, in the late summer of 1916. (Medical work would later take him to several other western cities in Canada and the United States before he settled in Oakland, California, in 1924.) That fall, he signed with the Vancouver Millionaires in the PCHA.

Art Ross.

By the time they reached Saint John, N.B., interest had been built up to the point where tickets were scarce. Both Art Ross and Tommy Gorman, who was in charge of the Maroons, were beseeched for passes, and both kept telling the pass-seekers that the other club had all the passes.

On the afternoon of the game, Ross called up Gorman and said it was Father Leveque speaking. Art can talk Habitant dialect with the best of them and Gorman went for it, particularly as "Father Leveque" kept telling him that he had admired the great job Tommy had done as a newspaper man and then as a

hockey manager. Tommy said yes, he remembered "Father Leveque" very well.

"Father Leveque" then said he was the principal of a boys school, and the boys were poor and he would like a few passes for the game. Could he possibly get them? Tommy said he thought he could handle it all right.

"Just a few passes," said Father Leveque. "There are 59 boys at the school and they all want to go to the game. Can I maybe have 59 passes?"

Tommy demurred … but "Father Leveque" again recollected the great job Tommy had done on the newspaper, and his glorious record in hockey. Tommy finally capitulated, saying he would pay for some of the seats himself.

"One more thing," said "Father Leveque. "Are you sure the boys will be able to see from the seats?"

"Of course they will," Tommy answered a little testily. "These will be the best seats in the house. They'll be able to see fine."

"That will be a miracle then," said "Father Leveque. "Because these boys are all blind."

Index